ADORNO ON MUSIC

Robert W. Witkin

London and New York

First published 1998
by Routledge
11 New Fetter Lane, London EC4P 4EE

Simultaneously published in the USA and Canada
by Routledge
29 West 35th Street, New York, NY 10001

Typeset in Garamond by Routledge
Printed and bound in Great Britain by MPG Books Ltd, Bodmin,
Cornwall

British Library Cataloguing in Publication Data
A catalogue record for this book is available from the British Library

Library of Congress Cataloguing in Publication Data
A catalogue record for this book has been requested

ISBN 0–415–16291–2 (hbk)
ISBN 0–415–16292–0 (pbk)

CONTENTS

ACKNOWLEDGEMENTS

The suggestion that I should write a book on Adorno's studies of music initially came from my colleague at Exeter, Tia DeNora. I am grateful to her for the push she gave the project by generously handing me her considerable file of bibliographic materials on Adorno's work. I wish to express my warmest thanks to Martin Jay who very kindly set aside time in the busiest of schedules to read and comment in some detail on earlier drafts of three of the chapters. I am grateful, too, to all my colleagues in the Department of Sociology at Exeter for helping to provide the study leave in which the book was written. Finally, I would like to thank the Senior Sociology Editor at Routledge, Mari Shullaw, for believing in and supporting the project even after it was apparent that it had grown, like Topsy.

1

MUSICA MORALIA

There is a Zen Buddhist description of Zen truth as being 'like a ball of fire stuck in your throat: you can't get it up but neither can you get it down'. This uncomfortable image can easily be fitted to the idea of truth which informs the work of Theodor Adorno. It is impossible to read Adorno without hearing, in the authorial voice, all those signs of high bourgeois cultural sensibility, of a bourgeois sense of truth, individuality, freedom, humanity, suffering. But in Adorno's writings, the world which might make sense of that authorial sensibility, the world of the 'heroic' phase of an entrepreneurial capitalism, is fast disappearing and is being supplanted by a monolithic, rational-technical commodity capitalism. The poisonous gas of that 'totalitarian' world, its *an*aesthetic, is the dream-stuff pumped out by the culture industry, by the Hollywood dream machine, Tin Pan Alley, advertising jingles, 'lollipop' music concerts, jazz, radio and so forth.

Adorno was closer than his modern readers to Auschwitz and to all which that implied. For him, Tin Pan Alley, Stravinsky, Hollywood, jazz and the culture industry belonged – however bizarre it might seem to many modern readers – in a configuration which included Auschwitz. In his aesthetic sociology he set, in powerful opposition, all those products of mass popular culture on the one hand, and the works of avant-garde musicians in the 'classical' tradition on the other. Within the latter category, he set up a further opposition; on one side there was serious and responsible music – true music – which developed, to the highest degree possible, the historical tendencies inherent in the 'musical material' and which conveyed the truth of the human condition – the suffering of the subject – in late capitalist society; and on the other side, the enemies of musical truth, musicians who did not acknowledge the obligations imposed by the historical demands of the musical material, musicians who retreated behind some notion of a world of pure musical effects and who sought musical models that were remote from the demands of the present, embracing 'primitivism' and 'neo-classicism'. Adorno saw these latter musicians as annihilating the subject and extinguishing genuine expression, ultimately as collaborating with the forces of oppression and alienation. Mahler, Schoenberg, Berg, Webern and the second Viennese school of composition provided him with his principal exemplars of music high in truth-value, while Stravinsky, Hindemith and the neo-classical composers were assigned to the camp of the enemies of true music.

More than half of Adorno's published works were devoted to his studies in music. Arguably, these studies represent the most formidable contribution so far to the development of a sociological theory of modern music and, more widely, of 'aesthetic modernity'. As Harold Blumenfeld put it:

> The writings of Theodor Wiesengrund Adorno have stirred up a whirlwind which has cut a widening swathe across the musical thought of the entire middle half of this century. Adorno – always provocative, sometimes provoking – places the musical act under a scrutiny which is at once exhaustive and multidimensional. His critique remains unexampled in terms of the sheer multiplicity of vantage points from which it probes its subject. Rooted in Hegel, Marx and Freud, his thought is often complex and complicated in expression – factors which have tended to make it stick in the throats of friends and foes alike.
>
> (H. Blumenfeld 1991: 263)

Belonging, as he did, so completely to music, philosophy and sociology, Adorno possessed all the cultural capital necessary for the task of constructing a sociology of the musical art work. Moreover, his credentials could not easily be challenged by musicologists. How many of them could boast, as could Adorno, of a sophisticated musical training as a pupil of the best teachers – among them Alban Berg – of membership of the avant-garde Viennese circle surrounding Schoenberg, of being in touch – often having close personal contact – with some of the foremost philosophical and musical talents of his day and of being a practising composer and a skilful instrumentalist for whom the choice between philosophy and a career as a professional musician had been a real one? Adorno's credentials for writing about music were clearly beyond question and his name, at least, is widely known among music specialists.

Of all the arts, music is perhaps the most profoundly sensuous in its capacity to stimulate emotions and feelings. But the power of music to excite or to gratify or to engage our sentiments is not, of itself, life-enhancing or a moral good. Adorno was surrounded by musical models in both the classical and the popular or light music traditions, which were regarded by their devotees as exciting and as appealing to the emotions; many of these models he despised and rejected. His rejection of music ranging from Stravinsky to Louis Armstrong was not based upon the fact of their popular appeal nor their power to stimulate emotion or to excite; it was, rather, based upon his belief that such music was 'manipulative', that it colluded in the weakening and undermining of the subjects it appealed to, that its claim to spontaneity or genuine expression was untrue. While he was unstinting in his admiration for many composers from Beethoven to Schoenberg, from Mahler to Boulez, the music against which he declaimed knew no more devastating or relentless a critic than Adorno. He despised any music – compositions or performances – that he saw as being in league with the inherently totalitarian tendencies of late bourgeois society, and he supported his arguments with analytical discussions of specific musical works.

Such a fierce stance presupposes that music has some serious function, that it is not simply diversion or entertainment, that it can even be judged and found wanting over the heads of its devotees or, in the case of a great composer like Bach, it can even be rescued from its devotees (T. Adorno 1982a). Inevitably Adorno ran the risk of being dismissed as an intellectual mandarin, a European dinosaur, legislating aesthetic choices for the rest of mankind. Such a judgement would not only be unjust to Adorno: it would miss the point altogether. In a world in which art and the aesthetic domain had been marginalised and their products trivialised, Adorno did more than any other philosopher to raise their profile and to establish beyond all doubt their right to be taken seriously, to be acknowledged as a moral and critical force in the development of a modern consciousness and a modern society. As Martin Jay pointed out (M. Jay 1973), Adorno viewed intelligence as a moral category. He deplored the tendency to separate feeling from the understanding and believed that philosophy must return to its original intention, 'the teaching of the correct life'. I seriously doubt that Adorno's will be the final judgement on Stravinsky's music or on jazz, but I am personally in no doubt that his arguments concerning both enlarge our whole perspective on the relationship between music and society.

The notion that artists have a moral obligation to reflect the truth of the subject's condition in society is a peculiarly modern one and has to be seen in the context of the historical evolution of art as an institution. In feudal times, what we recognise as art was not an autonomous social institution but was subsumed within other institutions – the princely courts or the Church. From the time of the Renaissance, art became progressively more independent as a social institution until by the nineteenth century it had virtually achieved autonomy status. The growing artistic freedom of the artist reflected the growing rationality of economic life, a rationality that squeezed out the elements of the non-rational – the sensuous, personal and aesthetic aspects of life. At the point at which art became more or less irrelevant to the service of the institutions and powers in modern society, the artist acquired freedom from the interference of the state; the artist could henceforth compose or paint in whatever ways s/he chose, provided of course that buyers could be found for the work.

The freedom of the modern artist is at the same time the mark of exile, of separation from any personal fulfilment in the forms of official or public social life. This describes the condition not only of the artist but of the sensuous life generally. Modern rational-technical society is one in which the individual subject is said to be free to make value choices, to live as s/he chooses, and so forth. At the same time, precisely because of the condition of exile, the choices that the subject makes have no real import in the rational-technical machinery of social life; they find no fulfilment or meaning in the modern institutional order. It was this disjunction between the individual subject and the society which confronted him or her as an external force, together with the weakness of the former and the overwhelming domination of the latter, which Adorno saw as the crisis of modernity. The reproduction of this disjunction, together with the crushing disparity in power, in the inner cells of works of art and of music was seen by Adorno as being the real measure of their truth-value.

Because art's awakening to its autonomy was also an awakening to its exile, modern art necessarily stood in a critical relationship to modern society. Criticism, here, did not mean that art preached or propagandised or offered a message of any kind; rather, it meant that in depicting the objective truth of the power of the collective force of modern bureaucratic society and the weakness of the individual subjects who are its victims, an artist like Kafka struck from it an expression of the suffering of the victims, a sense of what had been done to them, of what was withheld from them, of loss and absence. In the presence of this absence, as disclosed in the sufferings of society's victims, the artist provided a *via negativa* from which to glimpse utopia. What was true of Kafka was true, too, of the music of modern composers such as Mahler, Berg and Schoenberg: a music of seismic shocks and of dark forces, a music in which the de-individuating, atomising and fragmenting forces of modernity permeated all its textures.

Given the moral significance that Adorno perceives in music, together with his insider knowledge as a musician, one might imagine that musicologists would have embraced him as a worthy champion of modern music. That is far from being the case, however. The sociological sophistication Adorno brings to musical analysis and the difficulties of his language and philosophical ideas render his work opaque to many music specialists. Commenting on the disjunction of conventional musicology and the wider social concerns of Adorno, Edward Said writes:

And while I am very far from rejecting all, or even a significant portion, of what musicologists do by way of analysis or evaluation, I am struck by how much does not receive their critical attention, and by how little is actually done by fine scholars who, for example, in studying a composer's notebooks or the structure of classical form, fail to connect those things to ideology, or social space, or power, or to the formulation of an individual (and by no means sovereign) ego. Theodor Adorno may have been the last thinker about Western classical music to attempt many of these bigger things. I have little idea what his influence or status is in musicology today but I suspect that his intransigent theorising, complicated philosophical language, and vast speculative pessimism do not endear him to busy professionals.

(E. Said 1992: 13)

Among musicologists, Rose Rosengaard Subotnik is one who stands out as a pioneer in the field of Adorno music scholarship, having produced a profound and philosophically informed appreciation of Adorno's contribution to musicology (R. Subotnik 1990, 1996). Her work has contributed greatly to the recognition of Adorno's importance to musical criticism with her lucid and sympathetic reading of Adorno's ideas concerning the late music of Beethoven. Her expositions on other aspects of Adorno's work have contributed to the growing frequency and respect with which Adorno's works are now translated and discussed in musicology journals.

However, it is important to acknowledge the boundaries of this interest. It may seem curious to the lay sociologist that in those modern books on musical analysis which deal with a topic that is central to Adorno's concerns – the modernist aesthetic revolution involving, in the case of music, the transition from tonal to atonal and twelve-tone serial music – and which discuss in depth the work of Schoenberg, Berg and Webern, very little use is made of Adorno's writings on these subjects beyond the occasional passing reference and the more or less obligatory footnote or endnote. In part this is due to the fact that Adorno's formal analyses of musical works are preoccupied with meaning in the context of a *hearing* of the works. Adorno's analyses develop a sophisticated appreciation of what he hears as 'significant' in the music. Typically, he will discuss the effect of a single chord or even a single note in a Beethoven sonata on the hearing of an entire movement. Sometimes, his analyses can, to the layperson, seem extremely dense and technically demanding, as in his book on Mahler; however, they are still analyses centred more on a 'composed hearing'. Such analyses may not be particularly illuminating to musicologists for whom an accurate, detailed and close *reading* of the score is closer to their ideal of formal analysis and whose analytical purposes are, in any case, usually quite different. Adorno brings to musicology a consciousness that has been formed in the discourses of philosophy and sociology, and his construction of musical projects and purposes still appears alien to many musicologists.

The book's project

The focal concern of my book is to explore, from a sociological perspective, Adorno's critical and philosophical texts on modern music. I have taken those which appear to me to be the most important among the many texts he produced on music and have sought to develop a reading of the texts themselves, drawing them closer to the concerns of sociologists and even (Chapter 5) to see the parallels at a structural level, between the development of modern music and the development of modern sociology. What my book does not attempt to do is to offer an exposition of Adorno's analyses of specific musical works. Wherever such works are referred to in the text it is solely to illustrate or support Adorno's line of reasoning concerning the relationship between music and society. I have tried to explore, for a sociological readership, some implications of Adorno's ideas about music in relation to society and, for a musicological readership, the implications of his ideas about society in relation to music. However, while I have made some effort to remain true to Adorno's most fundamental ideas about music, I have made no attempt to ground them in a comprehensive account of his vast speculative interests and his critical immersion in German idealist philosophy, or even to locate his work in the context of the history of the debates and discussions that constituted the intellectual life of the Frankfurt Institute. There is not one Adorno for a reader to discover, but many, and there are a number of works which treat Adorno's work contextually in terms of both his Marxism and his role in the Frankfurt Institute. Although what I have offered here is essentially a reading of primary texts (in translation), there is a select but very fine secondary literature on Adorno that has undoubtedly helped to shape my perspective; it includes some of the most comprehensive, scholarly and yet readable texts on Adorno's work. The most obvious to name here are a few of those I have particularly enjoyed: Martin Jay's brilliant study *The Dialectical Imagination* (M. Jay 1973) which is still the finest and most readable account of the Frankfurt school and Critical Theory; Susan Buck-Morss's *The Origin of Negative Dialectics* (S. Buck-Morss 1977), a work of brilliant scholarship and analytical depth which provides a real insight into Adorno's philosophical origins and ideas, his relationship to Walter Benjamin, Schoenberg and the many formative influences that shaped his consciousness and provoked his critical spirit; Gillian Rose's *The Melancholy Science: An Introduction to the Thought of Theodor Adorno* (G. Rose 1978), a wide-ranging and intelligent discussion which provides some useful sociological discussions of Adorno's ideas, particularly the concept of reification, as well as exploring both Adorno's language and his mode of expression; J.M. Bernstein's *The Fate of Art* (J.M. Bernstein 1993) contains an insightful analysis of Adorno's *Aesthetic Theory* in a book about aesthetic alienation in modern European philosophy. Two very different texts which readers will find particularly helpful regarding the ideas on music are Rose Subotnik's philosophically informed studies in two volumes, *Developing Variations: Style and Ideology in Western Music* and *Deconstructive Variations: Music and Reason in Western Society* (R. Subotnik 1990, 1996) and Max Paddison's *Adorno's Aesthetics of Music* (M. Paddison 1993) – wide in its coverage of the range of Adorno's music studies.

Bringing the relationship between society and music out of the texts themselves is not easy. Adorno yields little to a reader unwilling to engage creatively and dialectically with his thinking. His works are opaque to passive reception. They demand that one contribute some theorising of one's own to the encounter if one is to gain anything of substance from them. It was not until I had completed work on another book, *Art and Social Structure* (Witkin 1995), that I felt sufficiently prepared to engage with Adorno in this dialectic. My doubts at the time sprang from my lack of technical expertise in music and musical theory. I have always enjoyed listening to music and have an average listener's appreciation of the classical music repertoire, as well as some of the more popular forms of jazz and rock music, but no real technical knowledge. I had to teach myself as best I could. However, there were two things that I quickly discovered. The first was that Adorno himself could be a helpful teacher if one was prepared to be an attentive pupil. Guided by him, I listened to modern music in a way that I had never done before. My musical tastes are not the same and I do not accept all of Adorno's judgements – I confess to enjoying much music that he hated and to engaging in listening practices of which he would have disapproved. Nevertheless, there is no doubting the fact that my appreciation of music has been irrevocably changed as a result of reading Adorno. While typing the chapters of this book I frequently listened to the music of the composers I was writing about – a practice that he might well have deplored – although, with the exception of the late Beethoven quartets, I preferred not to match the particular composer listened to with the text being written about. Often I listened to music not discussed, such as Bach's Mass in B minor, simply because I enjoyed listening to it while working. And in the latter stages, when I was revising chapters, I listened to Adorno's own music, in a recording by the Leipzig String Quartet of some early pieces he composed between the ages of 17 and 21. I enjoyed particularly his Two Pieces for String Quartet Opus 2. Alban Berg wrote to Schoenberg of this piece following its first performance, recommending the talents of the young Adorno:

> The performance of Wiesengrund's incredibly difficult quartet was a coup de main for the Kolisch Quartet. . . . I find Wiesengrund's work very good and I believe it would also meet with your approval should you ever hear it. In any event in its seriousness, its brevity and above all in the absolute purity of its entire style it is worthy of being grouped with the Schoenberg school (and nowhere else).
>
> (J. Brand *et al.* 1987: 355)

The second discovery I made was that if I restricted my concerns to the sociological focus that was driving my project and constructed a dialectical relationship to Adorno on that ground, the rudimentary knowledge of music that I was acquiring would be adequate for my purposes. It is inevitable that, confronted by so rich a mind, Adorno's readers will reflect different facets and project different interests upon their subject. I have deliberately narrowed my intellectual focus to that of bringing Adorno's reasoning about developments in modern music, and the models of individuation to which they give rise, into some kind of relationship – albeit still somewhat loose and tentative – with developments in modern sociology and the models of individuation instantiated there. Inevitably this narrowing of focus is achieved through abstracting Adorno's ideas from the whole context of speculative German philosophy and the discourse of Marxist aesthetics and of Critical Theory which is their home. In the process, I am certain that I have sought to make them work for me in ways of which he would not have approved. The reader should perhaps be particularly on guard concerning the moves made in Chapters 2 and 5. The theoretical intervention on my part is a considerable one, in that I have sought to construct, behind Adorno's back as it were, a 'lock step' semiotic theory of presentational codes that binds the different arts and seeks to assimilate Adorno's arguments. I have little reason to believe, from his writings, that such a project would have commended itself to Adorno; he would no doubt see this as precisely the type of conceptual trap he was dedicated to avoiding. Nevertheless, the semiotic theorising in these chapters is key to my own project of developing a sociology of the art work that can more easily accommodate the rich vein of thinking represented by Adorno's writings on music. While I am sympathetic to his notion of the importance of the negative moment in dialectical development, I have always been personally inclined to a somewhat positive cast of mind. I am not sure that optimism or pessimism in a thinker – Adorno is undoubtedly pessimistic – tells us a great deal about the state of the world. These are qualities of temperament. Moreover, I am not even sure that I give to critical thought the paramount position that he ascribes to it. It is central, of course, but for me it is inextricably bound up with the less talked-about art of appreciation. I find it essential to my understanding of a serious thinker's ideas that I develop a sympathetic appreciation – something like a 'willing suspension of disbelief' – as a necessary prerequisite for any critical insight into his or her work.

A brief overview

The musical texts discussed in this book are among Adorno's most important, and they are the ones that are key to the sociological argument that is the focus of my book. It is this latter consideration which has been predominant. Chapters 2 and 5 develop the semiotic theory I referred to above and Chapter 10 offers a critical appreciation of Adorno's arguments. The other seven chapters deal with major music texts. In Chapter 3 I discuss Adorno's analysis of the beginnings of the crisis of modernity in the development of

Beethoven's late style. In Chapter 4 I discuss Adorno's treatment of Wagner's music. In Chapter 6 I discuss Adorno's appreciation of the music of Mahler and Berg. In Chapter 7 I discuss his arguments concerning Schoenberg and the development of twelve-tone music. Chapter 8 deals with Adorno's critique of Stravinsky. In Chapter 9 I discuss in detail Adorno's rejection of jazz. For each of the texts, I present arguments that I hope will prove sociologically interesting. However, Adorno himself wrote about the work of many other modern composers who are not even referred to here, and his purposes, both philosophical and musical, were a great deal wider than mine. Even in the case of the texts I discuss, I have not attempted to provide the kind of exposition that would justify one in not reading the originals.

The barriers to an 'easy' reading of Adorno

There are certain impediments to an easy reading of Adorno's works on modern music. The following are perhaps the most obvious: (a) The technical difficulties of the text, which include the use of formal musical analysis in the development of argumentation. Adorno viewed technical analysis of musical compositions as being essential to his sociology of music. His project could scarcely be realised without such analyses and they are dotted throughout his writing on the works of particular composers. (b) The taken-for-granted presumption of a sophisticated readership with an in-depth understanding of German philosophy (Kant, Hegel, Schopenhauer, etc.). (c) The formidable difficulties posed by modernist works of art, difficulties which are reflected in theorising about them – Adorno saw the forbidding obstacles to accessibility in modern works of art as intrinsic to their critical force. (d) The aesthetic project of Adorno himself, who at one level appears mired in the densest of philosophical prose yet is, at another, the poet wrestling with the volatile fissionable material of shattered language, imbuing his writing about musical compositions with the same critical and *aesthetic* force as the musical works he discusses. He is happy to weaken the boundary between doing philosophy and doing music, and his language, style and ideas, as a consequence, are as difficult to grasp as a guitar in a Cubist canvas – now you see it, now you don't. (e) Finally, Adorno's tendency to engage with his subjects dialectically means that he appears at times to contradict himself; all too frequently, the reader finds him treating what appears to be the same phenomenon differently on different occasions or with reference to the work of different composers. It is instructive to watch him in *Aesthetic Theory* dismiss Brecht's work as superficial, didactic and artistically inferior, only to find him elsewhere in the same text praising the profundity of Brecht's poetry or appreciating aspects of his dramatic technique. One can find the same extremes of judgement applied to the same composer. Admiration and disdain are mixed even in his treatment of musicians close to him, for example Schoenberg and Webern; and, while one can be in no doubt as to his hostility to Stravinsky's music, close examination of the relevant texts finds Adorno unselfconsciously writing with a genuine admiration for certain specific works of Stravinsky's. Of course, Adorno's stock of basic concerns recurs throughout his analyses, but his analyses take on new colours and tones as a given phenomenon is 'rotated' through different contexts. Also, Adorno does not seek to cover the contradictory and ambiguous aspect of reality with smooth writing, and this often makes his theoretical meaning difficult to clarify. Such apparent contradictions recur throughout Adorno's writings, but they are only apparent. When Adorno's dialectical method and his notion of truth as relational is taken into account, his writings can be seen to maintain an impressive degree of self-consistency and coherence. Life is movement, change, motion; for an analysis that is equal to life to be self-consistent it must have the motility that Adorno's analyses have.

Said identified two impediments to a sympathetic reading of Adorno's work by either sociologists or musicologists, namely Adorno's 'complicated philosophical language' and his 'vast speculative pessimism' (E. Said 1992: xiii). Certainly, the difficulties of fusing musicological analysis with sociological speculation, together with the difficulties posed by Adorno's deliberately anti-systematic use of language, his exploitation of ambiguities in language and expression and his bleakly pessimistic outlook, may well discourage a sympathetic reading of his work. However, it is perhaps profitable to see Adorno's writing strategies as integral to his project. A philosophy whose central purpose was to profess the truth of a fragmented and transcendentally homeless subjectivity could not slyly seek to provide shelter and consolation for it in the architectonics of traditional linguistic and conceptual structures. Adorno was not the first to realise this. Nietzsche's aphoristic language and that of Wittgenstein, not to mention the opaque language of his friend Walter Benjamin, were all instances of language 'taking the strain' of modernity.

'Taking the strain' of modernity meant realising in the very construction of utterance the broken fragmented condition of the language through which the subject must express itself in late capitalist society. In an instrumental world dominated by markets and exchange values, a world in which the spiritual life could find no home, each utterance that aimed to be a vehicle for truth, each serious work of art, each musical composition and each element within a musical composition, had to form itself – in and through its brokenness as the authentic voice of suffering – as a critical opposition to the death star of modern culture. A book of Adorno's (especially a late work such as *Aesthetic Theory*) might be likened to an archipelago. There is no systematic argument which builds to a conclusion, no architectonic scaffold, just a string of islands, leaving the reader to navigate from one to another as s/he is able (T. Adorno 1984).

Adorno celebrated the idea of the inaccessibility of modern music, he did not apologise for it. He believed the 'languages' of modern art and modern music were necessarily difficult and inaccessible to the mass of people, not because the latter were intellectually incapable but because they were victims of a false consciousness, fetishising commodities, hypnotised by the lies, false promises and seductions of a modern materialist culture, with no desire to be awakened and preferring only to have their comforting illusions confirmed. In contrast, the utter bleakness and remoteness of so many works of modernist art were integral to their truth-value, as Adorno saw it. The music of the second Viennese school of Schoenberg and his circle, as much as the plays of Samuel Beckett, was seen by Adorno as an art of *resistance* and of critical negation; the very autonomy of serious music, its potential for critical opposition to modern society and to the ideological underpinning of that society depended crucially upon its inaccessibility. Music's active distancing of itself from mass culture and the products of the culture industry, from musical forms that were seductive, accessible or pleasing, was a distancing which marked the alienation of music from all that collaborated with the suffocating tyranny of modern instrumental culture.

Inevitably, this exclusivity was, in a very specifically modern sense, 'aristocratic'; the new advanced music was the cultural capital of the cognoscenti and of the avant-garde artistic and musical circles from which it emanated. Adorno's celebration of inaccessibility is made from the standpoint of an insider, a member of such an elite circle. For Adorno, the truths of modern music were not only hard won, they were themselves hard, bloody, negative truths, and they did not exercise their cleansing and redeeming power by falling lightly or sweetly upon the ear as did the 'hit tunes' with which, he claimed, Tchaikovsky had rendered despondency. It is a mark of that self-same avant-garde modernism that Adorno approached the business of philosophising in a similar way. One cannot imagine Adorno being fazed or even apologetic were he to be confronted by I.A. Richards' despairing student who once exclaimed to him, 'Gee whiz, Prof, your words sure skid off my cranium!'

However, over and above all such arguments about Adorno's choices and preferences (or those of modern artists), there is a sense in which the very historical conditions to which he refers control the degree of distance between the languages of art or of aesthetic discourse and everyday communication. The rational-technical forces that make modern society what it is condition the material with which artists work. These forces are appropriated in so-called serious art as a vehicle for expressing the subjects wrecked by them. The image of its own expressive import, held up to a society which has exiled the expressive, is necessarily opaque. It is the treatment of modernity itself in the languages of modern art which has distanced them from everyday discourse.

The point can be elaborated with respect to Adorno's general philosophical critique of the Enlightenment. It is a critique which acknowledges the complicity of the most esteemed models of language itself in the perpetuation of violence and exploitation. Adorno was a child of the Enlightenment. *The Dialectic of Enlightenment*, which he wrote with Max Horkheimer, is widely recognised as a major contribution to twentieth-century critical philosophy and a profound analysis of the crisis of modern culture. Adorno and Horkheimer establish, at the outset of that work, their own commitment to enlightened thought. 'We are wholly convinced – and therein lies our *petitio principii* – that social freedom is inseparable from enlightened thought.' In the same breath, however, the authors argue that the ways of thinking we associate with the Enlightenment – reason, science, progress, etc. – together with the entire framework of social institutions with which these modes of thinking are connected, are the very crucible in which modern barbarism and terror have been formed (T. Adorno and M. Horkheimer 1986). The prospect of total mastery of the world through the power of objective knowledge and reason – through developing a consciousness that is dispassionate, impersonal and objective – belongs to a society in the process of transforming itself into an instrument of world domination, a 'machine' consciousness.

The self-mutilation involved in this process – above all the destruction of spiritual and sensuous values – threatens to extinguish the subject altogether and deliver what remains to the barbarism of totalitarian administration. The only hope of finding a way out of barbarism lies in the development of the critique (and therefore the self-understanding) of 'enlightened thought'.

While the critical element is certainly itself an aspect of enlightened thought, Adorno and Horkheimer argue that the more advanced the development of the rational-technical world of modern society, the more effectively does that society absorb and defuse all genuinely critical thought and harden itself against any true self-understanding. There is no doubting the efficiency and the effectiveness of this rational-technical machinery. The world we live in is filled with commodities, skyscrapers, jumbo jets and shopping malls; their very existence testifies to the exploitative power of society in its domination of nature; this same exploitative power is reproduced in the relations of social production, in the hierarchical structure of organisations and in the inequalities of social class, gender and ethnicity.

In the classic Marxist conception, material, sinewy labour is subsumed in the abstract equivalence of capitals. The corresponding antagonistic relations and forms of domination appear at the level of thought. Hierarchy and subsumption define the systems of generalising abstraction through which experience is 'brought to mind'. The shiny, wet-nosed, jumping-up form that we call 'dog' is subsumed within the class of canines, then the class of mammals, the class of living things and so forth. With each step up the ladder of hierarchy we move towards more and more comprehensive levels of ordering, towards 'totality'. The 'violence' of the process is to be seen in the 'systematic' destruction of sensuous particulars, of the specifics, elements or details and their 'subsumption' within an abstract totality.

> Abstraction, the tool of the enlightenment, treats its objects as did fate, the notion of which it rejects: it liquidates them. Under the levelling domination of abstraction (which makes everything in nature repeatable), and of industry (for which abstraction ordains repetition), the freedoms themselves finally come to form that 'herd' which Hegel has declared to be the result of the Enlightenment.
> (T. Adorno and M. Horkheimer 1986: 13)

Because this same subsumption of particulars is the very form of so-called scientific and rational language – a language that corresponds to a particular stage in the development of social production – critical thought must turn itself into the critique of the very language through which it is advanced, not just at the level of natural language but also the languages of the arts. In music this can only serve to produce the discomforting fragmentation, the lacunae and discontinuities that one finds in modern musical language since late Beethoven (T. Adorno 1993: 102–7).

Making music from congealed history

The composer works with *inherited* musical structures, with 'historical' forms that are the building blocks of the musical culture into which s/he is initiated. These building blocks consist of such things as, for example, the principles of 'tonal' music, accepted practices in harmony, counterpoint, homophony, polyphony and so forth (T. Adorno 1994d: 281). They are the cumulative results of a long process of historical development. No matter how individually creative a composer such as Mozart may have been, he still composed music in a way that was recognisably similar to the music of his contemporaries. In Adorno's formulation, therefore, the musical material with which the composer works is both 'congealed history' and 'language' and the business of composition itself has to be seen as an historical process, a dynamic engagement with history. Far from being free to combine sounds at will, Adorno's composer entered into the further historical development of the already historically formed musical material which he inherited from his predecessors. Thus a twentieth-century composer such as Schoenberg grappled with the particular problems of developing the *musical material* he inherited from nineteenth-century composers in the Viennese classical tradition, such as Beethoven, Brahms and Wagner, with bringing its inherent possibilities to fulfilment and realising a more complete, a more total domination of the material. He therefore took an active part in a project that was as social and as objective as it was historical.

The drama of part–whole relations

In painting and in literature it is frequently possible to discuss the integrity of the work in terms of its representation of something, its correspondence with an external reality. In modern abstract painting, where that may appear to be less relevant, painting is seen as allied less to literature and more to music, which provides an ideal with which many modernist art projects had an affinity. The truth of music seems to be more bound up with the integrity of its own internal relations, its structural integrity. For Adorno, the dream of truth and integrity is to be sought here, in the structure of music. As Rose Subotnik puts it:

> In an age of disintegrating artistic and moral consensus, the musical structure becomes a perfect paradigm for the concept of integrity, in the sense not only of wholeness but also of honesty based on inner conviction. . . . Given the theoretical incorruptibility of self-knowl-edge, the individualistic structure, such as the musical artwork, came to seem the last remaining safeguard for the possibility of integrity in society.
>
> (R. Subotnik 1990: 268)

This integrity was seen by Adorno in terms of an 'isomorphism' between the structural condition of society and that of the art work. Commenting on the similarity between the form of the drama and that of the sonata, Adorno writes:

> The sense in which a drama, a sonata-like product of the bourgeois era, is said to be crafted – i.e. composed of tiny motifs that are objectified by dynamic synthesis – has echoes of commodity production. The link between technical-artistic procedures of this kind and material ones belonging to the industrial era is obvious, although it has remained obscured thus far.
>
> (T. Adorno 1984: 317)

Elements and relations and events within the musical work, the drama of its development and so forth, can be seen as having their counterparts at the level of social systems. Most obviously, the units, elements or 'motives' in the music can be identified with the individuals who make up a society, while the totality comprising the composition can be seen to correspond to society. Just as individuals can be spontaneous, subjective beings expressing themselves – and therefore objectifying their 'inner experience' – in their actions and relations with others, so society can be seen as an external and objective force which organises the actions of individuals from the outside. The same contrast between an expressive subjectivity and an external rationalising power can be drawn in respect of the arts. In music, the drama of part—whole relations is seen by Adorno in terms of the equilibration of two distinct processes, *mimesis* and *construction* (T. Adorno 1984: 65). The mimetic element in art is identified with the expressive impulse, with the reciprocity and primitive sympathy with which the subject discovers itself in outer forms, in objects. Mimesis is the process by which the sensuous experience of the subject seeks to assimilate objects, discovering their likeness in itself. By construction, Adorno refers to the external power of organisation, to the process by which sensuous elements are structured from the outside, as it were, and thereby made to correspond with objects. The playful and the imaginative are associated with mimesis, while the drive to conformity is associated with construction.

Modern society was seen by Max Weber as increasingly dominated by rational-technical organisation, of which the development of bureaucracy was an instance. The more the power of objective organisation garnered by the collective machinery of administration, the less room is there for the subject and the less tolerance for subjective expression. Thus, at the social level, modernity is associated with an excess of external force, of rationalising power, over subjectivity and expression. Modern music, too, precisely because it is grounded in modern society, must also manifest – as it does, for example, in serialism or in neo-classicism – an excess of construction over mimesis, of outer force over inner expression. Adorno gives this manifestation a special twist, however. He distinguishes between modern music which surrenders to this external domination of the subject and modern music which uses that domination as a means of expressing the suffering of the subject affected by it – in the latter case, *mimesis in and through construction*.

Hierarchy and privilege can describe structures in music as well as society. In homophonic music it is the melody that can be seen as privileged, with all the other musical elements working in harmony to support it. Counterpoint, on the other hand, preserves the independence of melodies that work together and against each other; polyphonic music might be seen as a 'democratic' interaction of individual musical subjects; hierarchy, power and privilege can be seen as present, too, in the formation of the musical material, in the themes and larger forms and in the subordination of the motives and details within the work. The orchestra itself, with its hierarchies and its privileging of certain instruments over others, can be described in these terms. And then there is the role of the conductor, who becomes the commanding presence and symbol of order. Adorno did not hesitate to draw an analogy here between the modern conductor of the orchestra and 'the Führer'.

This is not just a convenient language or set of metaphors with which to refer to musical processes. Adorno really means something much stronger than that: music is a social praxis, a mode of agency which participates in the same degree and kind of technical development as social praxis generally.

The organisation of social production, in mass assembly factories for example, represents a particular development of the technical division and organisation of labour, one in which the exploitation of nature and material has advanced to such a degree that the total mastery of the constituent elements – individual workers and work itself – can be clearly anticipated. Music that is made in such a society also tends to the same rational-technical mastery of its constituent elements, to the same ubiquitous constructivism. Thus, if modern social structures are increasingly rational-technical in character, as Weber argues, then modern music has this character, too. If factory production and the micro-division of labour reduce individuals to fragmentary beings, mere cogs, dividing labour by a process of endless fissiparous differentiation, then we should not be surprised to discover that there is an analogous process of fragmentation which occurs in modern music. Here, too, as in modernist art and literature, there is a relentless process of fragmentation. Thus, Adorno's notion of homology identifies the correspondence between music and society as occurring at a morphological level – the 'elective affinity' between them is primarily one of structure rather than content, and of formal means rather than substantive ends. Likeness to society can therefore be exploited in music to realise opposition to society.

Modern classical music, especially the music of Berg and Schoenberg, provided Adorno with his theoretical keystone. He saw modernist works of art and of music as 'autonomous' constructions, distanced from the functional demands and the practical concerns of everyday life. The subjective life of the individual was seen by Adorno as trivialised and corrupted by the instrumentalities of capitalist market society. Modernist music, in its innermost cells, reproduced the monolithic force of modern society as refracted in the sufferings of a life process wrecked by it. In music, the condition and 'suffering' of the subject could find a vehicle for expressing itself, for achieving 'wholeness', for perfecting its self-understanding. To the extent that a work of music achieved this, it constituted a critique of society and it did so, immanently, *by virtue of what it was in and of itself* and not through any attempt on its part to criticise society or to propagandise it. In this sense, music's 'likeness' to society has to be seen, paradoxically, as underpinning its function as critique of society.

Adorno's very notion of truth in music derives from his claim that the structural 'drama' of part–whole relations in music should reflect the objective condition of the individual subject in society. The fate of the elements, the musical details, 'motives' and 'themes' within the totality of the work, becomes a kind of formal analogue of the condition of the individual subject in society. The system of rational-technical domination was one in which the individual subject was both isolated and alienated, cut off from all meaningful sources of action and expression. Lacking the means of positive fulfilment in the world, the subject could nevertheless turn this lack, this wrecked life, into expression in modern music.

In Adorno's theory, music is like society in its appropriation of technical means, and it is the antithesis of society in its deployment of those means to express the suffering (and disclose the true condition) of the subject in the modern world. The rational-technical organisation of society, in Adorno's perspective, has reduced life to market relations and exchange values and corrupted all purely human relations; music appropriates the same rational-technical organisational means in composition, but for the pursuit of its own very different ends. In the best modern music, the awful force of technological administered society is made to express the subject who suffers its absurdity, fragmentation and meaninglessness and yet who somehow endures, somehow resists being absorbed, refuses identity. The clarity and objectivity with which this suffering and this endurance is realised in music demands the most technically advanced use of musical means. It is this same advanced development of technical means – appropriated as a language of suffering – which sets modern serious music in an antithetical relationship to modern society.

Musica moralia

There is no dream that Adorno opposed more vehemently than the dream of purity in all its varied forms. The totalitarian ideology of the Nazi period in Germany, in which so many of his generation lived, was the darkest manifestation of this dream. Its roots go deep into the heart of European culture, a fact that is acknowledged in Adorno and Horkheimer's critique of the Enlightenment. The rise of Fascist political forms was not the only manifestation in modern society of the purity dream (or nightmare, according to one's point of view). The belief in the possibility of the completely objective and rational control of the labour process inherent in the ideology of Taylorism/Fordism was another. The similar and associated notion of a rational-technical administrative machinery – bureaucracy – which would be free of any arbitrary or subjective element was a third; we can add, too, the vast impersonal machineries of economic life that made up the atomised metropolis as a fourth. In all of them, the project of purity demanded the annihilation of the subjective, personal and arbitrary element in human affairs in favour of an external, objective and rational-technical force. In each of them the 'agentic' individual is confronted by an overwhelming organising force – objective, impersonal and collective. The ideal of purity is realised to the extent that this ideal-typical individual manifests in thought and action the programme projected in that organising force, behaving exactly as s/he is required to behave without succumbing to arbitrary, subjective or non-rational impulse. Purity resides in the utter clarity with which this totally socialised, totally programmed being functions as a cog in this vast machinery. It is the horror of such a future that has motivated some of the best-known literary distopias of the century, such as Huxley's *Brave*

New World or Orwell's *1984*. Impurity, by contrast, resides in subjectivity, in the non-rational, in any free choice, spontaneity or act of will or whim on the part of the subject.

The dream of purity is not new, nor is it restricted to modern societies, but it has recurred in widely disparate societies at quite different levels of technological development; it does not necessarily or typically take the forms referred to above. However, taken together, the four manifestations of the dream of purity referred to here (totalitarianism, scientific management, bureaucracy and the metropolis) make up the oppressive force of a modernity against which the modernist subject has struggled to survive. The technical and structural features of these manifestations are key to appreciating Adorno's analysis of modern music, even though he himself never attempted to formulate them in a systematic way.

Totalitarian society   The totalitarian dictatorships established in the second and third decades of the century, in Nazi Germany and Stalinist Russia, provided powerful images of social control. Moreover, it was a mode of social control in which the state, its ideology and its leader sought a monopoly over the production of culture and the power to define situations or construct social and personal identities (Hannah Arendt 1973).

Structurally, the reality of a Fascist or totalitarian society approximates to the ideal of a society mobilised as a unitary and focused crowd of co-actional but not inter-actional (and therefore de-individuated) individuals. The Nuremberg rallies of the 1930s concretely manifested such an ideal. In contrast, the ideal of a pluralist society or a liberal democracy is one in which individuals are members of multiple reference groups – families, trades unions, work groups, golf clubs, learned societies, working men's clubs and voluntary associations and special interest groups of all kinds – in and through which they construct their identities as individuals. These cross-cutting memberships vary in some degree from person to person and are the basis of individuation and social differentiation. The multiplicity of groups in which these memberships are held are themselves elements or parts in the construction of the larger society. The specific identities of each individual are therefore constructed as configurations of the general – that is, as specific configurations of relations among the various groups in which they are members and which are themselves constitutive parts of a larger social order. The principle of centricity here is easily identified, at a formal level, with that governing part–whole relations in tonal music.

A totalitarian society is one which aims at the systematic destruction of all such sources of independent and multiple reference for the construction of personal identities. Ideal-typically, such a society sets out to destroy or to infiltrate and permeate all groups that mediate the individual's relationship to the state and to the totalitarian ideology. The (impossible) end of such an ideal is a situation in which every individual is isolated from every other individual, each with a precise value and location in a relational scheme ordained by the state and prefigured in its ideology. Each individual becomes indifferent to others (as individuals) and is no longer connected to them by 'organic' relations. Devoid of spontaneity, mechanically programmed and co-ordinated; all such individuals become atomised and rendered susceptible to the overwhelming force of total organisation. Adorno's critique of certain modern composers centred on disclosing the totalitarian tendencies in the music that were associated with the dream of a pure music. He found them not only in the musical movements he opposed, such as neo-classicism or jazz, but even in key developments in the music of composers he admired, such as Schoenberg.

The industrial division of labour   The same period in which totalitarian dictatorships emerged saw the development of industrial organisations of great size and complexity. It was the time of the worldwide dissemination of Taylorist 'principles of scientific management'. Industry was developing a micro-division of labour in which the mental and spiritual component – conception, design and initiative – was being stripped out of the work process. The operations left to each worker were a mere fragment of the previous task. Taken to its extreme, as it was in the case of Fordism, such a process radically de-sociates as well as de-skills the work process. It might have been claimed, in an earlier society, that work mediated social relations in a meaningful way. However, in a Fordist world, work could no longer support any such meaningful mediation. Drained of meaningful mental content, of the power of self-direction, of autonomous responsibility, of creative self-expression, work becomes subject to the mechanistic ordering and direction of a monolithic organisational machinery. This image – *qua* image – shades easily into that of the totalitarian society described above, as do its analogues in respect of modern music.

   For many intellectuals, the industrial system imaged the disaster facing a subject whose possibilities for meaningful social life were being reduced to rubble by the outwardly rational and progressive development of the technical forces of production. Such a view of the industrial order recurs as a kind of sociological 'motive' in Adorno's studies of music. It is there, too, in the work of his most admired composer, Schoenberg. The latter makes it the subject of his music drama, *Die Glückliche Hand*. In the third scene of the drama, the workers are shown performing their different tasks. The hero has discovered a way to make jewellery more simply. The workers turn on him. The situation is paradigmatic. Technological progress weakens the power of the workers; it threatens their jobs and they resist. Adorno comments:

> Chaos defines the law according to which market-society blindly reproduces, with no consideration for the individual. It includes the continuing growth of power in the hands of those in command over

all others. The world is chaotic in the eyes of the victims of the law of market value and industrial concentration. But the world is not chaotic 'in itself'. It is the individual – oppressed inexorably by the principles of this world – who considers it such.

(T. Adorno 1980: 44–5)

Rational-technical administration (bureaucracy)   A third and related source of imagery that Adorno drew upon was that of the administrative apparatus – the image of rational-technical bureaucracy – as depicted so starkly by Kafka in 'The Castle' and 'The Trial' and analysed sociologically by Weber. Adorno frequently refers to the condition of modern society as 'totally administered'. Everywhere, at this time, one could observe the growth of office space, of huge concrete and glass structures filled with armies of people dressed more or less alike and working with the endlessly proliferating paper, filing cabinets, formal rules and regulations, and so forth. If the image of the industrial process depicted the separation of intelligence, initiative and control from the worker, the image of the bureaucracy celebrated the impersonality of officials, the expropriation of the personal and private life of the individual from the means of administration, the subordination of the fragmentary individual to the chaotic and insane domination of a rational-technical machinery.

The image describes the situation of the functionary in an administrative order from which the sensuous life has been virtually expunged. Depersonalisation and objectification, a reduction of the compass of life's concerns to the pettiness of administrative routines, a growing submission to the power of algorithms and systems of formal rules, all are consequences of the development of such administrative machineries. Again, the image dovetails into those of the totalitarian society and the division of industrial labour, and with the same associations at the level of musical structure.

The metropolis   A final source of imagery was provided by the vision of the metropolis and of metropolitan life, an image explored by Fritz Lang in his film *Metropolis* and theorised by Georg Simmel in his essay 'The Metropolis and Mental Life', an image of the loneliness of individuals in close proximity to others who remain oblivious of their existence – proximity without interaction or meaningful relationship. The city is also the site of dirt, poverty, disease and pollution, the detritus heaped up on the boundaries of its clock-governed, synchronised and impersonal order. Simmel captures the growing impersonality of city dwellers, their fragmentation in the labour process, their obedience to the demands of a vast system of clocks and timetables. The blasé attitude of the city dweller, his or her social indifference to most others, the growth of cognitive calculation, the reduction of life to 'averaging, calculating and weighing', all are clearly identified by Simmel with the growth of a money economy and a construction of life that follows the flow of money rather than the flow of the seasons (G. Simmel 1950). The same, too, can be said of the loneliness of the metropolis, captured in Reismann's phrase 'the lonely crowd'. The disruption and disorganisation of personal and communal relations in the city was a theme of urban sociology in the early decades of the century. The new metropolis was founded on the decaying of traditional patterns of association and ordering. What was true of the new metropolis was true also of its new music. Traditional tonal means of organisation were being undermined and the residues of tonal structures in the work of modern composers were gradually being eliminated.

Each of these images is dark, and together they construct modern society as a vision of bleakness, a wasteland, as a ruin or disaster-in-the-making. For Adorno, a modernist music could not ignore this oppressive force, could not pretend it did not exist or seek to bypass it as some twentieth-century composers had done. If music was to have truth-value it must take this rationalising, objectifying force into itself and draw from it an expression of the condition of the human subject so disfigured by it. This was the task of all the authentic works of modernist art from the time of Beethoven's late style. Modern music, in Adorno's philosophy, takes disaster into itself. It inscribes it in music, finds its structural analogues in music; music becomes a means for envisioning disaster, for truthfully perceiving it. In doing so, modern music approaches true knowledge; it eschews all illusion and declines to provide, as had an earlier art, consolation for this 'vale of tears'.

> The shocks of incomprehension, emitted by artistic technique in the age of its meaninglessness, undergo a sudden change. They illuminate the meaningless world. Modern music sacrifices itself to this effort. It has taken upon itself all the darkness and guilt of the world. Its fortune lies in the perception of misfortune; all of its beauty is in denying itself the illusion of beauty . . . modern music sees absolute oblivion as its goal. It is the surviving message of despair from the shipwrecked.
>
> (T. Adorno 1980: 133)

To take these oppressive forces into the work of art was to gain the type of rational-technical control over the elements of musical material that the machineries of modern production had over those who worked in them. Such rational-technical control over the material easily led to the temptation to install the dream of purity itself at the heart of the art work, to make music itself pure, objective and rational, like mathematics, and unsullied by any real subjective expression or intentionality. That, for Adorno, would be a betrayal of the subject and of all authentic expression, a capitulation of art to the forces of oppression. Some of the complexities of Adorno's work are to be found in the fact that his critical thought is engaged in doing battle on more than one front at a time. His enemies are not only without; they are within, too. Where they explicitly espouse the ideal of purity as a project, they are more readily identified and opposed. Stravinsky and the neo-classicist composers espoused a philosophy and musical praxis which Adorno abhorred. He made Stravinsky the pivotal antagonist – in his *Philosophy of Modern Music* (1980) – to Schoenberg, whose music he saw as profound and progressive. However, it is impossible to read Adorno's discussion of Schoenberg, both in that book and elsewhere, or the treatment of Schoenberg's twelve-tone system in Thomas Mann's *Doctor Faustus* (for which Adorno was the musical adviser), without realising that Adorno sensed and feared the presence of the same oppressive forces and the same capitulation to the dream of purity behind Schoenberg's revolution in modern music. Of course he did not attribute such a project to the purposes of the 'revered master' himself, nor to Schoenberg's own use of his technical discoveries in his compositions, but rather to the dreams of purity to which his twelve-tone technique gave rise, and also to what he perceived as the inherent limitations of the technique: its destructiveness of a genuine spontaneity, historicity and expressivity (see Chapter 7).

Simmel had described the personality of the city dweller as calculative, rational and instrumental; these characteristics had evolved at the expense of the sensuous and emotional life which had become in some sense impoverished. As Wordsworth put it, 'Getting and spending, we lay waste our powers'. The metropolitan man or woman resists this spiritual impoverishment and struggles against becoming a mere object, a mere cog in a machine. It is this inner resistance which causes the city dweller to cultivate personality and distinctiveness, to project an image of himself or herself as a sensuous subject, as being something other than a mere object. Fashion, style, trendiness, personal exaggeration and the cult of personality become important here (G. Simmel 1950). The city dweller is drawn, too, to the embrace of the subjectivist literatures, those that valorise the subject confirming that s/he is absolutely significant, the existentialist and phenomenological literatures.

As the creature of the system, an 'element' or cog in modern production processes, each man or woman is an object rather than a subject, with little freedom of action; but as a consumer, a private individual, enjoying interpersonal relations, leisure time and so forth, each man or woman can fancy himself or herself to be a free, choosing subject. The products of the culture industry flatter this fancy, this sense of sensuous being as 'authentic', as being in possession of itself. It is necessary to arouse and reinforce sensuous subjectivity continuously in order to sell everything from toilet paper to cars. The culture industries organise, through their effects, the sensuous body of the subject; they shape belief in the possibilities of a meaningful sensuous life which is not available to the subject in the spaces of social production. All can be called in aid – the wailing of saxophones, the brushing of timpani, the rhythms of the night and of the leisure spaces of bourgeois society.

This rupture between subject and object threatens the moral integrity of the individual; there are terrors enough for a subject who confronts in himself a world that is no longer his world. Such a subject is not a complete or full subject, one that is at home in the world – that is, one whose spiritual integrity is grounded in society. There is a moral choice to be made here: either one can face up to one's responsibility to struggle with the world, to be fully historical, or one can retreat into a so-called realm of pure subjectivity – a realm in which Adorno located the products of the culture industry no less than those of so-called serious art and music and modern subjectivist philosophies. For Adorno, to choose the latter was to abdicate from responsibility for the world; it was a cowardly way out of the demands of becoming historical under modern conditions. The choice extended from the praxis of everyday life to the praxis of the arts. In Adorno's *musica moralia*, it was a matter of choosing life or choosing death. If he could not acknowledge the existence of heaven, he was certain about hell; neo-classical music, jazz, Toscanini and existentialism were among the routes to it.

When Adorno turned his critical knife on Stravinsky it was to accuse him of siding, in his music, with the dominating force of society which would extinguish the individual and annihilate the expressive life. In setting himself against 'the filthy tide' of popular music and the claims of jazz music, the same considerations are to the fore: music can either be a force for truth or it can be an instrument of repression and concealed domination. Society as a moral agency and the problematics of moral action have always been important topics for sociology as a discipline; with Adorno, they are absolutely central. In him, a keen sociological insight is an integral part of a critical moral philosophy.

Domination is not, of course, restricted to the domination of capitalist societies. Rather, antagonistic relations are more or less endemic in some degree in all societies which must struggle for self-preservation. Domination is intensified in the modern world because the instrumental aspect has, for the first time, broken free from the spiritual and sensuous life of community. This is reflected in the growing independence of the economic sphere in which, for the first time, it becomes possible to conceive of all 'values' as subject only to rational calculation. The very character of domination and exploitation, which constitutes the external relationship of society to nature, is reproduced in the specialisation of individuals in the division of labour and in the hierarchies through which the labour of the masses is exploited by the few. This same division of labour reproduces itself at the level of the knowledge systems – the division into specialised disciplines – which supply the consciousness through which society reproduces and develops itself. The latter, too, are organised hierarchically.

Implicit in the hierarchy of knowledge systems is the claim of superiority for 'scientific' knowledge – objectivity, facticity, rationality – over all other types of knowledge. Such a claim reflects the dominance of an autonomous economic and instrumental sphere over, for example, the aesthetic and the spiritual. This same domination reproduces itself at the level of the consciousness of the individual; it is constitutive of his or her personality, as Simmel argued (G. Simmel 1950). The strong boundary between work and leisure, between home and work, between production and consumption, is instantiated, at the level of consciousness, in the separation between on the one hand the cognitive, instrumental, conformist and blasé attitude of the city dweller, who fits like a cog into a vast machinery, and, on the other, the city dweller's indulgence of a cult of personality, a 'show business' outlook on life and, intellectually, an increased concern with the problem of subjectivity, together with a partiality for existentialist philosophies and all varieties of radical individualism.

In Adorno's sociology, however, this cult of personality, of the sensuous life and of subjectivity is not the antidote to calculative and instrumental rationality but one of its deadly manifestations. The calculative rationality of capitalism turns its instrumentalism upon the sensuous life of the subject, transforming all sensuous values and meanings into 'motives' (the terminology and description is mine but the meaning is consistent with Adorno's). The spiritual, sensuous and expressive life of the individual, which is felt as the 'within' of the subject – true sociality, genuine reciprocity – finds its compass squeezed until it is actually threatened with extinction. It is progressively appropriated by the rational-technical machinery of modern society and instrumentalised. The spiritual life of whole communities is quickly reduced to the 'motives' and manufactured needs of individuals, to the 'affects' that can be produced in the 'bodies' of individuals through the impact of commodities, pop music, mass culture, propaganda; that is, through the application of external force, the corporeal disciplines of an objective, collective 'without' that impinges upon the individual.

The body of the individual and its 'needs' come to assume a special significance in the instrumentalisation of all life. The body can be made to 'feel', to register the implosive force of a stimulus. In contrast, true sociality is always expressive. It is the spark of reciprocity through which the subject, immersed in social relations, brings social life bodying forth 'from within'. Instrumentalism reverses the direction of force in the sensuous life; it delivers the subject into the power of a totalitarian and external collective; it is de-sociating and, as such, reduces the sensuous life of the individual to a 'manufactured' affectivity – that is, to an abstract subjectivity. When Adorno rails against the products of the culture industry, against jazz and popular music, he is thinking of them in some such relationship to the individual, as manifestations of objective and external force, as oriented to the bringing about of affects in the body of the subject and as undermining the subject at the level of the latter's expressive agency.

Nominalist philosophies and individuated societies

The line of social development in Adorno's sociology is consistent with the dominant ideas of classical sociology. Society becomes progressively individuated. The locus of order, in social action and social organisation, shifts from the level of the collectivity to that of the individual. Such a development is one which increasingly emphasises the primacy of the parts, the individuals, the particulars or details, in realising the whole. Corresponding to this progressive individuation of society is the rise of Nominalist philosophies and epistemologies – e.g. existentialism and phenomenology. These, too, seek to absolutise the subject, which then ceases to be a relational structure constituted through interaction with others and becomes, instead, an 'in-itself', its claim to 'authentic being' resting upon the extent to which it is autochthonous and entirely and sovereignly at its own disposal, free of all determination by others. This Nominalist disintegration culminates, for him, in the advance of various twentieth-century philosophies, most noticeably existentialist and phenomenological philosophies such as those of Husserl, Heidegger and Kierkegaard. The retreat of these philosophies into some (false) in-itself being or subjectivity was the same process of fragmentation and cultural pathology that he saw occurring in some forms of modern music.

> Authenticity is ascribed to the being-a-subject of the subject, not to the subject as a relational factor. . . . The findings of Heidegger's existential analysis, according to which the subject is authentic insofar as it possesses itself, grant special praise to the person who is sovereignly at his own disposal; as though he were his own property; he has to have bearing, which is at the same time an internalisation, and an apotheosis of the principle of domination over nature. . . . Subjectivity, Dasein itself, is sought in the absolute disposal of the individual over himself, without regard to the fact that he is caught up in a determining objectivity.
>
> (T. Adorno 1973: 127–8)

Adorno reserves some of his most trenchant criticism for those whom he sees as the purveyors of what he terms the 'jargon of authenticity'. He tackles it in some of its most advanced intellectual formulations, for example the philosophies of Kierkegaard and of Heidegger. While these intellectual constructions may seem light years away from the problems of jazz or the 'variety act', they are clearly connected in Adorno's analysis. They, too, are oriented to the reduction of the individual to an abstract or pure subjectivity, to a complete disjunction of subject and object.

True subjectivity for Adorno is always an historically constituted subjectivity. It is a subjectivity in which subject and object, individual and society, mediate one another, constitute one another; there is no realm of pure subjectivity which is 'in-itself' and distinct and different from its objects; subject and object tango together in history but not without a struggle for hegemony, not without one or other appearing, sometimes, to get the upper hand – more subjectification, more objectification, etc. Because its mode of becoming is in and through a dialectical relationship with its objects, such a mediated subjectivity is always able to ensure – through the possession of a critical and discriminating 'distance' from its objects – that it is not assimilated or overcome by them. In the very process of actively mediating (and being mediated by) its objects – in being historical – the subject continuously realises its own non-identity which, for Adorno, is the ground of its becoming, its freedom, autonomy and spiritual integrity. The more that the subject seeks to de-sociate itself, to empty itself, the less does it possess within itself the wherewithal to resist the total domination of the 'external' – that is, the domination of the collectivity – and the more it gives itself over to the latter in an act of self-immolation.

In Adorno's view, philosophies such as Heidegger's and Kierkegaard's – philosophies which seek to lay claim to some privileged realm of subjectivity, to carve out a space outside of historical entanglement, under the illusion that they thereby attain to self-possession, *authentic being* and an enrichment of the life of the subject – are, in reality, an impoverishment of subjectivity. They represent the subject's loss of all power to hold its distance from the world and, through its lack of mediated relations with objects, the loss of its power to change the world and be changed by it. At one pole, this 'pure' subjectivity engenders an identity of the innate principles of reasoning with the 'in-it-selfness', of mind (absolute idealism). At the other pole, subjectivity surrenders itself to the 'in-it-selfness' of the facts (positivism). In either case, the free historical individual is lost.

When Adorno lines up his champions of truth in music against the enemies of that truth, it is on the basis of that same dark choice between a music that, he claims, truly reflects the human condition – a music that is the result of an historically constituted and mediated social praxis, a music which refuses identity and resists oppression – and a music which seeks to escape from entanglements, to lay claim to an unmediated realm of pure musical experience and which, whether it retreats into inwardness or escapes into outwardness, is a music which collaborates with oppression. In a world in which the spiritual, sensuous and expressive life of the subject is so threatened – and with it, all true sociality – the serious artist assumes a special significance. A 're-valuing' of experience under the conditions of barbarism, a re-sociation of life, becomes the special province of the artist in the modern world.

Serious art is never secure in Adorno's modernity; it is an organ of truth but it is beset with corrupting forces on all sides. Modern art is subject to the division of labour which assigns to the artist the role of being an autonomous own-account worker – an entrepreneur of 'sensibility' – and in that role banishes him to the periphery of the institutional order of modern society. Thus, the division of labour sets the modern artist free and thereby places him or her in a critical relationship to society, and yet, in the same moment, renders art inconsequential, as no longer of any importance in the praxis of everyday life. Even so, society does not truly leave the artist to his or her own devices. There is always social pressure to subvert or divert art into serving the goals of mass culture and the culture industry. Late capitalist society has an endless capacity to absorb criticism, even to indulge it as 'style'. Corruption and infection are ubiquitous and demand an ever-sharpened critical philosophy in order to combat them. Precisely because the artist is an own-account worker, dependent for a living upon selling art works in the market, s/he must sup with the devil using a spoon that is never quite long enough to ensure s/he remains out of reach. Moreover, art, both as practice and as product, is an embodiment of the division of mental from manual labour; insofar as art seeks to spirit away its origins in labour and to pass itself off as a self-contained world of spirit, it partakes of the 'magical' character of the commodity.

Adorno's commitment to struggle in the face of what appeared to be almost certain defeat seems to justify the label 'tragic' that Gillian Rose has attached to Adorno's vision (G. Rose 1978). Certainly, such a reading can be recovered from Adorno's writings. I would suggest that a different reading of Adorno's posture can also be justified. Adorno's pessimism is everywhere in evidence but I do not perceive it as 'tragic'. It makes as much sense to me to see this extraordinarily resourceful and restless thinker as sharing some of the characteristics of a modern Odysseus, rather than as a tragic hero or as a Cassandra prophesying doom. A pessimistic Odysseus, perhaps, and yet I cannot read his late essays without feeling that the memory of Ithaca is strong. He is sometimes dispirited and he is often far-seeing, concerning the dangers ahead. But he *does* seek to steer around them, to find a way through; he never gives up believing that the knot can be undone, the disaster overcome and the ship steered back on course. In this he is quite unlike the tragic hero. The latter follows the relentless path laid out for him by destiny and crashes – 'the all against the all'. Even as a composer, Adorno did no such thing. He saw the price of progress and chose not to pay it. He did not follow Schoenberg into the rigours of twelve-tone method, and it is clear from his late essays (T. Adorno 1994d) that he continued, with all the 'cunning' of an Odysseus, to seek a way to liberate music without enslaving it.

2

SOCIETY IN SONATA-FORM

The texts of novels or plays would appear, on the surface, to offer more obvious possibilities for sociological analysis than do musical compositions. The biographical unfolding of individual lives in a social context is at the heart of the classical conception of the novel as a bourgeois form. Even closer to the construction of real social action is classical bourgeois theatre which achieved the zenith of its development in the nineteenth-century proscenium arch 'theatre of illusion'. The play comes complete and self-contained with its own lighting and simulates a slice of real social interaction *as though* the world shown was made up of real individuals, living their social lives and developing as historical personalities in real time. Where the nineteenth-century novel or play is concerned, there seems to be genuine common ground between the sociologist and the writer. The novels of Balzac are filled with the fine detail of Parisian bourgeois life, with meticulous accounts of hundreds of different occupations, of a teeming division of social labour. It is little wonder that many described Balzac's method as sociological, and social theorists such as Engels and Lukács have praised it as a model for a socially progressive literature (G. Lukács 1972).

The sonata was the predominant form in which instrumental music developed at the time of Balzac and the rise of the novel. The great symphonies of Haydn, Mozart and Beethoven can be thought of as large-scale sonatas for orchestra. The sonata does not describe and sociologise, as does the novel. It is true that some music occasionally invokes literal associations – the sound of cannon in the *1812 Overture* by Tchaikovsky or the cuckoo in Beethoven's 'Pastoral' symphony; also, music may sometimes bind itself to a given literary text such as the tone poems of Richard Strauss or narrative music such as Prokoviev's *Peter and the Wolf*. It is clearly the case that music has a direct power to be 'affecting', to 'simulate' mood, sensation and emotional tension, to bring the sensuous constitution of the subject 'to mind'. However, for all its associations and allusions, music has none of the power of concrete 'object' representation that literature possesses. If the 'sonata-symphony' is to be equated with the novel as a powerful means of inscribing social relations, the key to this equation is to be found in the *form* of the sonata, in its structural relations. Moreover, in Adorno's sociology of music, the morphology of sonata-form – like the morphology of the novel-form in Lukács's sociology – is directly linked to the structure of bourgeois society. It is the highest development of the sonata-form as achieved by Beethoven in his middle-period compositions which provides Adorno with the perspective from which he views the subsequent development of music in the twentieth century (T. Adorno 1994c).

In his *Analytical Study of the NBC Musical Appreciation Hour*, Adorno criticises the material published by NBC in 1939–40 in connection with a popular weekly radio programme which was aimed at developing musical appreciation in the young (T. Adorno 1994b). Here, where he seeks to prescribe a better pedagogical approach than the one used in the programme, his own views on the classical music tradition are formulated simply and clearly. In the following passage he objects to the teaching of music in a way which puts the principal emphasis on the themes which appear in the music without seeing those themes dynamically in terms of the part they play in the development of the composition as a whole. For Adorno, even a complex composition can be shown to have developed from the varied repetition and juxtaposition of a very few simple elements. The conjunction of overall unity (totality) and manifold diversity is the problematic which recurs throughout Adorno's analyses. It is nowhere more simply expressed than here, when he is imagining putting the matter for children:

> The following method is suggested: Play or sing some well known nursery rhyme such as 'London Bridge is Falling Down'. The children are able to follow the tune as a whole and to memorise it very easily. It would probably never occur to them that it has a 'theme' as distinguished from the development. *The next step is to analyse the tune and show that it is developed out of one fundamental motive which is repeated, varied, and so on, and show concretely how this is done* [emphasis mine]. Then explain that a symphonic movement follows fundamentally the same line, and that a symphonic theme basically plays no other role than the 'motive' does in the nursery rhyme. Of course the concept of theme from the very beginning would appear here, too, but only as a mere *material* of the movement and not as its aim or essence. What must be strictly avoided is the idea that serious music fundamentally consists of important 'themes' with something more or less unimportant between them.
>
> (T. Adorno 1994b: 332)

The fundamental unit or element of a musical composition is usually referred to as a 'motive'. It might consist of a striking chord or a rhythmic pattern or a brief recurring succession of notes as, for example, the famous opening notes of Beethoven's Fifth Symphony. The basic motives of a composition, such as those of a Beethoven sonata or symphony, are then repeated and varied in different ways: for example rhythmically, harmonically, through juxtaposition, inversion, modulation, melodic decoration, timbral changes and so forth. The composition as a whole is thus thematically *developed* through *repetition* and *variation* of the basic motives of which it is constituted. These terms – 'motive', 'theme', 'repetition', 'variation', 'development' – are all key concepts in Adorno's sociology of music. In his analysis, a composition in the European classical tradition – as exemplified by a Beethoven symphony – is seen as developing out of simple elements (motives) through a process involving repetition, variation and juxtaposition of such motives. This developmental process appears to proceed spontaneously and freely as though determined immanently from below (rather than transcendentally from above); that is, the composition appears to be the outcome of the free movement of the elements themselves.

But where can we locate 'society' or the 'individual' in the sonata? Because the 'thematic particles' – the motives – of a Beethoven symphony all develop into something and are in themselves 'identical' with that development – that 'something' – they become, within his music, *historical* figures. When Adorno analyses a piece of music he identifies the particle, the 'sensuous particular', the element, with the 'individual' or 'subject', and the total form of the composition with 'society' as a 'collective' and 'objective' constraining force. Part–whole relations within a composition thus play a central role in Adorno's musical analyses, and music itself is seen as capable, in its internal relations – its structural relations – of truthfully reflecting the human condition of the individual in society.

In both the novel and the sonata-forms, the 'subject' is marked by its historicity. We might say that, at any moment of existence, the 'subject' of the sonata or of the narrative is what it is by virtue of its 'historicity'; by virtue, that is, of its possessing a development, an unfolding biography or history in and through which its identity is conserved. Moreover, this development of the subject appears to proceed organically out of the subject's relations and encounters in the 'text' and yet to lead, with a certain inevitability, to the conclusion to which it is oriented as its fulfilment; that is, to the completion of its development as its *project*. A 'bourgeois' composer, as the god-creator of texts, whether narrative or musical, can so arrange things that the total structure of the composition appears to develop spontaneously from the basic elements or parts of the composition in their local relations – their juxtapositions, couplings, variations, 'blendings' and 'collidings' with one another within the text – as though this totality was somehow contained in or presupposed by these elements from the outset. For Adorno, it is in Beethoven's development of the sonata-allegri in his middle-period compositions – which include the great symphonies – that the very pinnacle of the bourgeois effort to reconcile individual freedom and collective constraint is achieved in the medium of art. The point has been succinctly made by Rose Subotnik in her pioneering study of Adorno's work on Beethoven:

> 'The musical individual which may be identified variously with the tone, the motif, the theme, or the part for the concert instrument, is able to develop from within itself and to organise the totality of the musical work from the inner dynamics of the participating elements' (quoting Adorno) . . . the principle of form through which Beethoven's second period subject asserts its freedom is that of 'developing variation' as embodied in the development and recapitulation sections of the sonata allegro in which the musical subject demonstrates its autochthony by going out from itself into the generalising world of other or object – through which it demonstrates, in other words, its freedom in objective reality . . . it is through the recapitulation that the subject demonstrates its power to return to itself no matter how far it has travelled . . . through the recapitulation, the subject seems not only to bring together within itself, but actually to derive from within itself, the principles of dynamic development (historical change) and fixed eternal order (unchangeable identity) and to synthesise the two in a higher level of reality.
>
> (R. Subotnik 1976: 248)

This equating of part–whole relations in musical compositions with the mediated relations of 'individual' and 'society' is fundamental in all Adorno's theorising of music. To repeat the formula described above, when Adorno seeks the individual expressive subject in music, he discovers it in the dynamic elements or parts (the motivic-thematic particles) which develop through repetition and variation; against them he sets the totality of the composition, the 'form' to which they give rise and within which they develop and which he equates with the objective (external) collective force of society. Just as the actions of the individual can be totalistically determined from above, in the most authoritarian manner, or can be organised from below through social interaction and negotiation among 'free' individuals, so, in music, the same poles exist in respect of the organisation of the musical 'material' which may be totally constructed from above – Adorno saw pre-classical music in this way – or spontaneously and expressively ordered from below, as (in appearance) was Beethoven's music.

There is a passage in Thomas Mann's novel *Doctor Faustus* in which one character, Kretschmar, plays Beethoven's Piano Sonata Opus 111 for his friends. Mann's prose serves as a fine literary exposition of Adorno's basic idea. Adorno had acted as musical adviser to Thomas Mann in the writing of this novel and had actually played the sonata in a private performance for the author, commenting throughout and in detail on the sonata's structure and development. Mann rewrote his original draft of this passage as a consequence.

> The arietta theme, destined to vicissitudes for which in its idyllic innocence it would seem not to be born, is presented at once, and announced in sixteen bars, reducible to a motive which appears at the end of its first half, like a brief soul-cry – only three notes, a quaver, a semiquaver, and a dotted crotchet to be scanned as, say: 'heav-en's blue, lov-er's pain, fare-thee well, on a-time, mead-ow-land' [meadow-land is a translation of Adorno's patronymic, Wiesengrund] – and that is all. What now happens to this mild utterance, rhythmically, harmonically, contrapuntally, to this pensive, subdued formulation; with what its master blesses and to what condemns it; into what black nights and dazzling flashes, crystal spheres where in coldness and heat, repose and ecstasy are one and the same, he flings it down and lifts it up; all that one may well call vast, strange, extravagantly magnificent, without thereby giving it a name because it is quite truly nameless. . . . Much else happens before the end but when it ends and while it ends, something comes, after so much rage, persistency, obstinacy, extravagance; something entirely unexpected and touching in its mildness and goodness. With the motive passes through many vicissitudes, which takes leave and in so doing becomes itself entirely leave-taking, a parting wave and call, with this DGG occurs a slight change, a small melodic expansion. After an introductory C it puts a C# before the D, so that it no longer scans 'heav-en's blue' 'mead-ow-land', but 'O-thou heaven's blue', 'Greenest meadowland', 'Fare-thee well for aye'; and this added C# is the most moving, consolatory, pathetically reconciling thing in the world.

> (T. Mann 1968: 56–7)

The poet in both Mann and Adorno has no difficulty in theorising this purely instrumental piece of music as having a 'subject', which they identify with the 'motive' that enters into all kinds of relations and undergoes all manner of changes and development – 'the black nights and dazzling flashes' – until it re-emerges, altered and yet the same, reconciled within the composition as a whole and restoring the equilibrium that had been disturbed by the development. It is easy enough to assimilate the idea of such a structural development to the *form* of the novel or of the drama. In a sonata-allegro, the 'main characters' – the principal themes or subjects – are introduced at the outset in the *exposition*; they undergo development through the relations into which they enter in the *development section* and, finally, the tensions generated by these encounters, relations and circumstances are

resolved in the *recapitulation*, a concluding section in which the main characters from the exposition are reintroduced, but with modifications which
reflect the development undergone and the new equilibrium attained. The
recapitulation, through identifying and reconciling part and whole, reinforces our sense of the *historical*, of the transformations undergone by a
subject that remains recognisably itself throughout such changes. The recapitulation affirms *symmetry* – that is, invariance under transformation.

The principle of suspense in the semiotics of bourgeois life

For all his insights into the semiotic construction of texts, Adorno did not
develop a systematic semiotics or a general theory of art and of art styles, one
that can effectively link semiotic developments in art, literature and theatre
as well as music. I have felt it necessary to carry out this constructive work
behind Adorno's back, as it were, in order to make the most effective use of
his own insights.

Adorno's treatment of European tonal music can be seen in the context of
the semiotic revolution that developed in all the arts from the time of the
Renaissance and which was more or less completed in the period from the
mid-eighteenth to the mid-nineteenth century. The necessity for such a
semiotic revolution lies in the need for an identity between the morphology
of social systems and that of the semiotic systems through which their relations and values must be thought. If the principles governing the ordering
of social life do not also govern the construction of texts, those texts will be
unable to bring that ordering of social life to mind; they will not be a means
of thinking it. As a semiotic revolution, tonalism could be said to have, as
its aim, the construction of music that inscribes the 'historical' as *suspense*. It
is seen at its clearest in sonata-form which is heavy with motivic-thematic
development.

The characters in a novel or in a drama have both depth and background;
they have inner lives and biographies that operate as a kind of 'suspended
reality' which is, nevertheless, present and effective in determining their
actions in the present, and they participate in an external situation which is
also experienced in terms of its cumulative suspense. In a painting we can
observe the same suspense, both in the depiction of the inner lives of individuals as reflected in their outer forms, movements and expressions –
personality as suspense – and also in the background in which events and
relations build cumulative suspense.

This vision of an *organic* development in aesthetic works was closely
bound up with changes in the social order itself, changes in the relations of
social production. Marx claimed that human societies are distinguished from
non-human societies by the fact that they must produce the means of their
subsistence. However, in the process of doing so, different types of society

clearly stand in different types of relationship to nature. We can differentiate among societies on the basis of the degree of embeddedness of social agency in nature. In a hunter-gatherer society, for example, the 'distancing' of social 'agency' from nature is relatively low. Such societies do not produce nature or even occasion it; they organise themselves to make efficient use of what nature produces. In a society based upon settled agriculture, there is a greater degree of distancing of agency from nature. Although such societies do not produce nature, they do 'occasion' it through the practise of settled agriculture, drainage, defence and so forth. Such societies can develop significant urban centres as was the case in all the great agrarian empires.

Where city-based production is decisively distanced from nature, where it involves a significant degree of manufacture, then society become a producer proper. Such production takes place at a remove from nature. It involves individuals not only in 'freely' initiating and developing production and commercial enterprise but also in entering into co-operative relations with others to produce the environment – political, social and economic – in which the projects of 'free' citizens can be fulfilled. That is, in truly bourgeois societies, the very construction of society itself is the construction of a 'second nature' which is the ground of all the projects of individual producers and merchants. Ideal-typically, this second nature must be constructed through negotiation and co-operation among free individuals. Bourgeois societies tend to 'democratic' political structures and the development of 'universalist' systems of law. It was the individualism and cultivation of personality emerging in the political cultures of the Italian Renaissance cities that so impressed Burkhardt (J. Burkhardt 1981).

It is inherent in the construction of bourgeois societies that individual freedom and social co-operation and constraint must somehow be harmonised, that the social order constructed through co-operation among bourgeois producers must be the means of realising and fulfilling the individual projects of those producers. The reconciling of individual and society, personal freedom and collective constraint, subject and object, part and whole, is not *merely* ideological; it is an urgent practical problem in the construction of bourgeois life. To some extent, bourgeois societies have, as a matter of practical daily life, to achieve an accommodation between these poles, a degree of equilibration, however tense or imperfect. Failure to co-operate adequately in the efficient construction of a social order in and through which the projects of individuals can be realised means the failure of those projects.

However, the fact that an ideology has some basis in practical life does not make it any less an ideology; nor does it mean that, as ideology, it does not involve a considerable degree of distortion in its representation of reality. These questions of the truth or falsity of ideology depend upon the historical context. In the making of a bourgeois society, the elements of bourgeois ideology constituted a set of formative ideals, of practical help in constructing society. They also constituted a mode of *critical* thought, an opposition to forms of traditionalism. It was not really until the late eighteenth and early nineteenth centuries that bourgeois societies might be said to have more or less decisively gained the ascendancy over traditionalist thought and practice (which is not the same as eliminating it) and in their internal relations to have reached some degree of equilibration between individual freedom and social constraint. Any such approximation to equilibrium was only partial and only transient. As bourgeois societies develop, the problems of constructing 'second nature' grow more complex and the organisational process develops to the point where it threatens to submerge individuals and to bring about an end to the antinomy of individual and society: not through an equilibration between the two, as sought in the earlier phase of bourgeois development, but through penetrating the boundaries of the individual and entirely subsuming its constitutive elements in the collective order — in other words, through becoming totalitarian.

Throughout the nineteenth century, the growth of rational-technical organisation — of bureaucratic forces — in the development of a new political and economic order preoccupied with a continuous reorganisation of productive forces and markets made the spectre of a despotic and totalitarian order — and, therefore, the ultimate irreconcilability of individual liberty and societal constraint — visible upon the horizon. In the face of these social developments, the continuing affirmation, in bourgeois ideology, of the reconciliation of individual and society loses truth-value even as a formative ideal. Its survival as ideology serves the negative purpose of disguising the totalitarian nature of the conformist pressure in modern society by making it appear to be the reconciliation between individual and society that was promised by an earlier bourgeois society. If, as Adorno believed, the progressive phase in which bourgeois ideology had a genuinely formative role was really over by the early nineteenth century, it is clear that in its 'reactionary' phase it has lasted well into the twentieth century. Under its spell, in Adorno's perspective, the self-deluded subjects of modernity enter the 'pen' freely, without struggling against the 'inevitable'.

Because, in the classical model of a bourgeois society, individuals must interact with others to construct the system of social constraints and conditions through which their free choices are exercised, social interaction has an inherently *teleological* character. The material order of bourgeois life, a teleological order, demands of its texts a historicity, a *textual suspense* with which to furnish itself with ideas, with consciousness and with reflections on experience. One implication of this textual suspense is that we cannot identify an element or part (a character in a story, for example) with its immediate appearance, presuming that what we actually see at one instant is all there is; what appears of the subject at any given instant only has meaning in virtue of its historical unfolding (retrospective and prospective) and that

35

historical development (suspense), which stands behind what appears of a subject's actions, shapes and determines them, imparts meaning to them. This suspense divides the world into *foreground* and *background*, into what we can immediately see and what we perceive to lie 'behind' what we see; suspense invests appearances, or 'surfaces' that are in the foreground, with *depth*. To the extent that a subject in a story has depth, s/he has an interiority, a *personality* which can be 'perceived' in appearance and expression. Thus, the 'depth' of the subject in a story can be thought of synchronically, as the *personality* of the subject, and diachronically, as the *biography* of the subject. Corresponding to the individual's personality and biography is a society's *culture* and its *history*.

In his monumental study of the representation of reality in Western literature, Auerbach begins with an analysis of Homer's *Odyssey* (E. Auerbach 1968). He argues that the world of Odysseus is one which is entirely foregrounded, a world lacking background and depth; Homer's characters exist in an eternal present without biographical suspense arising from their past and determining their actions. They appear, in Auerbach's memorable phrase, 'as though on the first morning of their lives'. Odysseus has a character – we know that he is cunning and brave – but he is without an interior life extending into the background. By contrast, the classical bourgeois novel is steeped in background, in suspense, both at the level of the personalities and biographies of its main characters and at that of the larger culture and history which shapes their existence.

The representation of reality in terms of an articulation of foreground and background, of *outer* appearance and *inner* meaning, makes of the immediate visible surface of a representation a sign of an underlying dynamic stretching back into the past and forward into the future. The 'whole' or the 'totality' – society, culture, history, personality – is identified with what lies 'behind', 'beneath' or 'within' appearances; that is, with the 'idea' disclosed in appearances or – to express it semiotically – the 'signified'. European societies from the time of the Renaissance developed in all the arts – in painting, architecture, literature, theatre and music – a systematic dialectics of foreground/background relations, of inner/outer. It was an art that aimed at disclosing the depth, the inner meaning of experience – its psycho-logic, its socio-logic – in and through the systematic articulation of 'external' or 'surface' appearances. This disclosure depended crucially for its success upon systematics, upon the rational articulation of all the differentiated elements in a work such that the entire work appears to arise organically from the movements and relations among its parts. It is this identity relation between whole and part which puts suspense or *historicity* into the work, making the development of the parts, in their mutual relations, unfold towards the completion of the whole. The refinements through which this systematicity was developed were centuries in the making, but the principal technical means appeared as far back as the fifteenth century.

The principle of suspense in bourgeois painting

As a pioneering defender of the new art at the time of the Renaissance, Alberti coined the term 'istoria' to mark its most important characteristic (L.B. Alberti 1966). The istoria is identified with the 'themes' the painter is seeking to realise in the work. For Alberti these would be suggested by the stories of antiquity as well as the stories of the Bible. In Alberti's guide, the painter must seek to construct a painting such that there is a 'fit' between the structure of 'optical values' in the painting and those which realistically reflect the structure of visual relations which constitutes the story that the painter is seeking to tell. However, Alberti does not mean to imply that the work of the artist is centred simply on illustrating stories. The istoria is brought to life in the painting and becomes a 'virtual' reality, permitting the emotions of its bodies and events to be projected onto the observer. Moreover, the construction of the istoria is here identified with the rational organisation of a three-dimensional pictorial space:

> The greatest work of the painter is not a *colossus* but an *istoria*. . . . Bodies are parts of the istoria, members are parts of the bodies, planes parts of members. The primary part of painting, therefore, are the planes. . . . Bodies ought to harmonise together in the istoria in both size and function. It would be absurd for one who paints the Centaurs fighting after the banquet to leave a vase of wine still standing in such a tumult. [We would call] it a weakness if in the same distance one person should appear larger than another, or if dogs should be equal to horses, or better, as I frequently see, if a man is placed in a building as in a closed casket where there is scarcely room to sit down. *For these reasons, all bodies should harmonise in size and in function to what is happening in the istoria* [my emphasis].
>
> (L. Alberti 1966: 72)

To realise this isomorphic relationship between 'what is happening in the istoria' and the internal relations among the visual elements in a painting, the artist had to have recourse to the invention of certain formal techniques. In painting, from the time of the Renaissance, an optical suspense was established by such techniques as chiaroscuro and linear perspective. While these are devices for achieving realistic modelling of objects and a realistic construction of space and depth in the picture, they accomplish these effects by subjecting all values in the picture to a rational and unitary order. In the case of chiaroscuro, light and shade are used to model objects in accordance with their orientation towards or away from a unified light source. Thus each 'tonal value' established by means of chiaroscuro is hierarchically ordered in terms of its relationship to this centre – that is, the light source. Similarly with linear perspective. The convergence of parallel lines to one of an infinite number of points on the horizon enables the artist to establish a means of opening up the deep space of a picture and to render objects in their correct size-distance ratios according to where they are located – near or far – in that optically coherent space.

As I have argued elsewhere, the semiotic significance of such a principle is that it enables one to depict values, not as absolute and self-contained – in archaic art, governed by an earlier principle of centration, the importance of a king was depicted by making him larger than everyone else – but as attributes that are determined *relativistically*, by their relations to others within an optically coherent space. In this way, the rational historicity of bourgeois social life could be said to have its structural analogue in painting in the techniques of chiaroscuro and linear perspective (R. Witkin 1995).

The idea of art as homology, as a structural analogue of social relations, was a very important part of the Germanic tradition in art history, a tradition stemming from Hegel's *Aesthetics* and his *Lectures on Fine Art* (G.W. Hegel 1975). Like many other German philosophers in the Hegelian tradition, Adorno tended to see all cultural processes and practices of a given epoch as governed by the same set of principles. That is, he expected to find the same inherent tendencies in the philosophy of the time that were present in the social institutions, the economy, religious systems or artworks of the period. Social and cultural relations were seen as manifesting, in all their various forms, what another German aesthetician, Erwin Panofsky, referred to as a distinctive 'mind-world relationship' (E. Panofsky 1972). It was, natural, therefore, for Adorno to move freely, in his critical thought, between society, philosophy and music, since all three were seen as aspects of the same phenomena.

A particularly apt example of this type of claim of cultural unity is to be found in Panofsky's exploration of the parallels between the architecture of Gothic cathedrals and Scholasticism in the religion and philosophy of the late Middle Ages (E. Panofsky 1951). Panofsky does not seek to argue that Gothic cathedrals inscribed scholastic arguments or content. His attention is focused upon the modus operandi or structural relations in both architecture and the Scholastic *summa*. It is the thoroughgoing systematicity – the complex articulation of individual elements governed by the whole – which Panofsky sees as characterising both Scholasticism and Gothic architecture.

> A man imbued with the Scholastic habit would look upon the mode of architectural presentation, just as he looked upon the mode of literary presentation, from the point of view of *manifestatio*. He would have taken it for granted that the primary purpose of the many elements that compose a cathedral was to ensure stability just

as he took it for granted that the primary purpose of the many elements that constitute a *Summa* was to ensure validity.

But he would not have been satisfied had not the membrification of the edifice permitted him to re-experience the very process of architectural composition, just as the membrification of the *Summa* permitted him to re-experience the very process of cogitation. To him, the panoply of shafts, ribs, buttresses, tracery, pinnacles, and crockets was a self-analysis and self-explication of architecture much as the customary apparatus of parts, distinctions, questions and articles was, to him, a self-analysis and self-explication of reason.

(E. Panofsky 1951: 58–9)

Moreover, Panofsky sees the emergence of this systematic individuation of the elements of medieval argument and architecture as reflecting a shift in philosophy away from a concern with Platonist universals towards Nominalist philosophies. Panofsky's intellectual history aligns him with other writers in that tradition, such as Burkhardt, who identify the Renaissance with the growing individuation of social life. It aligns him, too, with Adorno, whose aesthetic theories are also grounded in the premise of what might be termed a crisis of Nominalism and individuation (T. Adorno 1984).

The principle of suspense in bourgeois theatre

We can find the same view of the principle of centration at work in the development of modern theatre. Szondi's theorising of what he calls the 'drama of modernity', which came into being in the Renaissance, seeks to identify it in terms of a clear set of structural characteristics. These can be seen to echo those established in the other arts, in painting, music and architecture, for example. However, in drama there is a more direct and obvious simulation of social action. Writers have frequently used theatre as a metaphor for social life and sociologists have appropriated its terminology to describe social life. The structural conditions of the new drama are therefore closest to those that describe – ideal-typically – the individuated social relations of bourgeois society. According to Szondi (P. Szondi 1987), the absolute drama was 'the result of a bold intellectual effort made by a newly self-conscious being who, after the collapse of the mediaeval world view, sought to create an artistic reality within which he could fix and mirror himself on the basis of interpersonal relationships alone' (P. Szondi 1987: 7). To be purely relational – that is, to be dramatic – the drama must be absolute in the sense of freeing itself from everything external. It must be a self-contained world which develops entirely from social interaction among the characters. Like a Renaissance painting which was a kind of tableau drama, the stage appropriate to the new absolute drama was the 'picture-frame' stage. The audience sits in the dark, a 'lamed and silent' observer who is neither addressed by the action nor intervenes in the action. The drama is a self-contained dialectic, but it is one that is free and redefined from moment to moment. The internal time of the drama is always the present, but the drama is never static. The present passes and becomes the past. As it passes away, it produces change: 'a new present springs from its antithesis'. The drama unfolds as an absolute linear sequence in the present; it generates its own time. Every moment in it must contain the seeds of the future, must be pregnant with futurity. This reflects the drama's dialectical structure – its historicity – which is rooted in interpersonal relations:

> Ultimately, the whole world of the Drama is dialectical in origin. It does not come into being because of an epic *I* which permeates the work. It exists because of the always achieved and, from that point, once again disrupted sublation of the interpersonal dialectic, which manifests itself as speech in the dialogue. In this respect as well, the dialogue carries the Drama. The Drama is possible only when dialogue is possible.
>
> (P. Szondi 1987: 10)

In Szondi's theory of the Absolute Drama, the work appears to develop openly from the dialectical relations among its constituent elements; in reality it has been closed in advance by the author so that those interactions are predetermined by the end to which they are oriented. It is just such an apparently organic identity between whole and part which Adorno sees as the illusory achievement of bourgeois ideology in all its forms, including the classical development of sonata-form. The technical problems of achieving this historicity in music were comparable to those in all the other arts. It was a question of how to construct a self-contained world of musical events which was dialectical in the sense of the Absolute Drama: that is, which appeared to develop, in time, from the dialectical relations among its elements and to bring the whole out of itself. This required a principle of suspense – similar to chiaroscuro and linear perspective in painting – in terms of which all events could be relativised in a self-contained, rational and self-consistent totality. The technical means for achieving this in the case of music were the principles of what came to be known as 'classical tonality'.

The principle of suspense in the bourgeois novel

The period in which Beethoven was born was also the period of the birth of the novel as a literary form. Typically, the classical novel was a narrative, a biography or history of the life and condition of a 'problematic' individual. Sometimes, the individual's name constituted the title of the novel, as in *Robinson Crusoe*, *Moll Flanders*, *Don Quixote*, and sometimes not, as for example Raskolnikov in Dostoevsky's *Crime and Punishment*. A novel told the story of a particular life or lives marked by restlessness and search, of a striving to reconcile individual desire and will with the society in which it must express itself, in which it must somehow find a home or fulfil itself. To be truly at home in the world implies that there is continuity within and without, a continuity between the inner life of the individual subject and the outer world of objective social relations. The ground from which the 'classical' novel springs is one in which 'communitas' has been ruptured and a potentially fatal divide has opened up between the individual and society. The hero of the novel strives through his or her own will and actions to close that divide, to make the world answer to the will, to express and fulfil him or herself in society.

It was in essentially these terms that Lukács theorised the novel (G. Lukács 1978). The 'problematic hero' of the novel, he argued, was engaged in a more or less doomed search for meaning in a degraded world. If the novel recorded the individual's struggle and effort to achieve an identity between individual and society, it also registered the failure to achieve that identity, indeed the illusory nature of any attempted reconciliation between individual and society, between subject and object. The authors of *Don Quixote* or *Crime and Punishment* could, through the use of irony, deconstruct their characters and make the illusory nature of their efforts visible. There were limits, however, to the compass of their irony. Such a distancing unmasked the author's creatures but preserved the author himself – for whom the writing of the novel was a similar search for meaning and integrity – from the force of his own criticism. In Lukács's view, the great bourgeois novels were at once a flowering of bourgeois idealism and at the same time a critical insight into the contradictions of bourgeois society. He identified their method with realism and valorised a 'critical realism' as a model of all that he believed to be 'progressive' in literature.

The novelist Balzac was, for Lukács, the quintessential bourgeois realist. He depicts the richness of Parisian life, the intricate details of a great variety of occupations and trades, the absolutely particular personalities of his characters and their projects, and does so against the backdrop of the drama of a great bourgeois society in the making, with its stock markets, banks, industries, political and social institutions, the break-up of the great estates and centres of feudal power and so forth. In a Balzac novel, all of this evolutionary ferment is brought out of the particular lives and projects of individual human beings, each of whom is both an absolutely unique character and at the same time a typical representative of his class and – through the relations of the different classes and groups constituting society as a totality – is also a typical Parisian bourgeois. The background to each individual life is, therefore, the vast system of interests and relations which constitutes the bourgeois order and which manifests itself in the daily struggles of each individual. It is this system which is presupposed in the formation of the individual's ideas and projects and which is the ground of the individual's actions. Thus, in his novel *The Peasants*, Balzac can assert: 'Tell me what you possess and I will tell you what you think.'

The world of Balzac's novels is one in which an identity between part and whole (individual and society) is sought and in which society appears to develop from the actions and projects of its members, while those actions, in turn, presuppose the very social order to which they give rise. This is the formula which Lukács extracts from the bourgeois realism of the nineteenth century and which he hypostatises as the basis of all progressive methods in art and literature.

> Every cog in the machinery of a Balzacian plot is a complete, living human being, with specific personal interests, passions, tragedies and comedies. The bond which links each character with the whole of the story is provided by some element in the make-up of the character itself, always in full accordance with the tendencies inherent in it. As this link always develops organically out of the interests, passions, etc. of the character, it appears necessary and vital. But it is the broader inner urges and compulsions of the characters themselves which gives them fullness of life and renders them non-mechanical, no mere components of the plot. Such a conception of the characters necessarily causes them to burst out of the story.
>
> (G. Lukács 1972: 54)

The bond – 'provided by some element in the make-up of the character itself' and 'which links each character with the whole of the story' – also, through that link, unifies the other elements in the make-up of the character, ensuring that the character itself is fully-rounded, a three-dimensional being with a biography and an historical development which is connected to that of the larger story. Thus, each individual element participates in the construction of a dynamic hierarchy of relations – through interaction with other individuals – in which the more general levels of social organisation grow out of more specific levels of organisation, even from the level of concrete particulars.

It is instructive, in this respect, to compare Lukács's attempt in the early years of this century to theorise the organic part–whole relations of a Balzacian novel with Durkheim's attempt, a few years earlier, to identify the principle of social organisation in industrial societies as being one of 'organic solidarity'. In a 'division of labour' society, individuals interact with one another in ways which reflect their complementarity in the social systems in which they participate. By taking those systems and that complementarity into account in formulating his or her own individual actions and responses, each individual succeeds in helping to construct and to take care of the totality of the social order on which s/he is dependent in order to play a part as an individual.

What might be termed *the organic model of individuation* was central to the writings of both theorists. Yet there are important differences between them. Durkheim advanced this model as describing the mature form of social relations in a modern industrial society. Industrial relations did not, however, offer conclusive evidence of organic solidarity, and the degree of individuation in industrial organisations was far greater in the case of some occupations than others — for example white-collar rather than blue-collar occupations. Durkheim reasoned that where the necessary complementarity and co-operative social relations among individuals did not occur, it was simply down to certain pathological forms of the division of labour which could be overcome — through the formation of special intermediate organisations such as occupational groups, for example.

With Lukács, the situation is quite different. Critical Realism as a method for progressive art and literature did not serve to confirm or validate bourgeois claims concerning organic individuation, as Durkheim's notion of organic solidarity sought to do. Quite the contrary: a genuinely critical realism served to expose the cracks and fissures, the fundamental contradictions, of bourgeois society; it gave rise to the realisation that subject and object, individual and society, simply don't add up. In a cultural form such as the novel, for example, the ultimately unbridgeable gap between the spiritual needs of the individual and the bourgeois social order in which he or she must participate is itself a reflection of the alienation produced by commodification in the economic sphere. The inner structural principle of the system of social production under capitalism is the germ of all culture creation in capitalist society. The disjunction of subject and object, individual and society, which is the result of capitalist economic relations (commodification), reappears as the inner structural principle of works of art. In Lukács's penetrating analysis, the organic integration of bourgeois society was always exposed as illusory in the greatest works of bourgeois art and literature. In the novel, it frequently emerged in the form of the central character's realisation of the futility of his or her quest, a realisation that might come at the end of the history, as in the deathbed realisation of Don Quixote. This realisation of the degraded nature of the search for values through a late reflection on the part of the subject is exactly what Adorno attributes to those artists who themselves — like Michelangelo, Rembrandt or Beethoven — could be said to have produced a late style in which they deconstructed the 'illusions' of their own earlier works (T. Adorno 1994c).

The principle of suspense in bourgeois music

The development of *diatonicism* in music also dates from the Renaissance and again was not fully realised until the late eighteenth and early nineteenth centuries. Tonal music is organised by the distinctive intervalic progressions of major and minor scales. The character of a scale depends upon the distribution of semi-tones and tones. The first two intervals of a *major* scale, for example, are whole tones. The next interval is a semitone and it is followed by three whole tones. The final interval of the scale is a semitone. There are thus five whole steps and two half steps in each major scale. The fact that the scales used contain only a restricted number of the possible notes of the octave is important. There is a dynamic force within the scale, a gravitational pull – felt by the hearer – towards a central point, towards the first note of the scale, the tonic. The gravitational pull of tonal (diatonic) music depends crucially upon the hierarchically established pitch relations in the scale in which only a limited number of notes can be used in the progression. If all of the possible notes were used we would have the full chromatic of twelve semitones. In *chromaticism*, where all the possible notes are used, the functional hierarchy of notes established by diatonicism breaks down and, with it, the key system. Chromaticism is, in this sense, the antithesis of diatonicism and is associated with the development of modern music and the destruction of the principle of centricity constituted by diatonicism.

In the functional hierarchy of the diatonic scale the first note – the tonic – is the most important. The gravitational pull of the music, experienced as tension and as resolution of tension, is towards the tonic. The next most important note is the fifth note of the scale, the dominant, where this pull is strongly felt; followed by the fourth up and fifth down from the tonic, the subdominant. The seventh or 'leading tone' is the one which moves to the tonic. A new scale can be built on the dominant of a previous scale (five notes up from the tonic) or on the subdominant (five notes down from the tonic). The centricity of the tonal system is to be seen in the very imagery used to describe it. It is customary to represent the possibilities for scale building on both the subdominant and the dominant as the complete 'circle of fifths'. It is this which constitutes the *key system* of classical tonality.

Tonal music is music which is written within the tonal (or key) system and is, therefore, music which has a tonal (or key) *centre*. In a tonal composition there are clear relationships existing between 'pitches' grouped around a single tonic. The central harmonic unit of classical tonality is a major triad (a chord made up of a 'root' note, a note that is an interval of a third from the root and a note that is an interval of a fifth from the root). Its fundamental harmonic progression is from the tonic to the dominant to the tonic (IVI). The principle of centration which governs all elements and relations within a classically tonal composition is succinctly stated by Samson: 'However widely ranging the harmonic movement within this progression, it takes place against a background of hierarchical relationships between diatonic triads grouped around a tonic triad and between secondary tonal regions grouped around a central tonality' (J. Samson 1993: 2). The gravitational pull towards the tonic thus constitutes a principle of centricity comparable to that of linear perspective and of the unified light source in painting; it provides a means of ordering the 'values' of all the elements of the music in terms of their hierarchical relations within a unified totality. It is this system which emerged in the fifteenth century and was progressively perfected and rationalised by the late eighteenth and early nineteenth centuries. It is tonalism which is the central organising principle of Beethoven's music and, according to Adorno, perfected by him in his second period compositions.

The system of tonal relations, like the principle of suspense operating in each of the other arts, was aimed at ensuring that the freedom of the elements or parts was fully reconciled with the constraint of the whole, the latter being the very ground of the former's project. In music, tonality was a means of establishing a rational ground for reconciling the demands of subjective (individual) freedom and those of objective (collective) constraint. The sonata-form of classical tonality, with its exposition section followed by a development section and then its reprise, was a powerful means for reflecting just such a dynamic equilibration of freedom and constraint, of individual and society, subject and object, thus bridging the (inner) spiritual life and the (outer) material form.

Classical tonality, no less than linear perspective or the conventions of the absolute drama, was integral to bourgeois ideology. As ideology, it offered an *image* of reconciliation. In an antagonistic society constructed for the exploitation of nature, all social relations bear the scars of that antagonism and no identity is possible between the oppressive force of society and the spiritual needs of the individual. In that sense, bourgeois art is false and partakes in the construction of illusion and not truth. However, such art can be seen to have a critical function. Insofar as its idealised integrity was manifestly not realised in everyday life, art, even as bourgeois ideology, could hold up to a bourgeois society an image of how far short it fell of its own ideals.

Adorno's position concerning the sonata-form bears comparison with that of Lukács on the novel. The sonata, too, he saw as a means of developing a rich individuation of parts or elements, each of which unfolds organically from within itself towards the development of a totality with which it is integrally identified. Classical tonality was the means for achieving that. The hierarchical construction of music in which tones are related to one another through their tonal centres is paralleled by the structural ideal of a bourgeois society. Such a society, like the sonata-allegro, was both individuated and hierarchical. The sonata-form is a closed form; its illusory dynamism is achieved at the cost of a restriction in the openness of the 'sensuous particulars' to each other – a restriction inherent in diatonicism. The system of tonal relations which ensured the lawfulness of all relations among elements concealed the unfreedom of the individual tones and the force with which they were constrained in their relations. The individuated and hierarchical structure of the classical sonata-allegro made it an analogue of formal relations in bourgeois society. It is in that sense that one might claim that entrepreneurial bourgeois society was a 'society in sonata-form'.

For Adorno, the inherent historical development of bourgeois society was not towards more individual freedom and expression but towards totalitarian collectivist forms which threatened to annihilate the individual and all expression. That social and historical development was registered fully in the development of modern music from the time of Beethoven's Piano Sonata Opus 111, in which Adorno sees Beethoven as bidding farewell to the very sonata-form itself (T. Mann 1968: 57). Unlike Lukács, Adorno had no faith in the development of modern socialist societies, which he saw as governed by even more antagonistic relations. There were other important differences between the two thinkers. One of the most obvious, perhaps, is the fact that Adorno did not valorise the sonata-form and prescribe it as the measure of musical progress for the twentieth century in the way that Lukács valorised the bourgeois realist form of the novel. And this despite the fact that Beethoven was as central to Adorno's sociology of music as Balzac was to Lukács's sociology of literature. Nevertheless, the model of the sonata-form remains key to an understanding of Adorno's music analyses: certain principles that he holds to be central to sonata-form as an ideal provide him with a model of *sociality* which might be said to constitute a universalistic set of claims as distinct from being merely ideological. Also, it is clear that Adorno, like Lukács, found the price of progress in modernist music more than he was willing to pay. He indicated his preference for the earlier critical phase of modernist music, that which extended from, for example, late Beethoven to Mahler and Berg.

Individuation as sociality

In itself, any element in the music is more or less 'empty', a nothingness. It is only in virtue of its relations with other elements within the whole that it acquires its substantial individuality and its meaning. Thus Adorno writes of Beethoven's music:

> In Beethoven, the particulars have a momentum in the direction of the totality. For the most part they become what they are because of their relation to the whole. In themselves they are relatively unspecific, like the basic proportions of tonality, and tend to be amorphous. If you listen to or read Beethoven's most articulate music with attention, you will notice that it resembles a continuum of nothingness. The tour de force of every one of his major works lies in the fact that, to use Hegelian terms literally, the totality of nothing determines itself to become being.
>
> (T. Adorno 1984: 265)

What Adorno says here of music applies to his idea of individuals in society, too. The idea of an isolated subject or ego is for him a kind of emptiness, a nothingness. It is only as a being, thoroughly mediated by its relations with others, that the individual acquires any kind of mass or substance. The individual is, therefore, not defined as that which stands apart from others or from society, but as that which is constituted only relationally: that is, only in and through relations with others. The integral and social constitution of the individual is nowhere more strikingly asserted than in the opening lines of Raymond Williams' definition of the word 'individual' in his book *Keywords*:

> *Individual* originally meant indivisible. That now sounds like a paradox. 'Individual' stresses a distinction from others; 'indivisible' a necessary connection. The development of the modern meaning from the original meaning is a record in language of an extraordinary social and political history.
>
> (R. Williams 1976: 133–6)

This polarity is at the heart of Adorno's social criticism. He remains morally and implacably opposed to a Nominalism that destroys that integral sociality. For Adorno, the more comprehensive, fully developed and integral the social relations in which the individual is constituted, the more 'substance' s/he has as an individual. The isolated ego of individualism or of phenomenology was anathema to him. The sonata-form, as Adorno theorised it, could be said to aim at such an ideal of integral sociality, and when he looked beyond its demise he was even less comforted by what he saw ahead than was Lukács contemplating the demise of the realist novel. Lukács could at least look forward to an eventual liberation through socialism; no such comfort was available for Adorno. In the final analysis, the fact that Adorno was a subtle and yet vigorous defender of modernist art and Lukács was an implacable opponent of it may not truly place them on opposite sides of a debate. Both perceived the de-sociating forces at work in modern art and modern society even if they contextualised them differently.

Historicity as sociality

There are two further principles of sociality which inhere in the model of sonata-form. They are both really corollaries of the social constitution of the individual subject. The social constitution of the subject is the *self-development* of the subject. It is development, from within itself, through mediated relations with others towards the integral unity of the whole. That unity is its objective, its fullest development and its fulfilment. The mediated relations to be developed in order to reach that fulfilment construct *temporality* and *historicity* in both society and music – sonata and symphony both make

47

time their subject; through the substance they impart to it they force it to manifest itself (T. Adorno 1981: 37). It is this process of the subject's going out of itself to the larger whole which gives rise to the construction and meaning of temporality. Sociality for Adorno meant, therefore, the double mediation of the free development of relations among the elements or sensuous particulars and also between sensuous particulars and the totality. Without both – without, that is, the opening of the parts to being changed by each other as well as their opening to the whole – no temporal or historical experience was possible.

But this spontaneous development of the sensuous particulars reflects their openness to determination by social experience. History is immanent in the work of art, is its inner temporality. But the work of art is not a static thing which endures unchanged with its inner history congealed. It passes through real time. That is, the work of art enters into relations with society, it enters into an 'outer' history. Works of art are thus in a continuous process of becoming. The immanent history congealed in them as content is recontextualised in the commerce that society has with works of art over time. How we hear late Beethoven is not unaffected by our own history, associations, development:

> The work of art is not a being immune to change but an existent in the process of becoming. Its historicity is more comprehensive than historicism would have us believe, according to which art is what it is because of its relation to real history. What appears in the work of art is its inner time, and it is the continuity of this inner time which gets blown up in the explosion of appearance. The link between art and real history is the fact that works of art are structured like monads. History may be called the content of works of art. Analysing them is the same as becoming conscious of the immanent history stored in them.
>
> (T. Adorno 1984: 127)

Spontaneity as sociality

A third aspect of the principle of sociality is that the process must be controlled from below, from the spontaneous movement of elements or parts. Adorno conceives of works of art in terms of a polar opposition between a process of ordering which proceeds from the domination of the whole over the parts and one developed from the spontaneous development of the parts to the whole:

> We can typologise works of art in the following rather simplistic way. There is one type that moves downwards from the whole to the lower echelons; there is another type that proceeds inversely. These

48

two types have been fairly distinct throughout the history of art. Their distinctness is caused by the antinomy between unity and particularisation, which in turn is ineradicable.

(T. Adorno 1984: 264–5)

Examples of art in which the whole dominates the parts are to be found in archaic and primitive art as much as they are in modern art. Adorno's principle of sociality, however, requires that ordering should proceed dynamically and spontaneously from the inner movement or impulsion of the parts.

Nothing deserves to be called an art work that keeps the contingent at bay. For by definition form is form of something and this something must not be allowed to degenerate into a tautological iteration of form.

(T. Adorno 1984: 314)

Without contingency, the elements, as sensuous particulars, would not be open either to mediation by each other or to mediation through the subject's relationship to society. What is organised from above is necessarily closed. It can be arranged or assembled like the parts of machinery but it cannot grow organically, cannot be a form of life communing with life. It is Adorno's notion of a form of life freely interacting – integrally social – which is the very ground and condition of his vision of spontaneity. Thus individuation, historicity and spontaneity are all implicitly derived from Adorno's 'utopian' vision of the social. His critical sociology is a testament to the power of this utopian vision of what it means to be truly social. It is also a genuinely bourgeois utopia and one which bourgeois society sought to perfect at the level of ideology. In that sense, Beethoven's great symphonies are realisations of bourgeois ideology. The sonata-allegro represents the pinnacle of this development. It aims at the most complete appearance of a reconciliation between freedom and constraint, 'individual' and 'society', part and whole; but because the sonata is, in reality, a closed form, the appearance of spontaneity or genuine expressiveness becomes harder to achieve, as music develops, without breaking out of the straitjacket of diatonicism that had come to govern the development of European music since the Renaissance.

The transformations in modern music leading to the weakening and demise of classical sonata-form had their parallels in every aspect of modern social life, in the micro-division of labour and in the development of interpersonal relations in the metropolis. The musical watershed for Adorno was to be found in the transition from the sonata-allegri of Beethoven's middle period to the profound 'deconstructive' music of his late style.

3

BEETHOVEN LATE AND SOON

In his book *The Ritual Process: Structure and Anti-Structure*, the anthropologist Victor Turner counterposed the spirit of community – 'communitas' – to convention and order, to the normal institutional control of everyday life (V. Turner 1969). He drew on Martin Buber's distinction in *I–Thou*, in which:

> Community is the being no longer side by side (and, one might add, above and below) but *with* one another of a multitude of persons. And this multitude, though it moves towards one goal, yet experiences everywhere a turning to, a dynamic facing of the others, a flowing from *I* to *thou*. Community is where community happens.
>
> (M. Buber 1987: 51)

The spontaneous, immediate, concrete nature of communitas stands opposed to the norm-governed, institutionalised, abstract nature of social structure. Yet communitas, according to Turner, is only made evident through its juxtaposition to, or hybridisation with, aspects of social structure. It represents the 'quick' of human relatedness. 'It involves the whole man in his relation to other whole men' (V. Turner 1969: 127). Turner saw the work of artists and of prophets as an expression of communitas and of liminality:

> Prophets and artists tend to be liminal and marginal people, 'edgemen' who strive with a passionate sincerity to rid themselves of the clichés associated with status incumbency and role-playing and to enter into vital relations with other men in fact or imagination. In their productions we may catch glimpses of that unused evolutionary potential in mankind which has not yet been externalised and fixed in structure.
>
> (V. Turner 1969: 128)

Communitas, claims Turner, breaks through the interstices of structure, in liminality; at the edges of structure, in marginality; and from beneath structure, in inferiority. 'It is almost everywhere held to be sacred or "holy", possibly because it transgresses the norms that govern sacred and institutionalised relationships and is accompanied by experiences of unprecedented potency' (ibid. 128). Turner does not associate this liberation of affect as equivalent to some kind of expression of instinctual or biological drives released from cultural suppression. He sees it as feeling that is fully developed, the product of maturity and memory.

> I am now inclined to think that communitas is not solely the product of biologically inherited drives released from cultural constraints. Rather it is the product of peculiarly human faculties, which include rationality, volition and memory, and which develop with experience of life in society – just as among the Tallensi who undergo the experiences that induce them to receive the *bakalogo* shrines.
>
> (V. Turner 1969: 128)

In the dialectic of structure and anti-structure, Turner places the artist on the side of anti-structure, of liminality and communitas. However, it can also be argued that the very evolution of an artist's work can manifest, in its internal development, the dialectic of structure and anti-structure. The artist can develop a liminality in opposition to what he himself has produced. Moreover, in line with Turner's understanding, this tends to occur late in the artist's career. Some of the greatest artists have developed 'late styles' in which they have deconstructed the work of their maturity, opening what had formerly been closed and liberating forces that had formerly been suppressed.

Anyone who contemplates the late sculptures of Michelangelo cannot help but be struck by the powerful contrast they make with his earlier work. The late works – *The Prisoners* still emerging from the rock from which they have been carved, the *Palestrina* and Rondanini Pietàs whose grieving forms contrast with the sweetness and serenity of the Pietà in St Peter's in Rome – appear remarkable to the modern eye for their truthfulness, for the impression they give of confronting life as it is without glossing or framing it. The same impression of utter truthfulness is to be had from the late self-portraits of Rembrandt. The 'greatness' of the late styles of these artists can be measured by the degree of self-consciousness and self-mastery they attain in them. In a similar way many have marvelled at the profundity of Beethoven's late style and the beauty of the last quartets. In each of the examples given, the artist surrenders, in his late style, something that had been central to the mastery he attained in the works of his maturity. It is the sense that the spirit (which Turner identifies with communitas and with liminality) can master the world, that the spirit can be reconciled with the world and fulfilled in it. In each case this positive énergetique of the works of the artist's maturity gives way to a sense of the weakness of the subject in the face of elemental force. Moreover, this sense of weakness is paradoxically a manifestation of the greatest potency and mastery achieved by the artist; it is a breaking through of liminality, of communitas, and the radical deconstruction of his earlier work. The illusory depiction of the world as harmony – the reconciliation of world and spirit – is replaced by a vision dominated by the absence of reconciliation and the pain of that absence.

Beethoven was at the very centre of modern music for Adorno, and the transition between the works of Beethoven's maturity – his so-called second-period style – and the last works of his late style is key to Adorno's sociology of modern music. It is in Beethoven's late style that an anti-harmonistic music of deep suffering is born. Adorno generalises this situation to the late works of other great artists:

> The maturity of the late works of significant artists does not resemble the kind one finds in fruit. They are for the most part not round, but furrowed or even ravaged. Devoid of sweetness, bitter and spiny, they do not surrender themselves to mere delectation. They lack all the harmony that the classicist aesthetic is in the habit of demanding from works of art and they show more traces of history than of growth.
>
> (Adorno 1994c: 102–3)

Adorno explains this by arguing that the more completely these artists approached the integrative and harmonic, the more the 'lie' became apparent to them. The world – and the experience of the subject in the world – is not reconciled but rooted in antagonistic relations. Dissonance then becomes the truth about harmony, a true reflection of the human condition. The sense of this comes to the artist in and through his or her efforts to realise the harmonistic through shaping the aesthetic material with which s/he works. It does not necessarily reflect an insight into social or political life nor, argues Adorno, is it a statement about personal sufferings. It is a realisation of the lack of truth-value at the level of artistic creation:

> Aesthetic harmony is never fully attained; it is either superficial polish or temporary balance. Inside everything that can justly be called harmonious in art there are vestiges of despair and antago-nism . . . the antiharmonistic postures of Michelangelo, of the mature Rembrandt and Beethoven are all attributable to the inner development of the concept of harmony and in the last analysis to its insufficiency. *They have nothing to do with the subjective pain and suffering experienced by these artists.* [emphasis mine] Dissonance is the truth about harmony. . . . Harmony presents something as actually reconciled which is not. In so doing it violates the postulate of

appearing essence which the ideal of harmony aims at. The historical emancipation from harmony as an ideal has been an important
aspect of the development of art's truth content.

(T. Adorno 1984: 160–1)

However, while the realisation of truth-value in the late style of an artist
like Beethoven cannot be viewed as simply a reflection or record of his
personal sufferings, the artist's felt response to life and its challenges, his
sensibility as it has been shaped by experience, enters into the creative
process. Such a sensibility is mediated by the stages of the life-cycle of the
artist, each of which is distinctive, and none more so than the 'end-game'. In
Adorno's sociology, the material with which the artist works, and which is
the real source of the realisation of the impossibility of his project, is material that has been formed by society, and it is material in which the history
of that society is congealed. The discovery of the impossibility of a reconciliation of part and whole in music is thus a reflection of the impossibility of
reconciling individual and society. It is a discovery that is mediated by the
artist's personal life experience, his or her relations in society, and it is mediated, too, by the artist's attainment of considerable mastery in the handling
of the aesthetic material with which s/he works.

What makes the late style of Beethoven so significant is its relationship
to the times in which it developed. Thus, Adorno claims:

Subsequent to Beethoven there has not been a single work that
matches his late quartets in terms of truth content. But the reasons
for this are objective: the status of these quartets in terms of material, spirit and technique, was unique and will never be duplicated,
not even by an artistic talent greater than Beethoven's.

(T. Adorno 1984: 298)

But what causes a few artists to develop late styles that effectively deconstruct their earlier work, and why are such styles frequently marked by the
experience of dissonance, conflict and disorder? Adorno places the emphasis
on the artist's insight into the possibilities inherent in the aesthetic material,
in the resistance of the material to his efforts to realise his artistic objectives.
The material is already organised when the artist inherits it. The artist
engages with the material, seeking to bring out of the inherent dialectic of
subject and object, of spirit and form, a positive synthesis, a reconciliation of
part and whole of spirit and matter. The more that the artist pursues this
reconciliation the greater is the degree of resistance he meets with in the
material, and the greater is the corresponding constructive force or violence
that is required from him to formulate such a reconciliation. The artist is
thus brought, through his or her engagement with the material itself, to the
realisation of the artificial and illusionary nature of the reconciliation s/he is

seeking. Once that objective is relinquished, the artist realises the true condition of the subject, its homelessness in the world.

In Victor Turner's discussion of communitas, liminality is a universal feature of all social life and is not a dialectic attributable to one type of society rather than another. In that sense all varieties of social life manifest an oscillation between their conventional and liminal 'moments', as though social structures and aesthetic structures were subject to the equivalent of the second law of thermodynamics – the tendency to increasing entropy. We might express this as a process of continuous approximation to and departure from an equilibrium state, or, in Victor Turner's terms, structure and anti-structure. Paradoxically, the departure from structure can be seen as a response to disorder and as a call to order. It is the increasing entropy of structures which generates the move away from structure, and such a move is often experienced as a liberative high-energy moment, a liminal state. The liminality of an artist's late style can be likened to the high energy state of 'negative entropy'. The very equilibrium between subject and world which constitutes a successful adaptation in art or in life will, as a result of its very success, bring the subject into contact with experience that can no longer be ordered by these means. It is this which makes the falseness of convention universal and not just specific to a certain type of society. When such recalcitrant events proliferate, equilibrium gives way to its opposite, disequilibrium, before some new plateau can be reached and a (temporary) stability re-established. Such a way of thinking about development does not treat equilibrium or disequilibrium (as descriptive of the state of relations between subject and world) as absolutes or as permanent. The development of subject–world relations is, according to such a view, a continuous process of equilibration–disequilibration (structure and anti-structure).

Piaget's assimilation–accommodation model

The dialectical process of development, so characteristic of all varieties of Hegelianism, is realised in its modern biological form in the genetic epistemology of Jean Piaget (J. Piaget 1970, 1972, 1978). In Piaget's theory the development of the intelligence and understanding of the individual results from a continuous process of subject–world interaction through the twin invariant processes of *assimilation* and *accommodation*. These serve Piaget in a similar way to the Kantian *a priori* categories. They are not innate ideas or categories, however, but innate modes of functioning. By 'assimilation' is meant the process by which the subject assimilates the world to the self – that is, responds to the world in terms of its own schemata – which have developed as a result of past interactions – by acting 'as if' the world corresponded to those schemata. Play and make-believe, the life of the imagination, etc., involve an excess of assimilation over accommodation because play is a mode in which the subject goes out of itself to things.

When a child behaves towards a broom as though it is a person, s/he is assimilating the person-like characteristics of the broom to his or her person schema. By 'accommodation' is meant the process by which the subject changes and adapts those same schemata (the structures of intelligence and knowledge) to meet the demands of the external world. Whenever the individual is rigidly conformist or attempts to imitate others exactly or to model their behaviour, there is an excess of accommodation over assimilation. Put crudely, in assimilation there is a primitive sympathy between subject and world – the subject finds expression in the world which resonates to its schemata – whereas, in accommodation, the world impacts upon the subject – in all its difference and otherness and the subject reconstructs its schemata to make them correspond to the characteristics of the world.

Adorno, as a post-Hegelian thinker, also tends to treat subject–world relations in a similar way. His contrast between mimesis and construction, for example, captures something of Piaget's distinction between assimilation and accommodation. Mimesis is the subjective element, that primitive sympathy of the subject in respect of its objects which facilitates the expressivity of the subject, whereas construction has the sense of an external organising process (T. Adorno 1984).

In the modern world there is a more or less sharp bifurcation of mental life into the sensuous realm of subject–object relations – the province of the aesthetic and the arts – and the instrumental realm of object relations which is the province of ratiocination and science. At the level of the sensuous life, an equilibrium between accommodation and assimilation would imply that what Hegel called 'the world's course' would somehow express or realise the aspiration of individuals; that there would be some kind of mimesis of subject and object, individual and society. If modernist art manifests a disequilibrium between subject and world, it no doubt reflects the split between the two worlds of the sensuous domain and the domain of object relations. Science – and the Enlightenment project generally – abstracts the subject as a rational agent from the subject as a sensuous and feeling being. Assimilation and accommodation thus proceed at the level of object relations more or less independently of the process whereby the life process (subject schemata) of the sensuous subject seeks expression or realisation in that world. Piaget's understanding of intelligence, as I have argued elsewhere (R. Witkin 1995), is more or less exclusively concerned with the domain of object relations, and his epistemology takes no account of the meaning of this disjunction for the exercise of intelligence by the artist. This disjunction between the two worlds of subject and object engenders what one might call a crisis of subjectivity; an all-powerful and integrated world of objects confronts a subjectivity that is not expressed, realised or fulfilled in it; moreover, the very development of this heightened objectivity has been achieved through exiling the sensuous and non-rational, non-cognitive element in mental life. In response to that exiling of the sensuous dimension there were those in the Romantic tradition who made of it an absolute virtue and hypostatised both art and the sensuous life as a special mode of understanding distinct from and counterposed to reason. Such a position was strongly opposed by Adorno, who viewed it as merely reflecting the status quo and the current conditions of socio-economic life.

The fact is, however, that the 'truth-value' of Piagetian theory is not itself independent of the socio-historical conditions in which the theory is grounded. The ontogenesis of intelligence and of mental life reflects that historical development. Adolescence, in Piagetian theory, is the quintessential achievement of the hypothetico-deductive operations of scientific reasoning and the sixteen binary operations of logic. As a mode of intelligence that is dominated by rational cognition – one which banishes the sensuous and the aesthetic modes to the margins of intellectual life – modern adolescence bears the scars and wounds of the European Enlightenment. The ontogenesis of intelligence has to be seen, therefore, as itself constituted by a modernity that culminated in the abstract domination of economic and calculative values – of exchange values and market societies; as process it may be universal and invariant, but the structures that are realised in that process are conditioned by the systems of social relations in which they are grounded.

In Piagetian theory, the attainment of the stage of formal operations as the mature stage, which completes the development of knowledge structures in the individual, reflects the attainment of an equilibrium between assimilation and accommodation at a higher level of operation. However, that very equilibration might itself be said to precipitate a critical break between the sensuous and the instrumental life, a break which leads to a revolt of the subject against the structures which no longer realise the expressive life of the subject but exclude and impede it. Piaget has nothing to say about such a possibility, but his theory offers the prospect of conceptualising the specific form taken by the revolt against structure in the modern world. It was the advance of rational instrumentalism which was central to the sociology of the nineteenth century and, especially, the conceptualisation of the alienation of the subject. For such a subject, denied the possibility of self-actualisation in 'the world's course', a relentless process of accommodation (construction) of the subject to the world's course threatens the subject with extinction. The symbolic realisation of such a process of accommodation, however, can itself be made a means to express the suffering of the subject, mutilated by it as in Kafka's bleak tales or in the plays of Samuel Beckett. In other words, the most extreme constructivism – in Piagetian terms the most extreme accommodation – becomes in itself the vehicle of mimesis, of assimilation and expression.

Back to Adorno!

For those artists who were in the vanguard of intellectual developments in bourgeois society during the positive phase of its making (from the fifteenth to the early nineteenth centuries), the pursuit of a harmonising synthesis, an identity of subject and object, was key to their projects. The artist's material – material which is inherited and which is historically developed – is, in a sense, a 'simulacrum' in which are reproduced the structural relations governing action in society generally. Such a simulacrum embodies, as material, all the same limitations. It is, therefore, conceivable that the artist, relentlessly pursuing the possibilities for developing his or her material, may discover the falseness of the project of synthesis simply on the basis of the mastery of the aesthetic material alone. Just as Marx claimed that a revolution could not occur until all the forces had matured in the womb of the old society, so the deconstructive realisation of the limits of harmony depends upon the artist realising to the full the harmonistic possibilities in the material with which s/he works. Such a full development of the harmonistic possibilities comes only with the mastery attained in the artist's maturity. It is thus in the artist's late style (in the case of those artists who actually have a late style) that s/he can deconstruct the work of his or her maturity and unleash the dissonant, disequilibrating forces through which the subject is brought once more into an authentic relationship with the world.

It is possible, therefore, to imagine that artists like Rembrandt and Beethoven can, through their advanced development of the material with which they work, realise the failure of synthesis long before events in socio-political life correspond to or appear to confirm any such insight. Such artists are ahead of the game, but not in the sense of prophesying the future of socio-political life or even of developing a socio-political understanding: rather, in comprehending the very limits of the developmental possibilities of the aesthetic material which they have inherited from society. The insight itself remains bound to the aesthetic domain and to the conditions of the life-world of the artist. From the point of view of the analyst there is no need to posit a contemporaneous 'fit' between particular developments in economic life or in social production and particular developments in artistic form. On the contrary, there may be a considerable time lag between developments in the two spheres.

The banality of conventions

All artists make use of techniques and conventions that have been accumulated within the tradition: conventional ways of doing things, of solving problems and so forth. These learned solutions – the accumulated wisdom of the culture of pottery-making, poetry, drama, art or whatever – can be likened to all those accumulated forms in natural language; those ready-made forms of utterance, linguistic structures and conventions that we mobilise every time we speak. Words are not isolated elements which we combine at will. They are already organised as a body of accumulated forms in which the history of speech communities has congealed. In truly embodied or expressive speech, the deployment of such forms in the shaping of utterance is commanded by the subject, much as the master potter commands the techniques and conventions through which s/he makes pots or a pianist utilises the scales and routines s/he has practised. So long as speech or action remains embodied, then there will be no break between inner/outer, subject/object; there will be an experience of continuity throughout. Utterance will appear to be 'eloquent'.

When conventions become 'mere conventions' and are emptied of any kind of living expression – mere form – they can be subsumed within the category of *the banal*. As natural language, musical language or the language of painting, etc., grows more mechanical, more clichéd, more incapable of expressing, its conventions and forms take on the character of the banal. The banal is a key category in Adorno's discussion of modernist music and modernity (T. Adorno 1992). Just as the commodity appears as more or less disembodied, as abstracted from the sinewy social relations through which it is produced – a kind of 'reified' object – so language conventions which are emptied of the expression of the subject are equally ghostly, reified things. The formalists who spoke of life as a 'gasp between clichés' captured this notion. In everyday speech we frequently employ conventional and clichéd forms of speech as a kind of filler – 'in the final analysis', 'when all is said and done', 'at the end of the day', etc. However, when speech and action are no longer *embodied*, when the form of the subject's own actions no longer expresses or fulfils the sensuous life of the subject – as in the case of work that is mechanical and which reduces the individual to the level of an automaton or a manikin – then such forms appear to consciousness as alien, as superimposed.

The proliferation of structure within language (either natural or aesthetic language) which is disembodied utterance, mere form, is associated with the growing commodification of life. Indeed, commodification is really defined in an analogous way. The commodity is the very form of a product abstracted from the sinewy relations of production through which it was made and circulating in a system of exchange values. Just as the commodity instantiates the disjunction between the subject and the forms of its own activity, so in musical or natural language mere forms or conventions reflect the same disjunction between the sensuous subject and the forms of its utterance. Moreover, the disjunction represents not only the alienation of the individual in society but also the disparity of power between them. Commodification is the work of the machinery of social production as it impinges upon and uses the individual. It therefore represents force that is external and collective in character. The conventions of language are similarly the repository of the collective. They are the modes of inherited organisation from which the spirit of the subject is disjoined. The subject no longer finds fulfilment or expression in the meaningless and ceaseless activity of what Hegel called 'the world's course'. This crisis of modernity, a crisis that had its origins in the development of bourgeois institutions, bourgeois economic life and the labour process, extended deeply into the realm of the arts. It was quintessentially reflected in the emergence of Beethoven's late style.

Motives and values

'Mere' conventions may be disembodied, in the sense that they are no longer imbued with spirit nor expressive of the life process of the subject; but they are, nevertheless, repositories for the congealed intentions that are inherited from the past and which represent the presence and pressure of the world in its otherness. In commodities as well as in the conventions of natural and aesthetic languages, *desire* is inscribed as an externalised and reified 'affordance'; it is what conventional and commodified forms 'afford' the subject in use. Opaque to expression and to the sensuous fulfilment of the subject, these alien forms impinge upon the individual, constructing desire.

Desire belongs to the *discourse of motives* (R. Witkin 1997). The more developed the commodification of life − a development which reflects the rational-technical progress of the means of production and administration − the more does it shape the desires of subjects so as to make of them its creatures. In such a way, individuals are brought to desire what they are required to buy or to consume in order to feed the machinery of production, and to fear what they are required to reject and oppose in order to serve, preserve and defend the machinery of production. The totalitarian forces of capitalist society seemed to Adorno to be immense, and the power of self-expression to be correspondingly weak.

Self-expression, however, does not belong to a discourse of motives. As the process by which the subject externalises his or her social being, it is both the means of bringing the subject to self-consciousness and a means of realising sensuous coherence at the level of social life. As such, self-expression belongs to a *discourse of values*. The mode of analysis and use of terminology here are mine, not Adorno's, but my argument and conclusions are, I believe, consistent with his (R. Witkin 1997). In Adorno's vision of modern society, what I am calling a discourse of values is progressively being drowned out by an instrumentalisation of social relations. That is, social life is increasingly dominated by a discourse of motives. Adorno expressed this in the Marxian language of political economy in terms of the domination of 'exchange values'. The usurpation of value by motive led to the de-sociation of social life and to the annihilation of the possibility of the development of the subject, of change and of the historical. True sociality and history is grounded in the expressive relations through which social life is dynamically constituted by active subjects. Without the discourse of values through which this is realised, sociality and history are brought to a halt. Modern society and modern art and music confront this threat. Art, at its best, finds a *via negativa*, a way for the subject to express itself not positively but negatively. It is expression which manifests itself in and through its absence from forms, an *absence* which in itself constitutes a negative *presence* or indwelling in forms. It is from this negative presence that the artist strikes the expression of a suffering humanity, much as Kafka succeeds in doing in *The Trial* or *The Castle*, or Beckett does in *Waiting for Godot*, or Schoenberg in *Erwartung*.

The banal in art represents the appearance of the commodified world. For Adorno, therefore, this element is inescapable in an art that has truth-value in the modern world. The integrity of the modern subject must somehow be realised in art through 'acknowledgement' of the power of the banal, much as good is made to acknowledge the power of evil.

The subject of modernity, weak, overwhelmed and defeated – these are all descriptions which held truth-value for Adorno – survived, as in Beethoven's late style, not through its identity with the forms that constitute the banal but through its non-identity with them, its capacity to realise itself in mutually deconstructive counter-forms. The subject that moves in and out of forms, merging with them and emerging from them, can be characterised by the term Baudelaire used, *evanescence*. These two elements, the banality of the world and the evanescence of the subject, are key in modernist art. In the art of an earlier bourgeois society, the world is presented as mastered by the embodied subject; in a modernist art, by contrast, the subject's weakness is its power, its withholding of itself, its non-identity with the disembodied forms of an oppressive order. The world is not mastered by such a subject but undermined by it. It is the evanescence of the modern subject which ensures that – to quote Marx – 'all that is solid melts into air'.

The development of Beethoven's music is seen as encapsulating both the ascent of bourgeois idealism and its decline. What is pivotal for Adorno is the music of the middle (second) period compositions, which include the great symphonies, and the contrasting music of the late (third) period compositions, which include the late quartets and which, for Adorno as for many others, represent a pinnacle of achievement in European art music. The span of Beethoven's work is made, in Adorno's analysis, to encompass both the progressive phase of bourgeois ideology, which governs his middle-period compositions, and the progressive deconstruction of that ideology in his late compositions, a deconstruction which heralds the 'crisis of modernity'. Thus Adorno can accept both Beethoven's conformity with bourgeois ideology (in the age of its innocence) and his later critical relation to it when its illusory nature becomes apparent. Middle and late Beethoven can be seen as authentic and progressive because they possess truth-content: that is, they are true to the historical conditions governing their realisation.

There is, therefore, a dual face to ideology. On the one hand, it may have some real basis in the demands of practical daily life and be useful to the production and motivation of that life. On the other hand, it may describe an aspiration which is, in the long run, inherently impossible of achievement. Moreover, we need to distinguish between the illusionary nature of an ideological aspiration as it exists prior to the time when its character as illusion can be known, and the type of reactionary distortion that occurs at an ideological level after that time and for the purpose of defending against just such a penetration of its character as illusion. From a moral standpoint, we might be inclined to view an ideology as being progressive or reactionary, as possessed of truth-content or not, on the basis of its functional relationship to the development of practical action. In the making of a bourgeois society, the elements of bourgeois ideology constituted a set of formative ideals guiding the construction of society. They also constituted a mode of *critical* thought, an opposition to forms of traditionalism. In the 'heroic' phase of an entrepreneurial capitalism, the possibility of a liberation from tradition and a reconciliation of individual and society must have appeared real. To that extent, ideology and social formation converged. The convergence, however, was only partial and transient, and an ideology which appeared to clarify the world ultimately served to obscure it from view. In that sense, up to a given point in the development of bourgeois society, bourgeois ideology might be described as progressive, and after that time as reactionary. Although Adorno does not put the matter in this way, it is reasoning consistent with his treatment of Beethoven as a composer.

As a post-Hegelian thinker, Adorno subscribes to the idea of development as the progress of self-knowledge of the subject; his evaluation (not necessarily the same thing as his appreciation) of the music of past composers is always affected by where he sees them in terms of how far their music attains to this self-knowledge. Technique alone can never decide the matter. A composer more accomplished in technique may nevertheless be regressive in idea and expression as compared with a less technically accomplished composer. In this respect Adorno's reflections on the relative merits of Bach and Beethoven as composers is interesting. Although the two represent, for him, twin peaks of technical brilliance, he does not hesitate to accord Beethoven primacy because he believes that his music represents a higher level of truth-content:

> Progress is more than growing technical mastery and spiritualisation. It is also the progress of the spirit in the Hegelian sense of the term, i.e. an increasing awareness by spirit of its freedom. There is room for endless disagreement on the question of whether Beethoven was superior to Bach in terms of mastery of materials.

Each probably has mastered different dimensions of material, and each probably did so equally well. To ask which of the two ranks more highly is therefore a moot question. It is only when we use the criterion of truth content – the emancipation of the subject from myth and the reconciliation of both – that Beethoven emerges as the more advanced composer. This criterion outweighs all others in importance.

(T. Adorno 1984: 303)

Adorno continuously offers us 'hearings' of music in which his vision of truth-content is central. It is an approach that deliberately runs counter to an appreciation of music as an ahistorical culinary experience, to the type of hearing that, for example, can rove freely over different types and epochs of music and can judge this or that music to be superior because it produces a more enjoyable effect upon oneself as a listener than other types of music. It is truth and not enjoyment which Adorno sees as the raison d'être for modern music. He sees truth in the modern world as hard and bloody. Being true to a late capitalist society means, for Adorno, eschewing everything easy, warm or seductive and developing a music which is equal to what he sees as the immense threat to all spiritual life and expression posed by a commodified world.

The greater the autonomy of an artwork from social or institutional imperatives, the more precisely will its formal constitution depict the structure and conflicts of the society in which the artist works. Aesthetic form, the artwork's perceptual frame, is, as a product of consciousness, shaped by the social objectivity that mediates all consciousness; thus the more the artwork relies on its own autonomous form rather than trying to depict, immediately, social reality, the more distinctly will this reality and its antagonisms appear in cipher in the work's perceptual arrangements and the tensions they engender: 'It is as a dynamic totality, not as a series of images that great music becomes an intrinsic theatre of the world' (T. Adorno 1984: 76).

Mature Beethoven

In his critical reflections concerning the pedagogical approach of NBC's *Music Appreciation Hour*, Adorno does not hesitate to assert that Beethoven should be treated as the centre of musical history, as the standard or measure of what went before in classical music as well as what was to come after. The music of Beethoven's own maturity was the music of his middle or second-period compositions, which included most of the symphonies. Adorno associates this music with the attempt to realise, aesthetically, an integral relationship between the individual and society – a reconciliation between the freedom of the individual and the constraint of society – which is the dream of all bourgeois idealism. Adorno claims that the popularity of

Beethoven's second-period compositions with audiences in his own day was probably due to the extent to which they embodied, in music, the structural dynamics of just such an identity between individual and society – to the extent, that is, that they inscribed bourgeois ideology (T. Adorno 1994c). The music of Beethoven's second-period compositions celebrates the development of the bourgeois subject as secure in the mastery of his world.

In the great symphonies and sonatas of his mature style (as distinct from his late style), Beethoven achieves the appearance of a music in which the form of the music as a whole appears to be generated organically, from below, by the *becoming* of the parts or elements in their mutual relations. Adorno saw this as a major achievement and as the quintessential realisation in music of an apparent reconciliation between the collective force of society, which he identified with 'form' in music, and the spontaneous movement of free individuals – represented in music in the sensuous particulars or elements, the motives and material which the composer forms into musical works. It was Beethoven's special contribution to have produced a music which appeared to unify the particular and the universal – individual and society, subject and object – to harmonise them. This contrasted with an earlier music in which the parts were annihilated by the imposition of the whole, and a later music where the whole was annihilated in the most extreme assertion of the elements. Empty abstraction results from attempting to lose one or other pole of this antinomy. Beethoven's music achieves its plenitude through the dynamic mediation of part and whole. Moreover, because he sought to meet the criterion referred to above – that music and society should each be a continuum consisting in the becoming of their parts – he refined the elements or parts so that they would fit smoothly into each other:

> Instead of mechanically annihilating the individual elements, as was the standard practice during the age immediately before him, he [Beethoven] stripped them of their specificity, which is not unlike the approach the bourgeois spirit takes in natural science. Consequently he not only integrated music into a continuum of becoming, and spared form the dire fate of emptiness and abstraction, but he also made sure the individual elements would pass into one another, determining form as they vanish. In Beethoven, the particulars have a momentum in the direction of the totality. For the most part they become what they are because of their relation to the whole.
>
> (T. Adorno 1984: 264–5)

Repeatedly in his discussions of Beethoven, Adorno points to what he calls the 'nothingness' of the elements or parts in a Beethoven sonata or symphony, even as he shows us what an overwhelming effect a single chord or note can have when heard in the context of a specific composition. For example, just before the reprise of the first movement of Beethoven's 'Kreutzer' Sonata, there is what Adorno describes as 'an enormously effective chord in the key of the second subdominant'. Occurring anywhere outside of the 'Kreutzer' Sonata, the same chord would be more or less trivial (T. Adorno 1984: 130). The power of its effect is determined by its function within the composition as a whole. But the fact that the meaning of this chord cannot be understood in isolation from the whole is a result of its thorough 'sociation'. It is the whole structure of tonal relations which is immanent in this chord and which gives it its substance. As Adorno puts it:

> Yet the nothingness of the particular – that its meaning cannot be understood in isolation from the whole – makes conversely for its substantiality, since the whole structure of tonal relations is immanent in the particular melodic moment. Beethoven's success consists in the fact that in his work, and there alone, the whole is never extrinsic to the particular, but proceeds alone out of its movement or, rather, is its movement. In Beethoven, there is never mediation *between* themes; rather, as in Hegel, the whole, as pure becoming, is itself the concrete mediation.
>
> (C. Sample 1994: 383)

I have used the term 'sociation' in a broad sense to take account of something that language, music and society have in common. They are systems of relationships. Each word in a language, each motive in a musical composition, is 'sociated' to the extent that the system as a whole is somehow reflected in it. The quality of being an individual is that of being like an element in language or a citizen of a state – a society in one of its parts. Thus, as Colin Sample puts it:

> Just as the entire ethical substance of a citizen in an Hegelian state consists in his relationships within the social totality, so in Beethoven's music the meaningfulness of the particular moment is only to be made out in the light of its relations to the whole.
>
> (C. Sample 1994: 382–3)

It is this sociation, moreover, which provides the logical force of development, of history and biography; it is the inexorable unfolding of the totality through the development of its elements or parts:

> The first movements of the Eroica, the Pastoral, the Ninth, are ultimately only commentaries on what takes place in their opening measures. The mightiest intensifications that Beethoven has created – the lines from the beginning of the Fifth and Seventh symphonies

to their conclusions – unroll with the overwhelming logic that the revelation of an ineluctably self-consistent event implies. It has the imperturbability of a mathematical formula and stands before us from the first moment to its last ramifications as an elemental fact. It is precisely in the irrefutable logical force of this art that its power resides, the unparalleled effect that Beethoven's symphonies have even today. It gave rise to the fundamental organic law that Beethoven could not escape even in the Ninth, the law that forcibly concentrated the basic idea in the opening phrase, the beginning, the theme, and evolved the whole organism as something ready-made from the beginning.

(P. Bekker 1921: 16)

Late Beethoven

Language, whether natural or musical, can only be a vehicle for truth if the sociation congealed in its forms can answer to the social relations that bind the members of the community in the present. Where the congealed sociality of language is no longer capable of any true correspondence to social relations and conditions in the present, then it becomes worn out and clichéd. What is true of natural language is true of the musical material with which the composer works. A system of social relations – an historical development – is sedimented in all its elements and forms. To the extent that the social relations sedimented in the musical material have lost their correspondence and relevance to social life in the present, so musical life becomes increasingly mired in cliché forms. Its stock of truth-value dwindles rapidly to nothing. Thus, Adorno argues that it is ultimately the reality of social life and social experience which precipitates the crisis of utterance, of expression, and which makes necessary a thoroughgoing revolution at the level of the musical material. It is conceivable, as I suggest above, that the insufficiency and inadequacy of the inherited musical material, as language, may become apparent to a composer simply as a result of his own attempts to develop the possibilities of that material to the full.

In Beethoven's case, as Rose Subotnik points out, the extreme propulsion of the development sections in his second-period compositions belie the illusion that the part and whole can exist freely in his sonata movements. For that to happen, we must feel that the development sections of a musical work proceed freely in the filling out of the form as a whole. But the smooth 'fit' of the elements is not achieved without a great deal of hidden violence. The demands of the development process tend to grind down the musical materials until the individual elements fit smoothly into each other (R. Subotnik 1976: 252). Just as excessive socialisation can produce a conformist individual who is completely subservient to society's demands, so the advanced development of the system of tonal harmony can similarly undermine the freedom of the particular elements or parts of the music and subordinate them more or less completely to the dominating demands of the whole:

> In fact, according to Adorno, just as the work of society ultimately requires the sacrifice of individuality, so too, Beethoven's development tends to wear down its engendering material – the musical subject – to the point where the latter negates itself entirely in the service of the larger entity.
>
> (R. Subotnik 1976: 252)

The problem of the domination of the whole over the part can be put in terms of the two moments of aesthetic practice which Adorno labels 'expression' and 'construction'. Construction is the 'forming' of content but expression is the sensuous response of the subject. The exclusive preoccupation with either moment is a violation of truth-content since Adorno rejects both the notion of an absolute subject, self-contained and self-sufficient, and that of an absolute 'object', a totalitarian organising force – whether or not it conceals its domination. Truth, for Adorno, is bound up with the struggle against both these extreme tendencies which, for him, constitute the poles of pathology in the modern world – on the one hand, of an empty gestural anarchy and, on the other, of a Fascistic order. It is in the disintegrative work of their late styles that a few composers, such as Beethoven, achieve a quantum leap in truth-content and against the odds struggle to maintain the poles of the antinomy in the grip of a negative dialectics:

> Truth in art is no longer adequately articulated either by expression – for expression merely fills the helpless individual with a false sense of importance – or by construction – for construction is more than just an analogy to the bureaucratic world. Extreme integration is illusion pushed to the extreme. But there is the possibility of a reversal of this process: ever since the late Beethoven, those artists who had gone farthest along the road to integration were able to mobilise disintegration eventually. At this point in the career of an artist the truth content of art whose vehicle was integration turns against art. It is precisely at these turning points that art has had some of its greatest moments. What pressures artists into making such about-faces is the realisation that their works are overloaded with elements of organisation and control. . . . Before he reaches this disintegrative truth, the artist must traverse the field of integration with its triumphs and defeats. Akin to the concept of disintegration is that of the aesthetic fragment. . . . It is not some contingent particular, but that portion of the totality of the art work that resists being integrated.
>
> (T. Adorno 1984: 67)

The subject constitutes itself in social relations with others in the context of a shared world that is inherited and undergoing development, a world which is captured in the intentionality of forms. The loss of this shared inheritance prevents the subject from constituting itself as an historical and intentional being. Neither individually nor collectively can subjects undergo genuine change or transformation when their relations are no longer governed by intentionality. In such a situation, each element of a discourse – each note or element of music – would be independent of every other element and each individual subject independent of every other subject. Such a subject would be entirely susceptible to the imposition of order from outside, would be incapable of bringing order out of itself. This is part of the pathology that Adorno is criticising in the development of modern music, and he sees it as developing in both the 'reactionary' and the 'progressive' tendencies in modern music. Thus he opposes Stravinsky and sympathises with Schoenberg, but he sees both as converging from different sides towards an annihilation of the subject and of all expression in music (T. Adorno 1980). Both lead to an omnipresent constructivism at the expense of the expressive and 'mimetic' moment in music (see Chapters 7 and 8).

In the mature music of his middle-period compositions, Beethoven's advances in achieving the appearance of harmony were realised through an increase in the constructive force of the work to the point where the role of construction in undermining genuine expression could be perceived. This increase in constructive force was demanded by the condition of the inherited and developed material and was, therefore, real. It marked the true condition of the subject confronted with the monolithic administrative force of modernity, of bureaucracy. From this point on, a music that had truth-value could no longer be governed by the illusion of harmony, but would have to recognise the true nature of force in the condition of the subject dominated and even overwhelmed by it. From now on, for the serious modern artist, there could be no more pretence that individual and society were reconciled or that the sensuous life of the subject could find its fulfilment and expression in society; the authentic work of art would henceforth have to reproduce the rupture of subject and object, of individual and society, within itself.

In Beethoven's late style, the composer's recognition of this rupture is, for Adorno, the key to understanding his music and its relationship to society. Adorno rejects psychologistic explanations and denies that Beethoven's music is narrowly expressive in the sense of being concerned with personal biography. The formal law of the late works, Adorno argues, is not capable of being subsumed under the concept of expression. The late works of Beethoven are extremely distanced, expressionless works (at least in the sense in which the term 'expression' applies to the middle-period compositions). Subjectivity operates in these works, not so much by breaking through form but, rather more fundamentally, by creating form (T. Adorno 1994c: 103).

If the late works were truly capable of being subsumed in a subjectivist methodology, then the subjective elements would dominate all conventions and forms within the work. 'The first commandment of every subjectivist methodology is to brook no conventions, and to recast those that are unavoidable in terms that are dictated by the expressive impulse' (T. Adorno 1994c: 104). But everywhere in the formal language of Beethoven's late style one finds formulas and phrases of convention scattered about. The works are full of decorative trill sequences, cadences and fiorituras (T. Adorno 1994c: 104). The omnipresence of formulas and conventions in the music is the sign of the withdrawal of the subject from identity with them; it is a mark of the subject's separation from the object.

The realisation of the unreality of the identity of subject and object leads to their parturition, to the subject's abandonment of the forms that it had once inhabited and filled out as living language. Just as a word or phrase can suddenly appear to the mind as a sound pattern emptied of all meaning and therefore as isolated and split off from other phrases in the language, so the conventions and forms of music – the phrases and forms that have been abandoned by the subject – are splintered and fragmented; they move off, as the subject withdraws from them, like icebergs adrift in an ocean. These husks or shells emptied of the subject correspond to the 'banality' of the appearances of the commodified world. It is from these fragmented forms that the composer seeks to strike expression anew; not the expression of an isolated subject but the condition of a world caught in the light of its abandonment, a world in which is refracted the infinite powerlessness of the subject:

> The power of subjectivity in the late works of art is the irascible gesture with which it takes leave of the works themselves. It breaks their bonds not in order to express itself but in order, expressionless, to cast off the appearance of art. Of the works itself, it leaves only fragments behind and communicates itself like a cipher, only through the blank spaces from which it has disengaged itself. Touched by death the hand of the master sets free the masses of material that he used to form; its tears and its fissures, witnesses to the infinite powerlessness of the I confronted with Being, are its final work. . . . With the breaking free of subjectivity they splinter off. And as splinters, fallen away and abandoned, they themselves finally revert to expression; no longer at this point an expression of the solitary I but of the mythical nature of the created being and its fall, whose steps the late works strike symbolically as if in the momentary pauses of their descent.
>
> (T. Adorno 1994c: 104)

In late Beethoven the phrases, conventions and forms, the trills and cadenzas and flourishes, are freed of the appearance of having been mastered by the subject. The subject's absence from them is, of itself, a palpable negative presence, an indwelling. However, these 'empty' phrases do not simply speak for themselves. The subjectivity that abandons them provides the light in which they are seen; the sufferings of the subject are projected in that light. Adorno notes the disjunction within the music between the musical construction itself and the extremes of expression that are developed in the music – such as crescendi and diminuendi – and which seem to be independent of the construction. The subject's intentionality thus makes itself felt both negatively – in its absence from form and in the silences, discontinuities and spaces in the music – and positively – in its efforts to break through the forms that make up the walls of its prison. This effort of the alienated subject to fill the musical structure with its intentions breaks up that structure; the subject then withdraws, leaving the petrified material, the abandoned forms behind:

> On the one hand the monophony, the *unisono* of the significant mere phrase; on the other the polyphony which rises above it without mediation. It is subjectivity that forcibly brings the extremes together in the moment, fills the dense polyphony with its intentions, breaks it apart with the *unisono*, and disengages itself, leaving the naked tone behind; that sets the mere phrase as a monument to what has been, marking a subjectivity that has turned to stone. . . . Objective is the fractured landscape, subjective the light in which, alone, it glows into life. He [Beethoven] does not bring about their harmonious synthesis. As the power of dissociation, he tears them apart in time, in order, perhaps, to preserve them for the eternal. In the history of art, late works are the catastrophes.
>
> (T. Adorno 1994c: 107)

In Beethoven's late style, the forms and conventions of music unmediated by subjectivity become the content of the work. They represent the principle of domination and in being brought into relationship with an alienated subjectivity are made to express the human condition. The authenticity of modern works is bound up with this heightened objectivity. Through objectively realising the principle of domination in the aesthetic form, the repressed subject finds a way of expressing itself. Emptiness, ghostliness, banality, every token of the absence of a departed subject fills the works of modernist art with an incandescent suffering.

4

WAGNER

In *The Dialectic of Enlightenment* (1986), Adorno and Horkheimer present the Enlightenment, not as the liberation of the world through the power of reason, but as the enslavement of the world through society's antagonistic and alienated relationship to nature. It is an antagonistic relationship that penetrates all social relationships and hardens them into a rigid prison from which true spontaneity and sociality have been expunged. The conceptual 'grasp' of the Enlightenment – thought as 'the belly turned mind' – subsumes and devours all sensuous particulars, all free spirit. In the conceptual hierarchies of reason, sensuous details and particulars are subsumed by an abstract conceptual order imposed from above. Instrumental reasoning and the calculative mentality take precedence over all else. Such conceptual hierarchies are rooted, argue the authors, in the development of a capitalism in which all things are subordinated to the (abstract) power of money exchange values.

> Even the deductive form of science reflects hierarchy and coercion. Just as the first categories represented the organised tribe and its power over the individual, so the whole logical order of dependency, connection, progression and union of concepts is grounded in the corresponding conditions of social reality – that is, of the division of labor. But of course this social character of categories of thought is not, as Durkheim asserts, an expression of social solidarity but evidence of the inscrutable unity of society and domination. . . . In the impartiality of scientific language, that which is powerless has wholly lost any means of expression, and only the given finds its neutral sign.
>
> (T. Adorno and M. Horkheimer 1986: 21–3)

In the bleak poetics of Adorno and Horkheimer's dialectic, hope of redeeming the promise of the Enlightenment has all but vanished; the flaw appears to be more or less fatal. Only in the utopian dream of a society which is not founded on antagonistic relations, a society in which 'man' lives as an integral part of nature, is it possible to imagine a liberated world made up of individuals who develop in mutual relations that are freely initiated and ordered from below and not (externally) from above. Such a world would be served by a consciousness in which the sensuous particulars of experience predominate.

The 'story' told by Adorno and Horkheimer of the Enlightenment has some structural resonances with that told by Wagner in his giant music-drama – the cycle of four operas known as *The Ring*. There, an act of theft from nature takes place when the Ring of the Nibelungs, which gives to whoever possesses it power over the world and access to the Nibelung treasure, is stolen by Alberich and then taken from him by Wotan, the chief of the gods. The evil cannot be expunged until the gods have fallen and the Ring has been returned to nature. Wotan seeks with every means possible to extend his power and, by subjecting others to his will through calculative reasoning and the making of alliances and treaties, to impose an everlasting order on the world. His project is mired in the sin he cannot expiate, and he ultimately resigns himself to his doom.

In his *Opera and Drama*, Wagner described *The Ring* as 'an understandable image of the whole history of mankind from the beginnings of society to the requisite collapse of the state' (R. Wagner 1995). In a letter to Agust Rÿouckel dated 25 January 1854, Wagner comments on his deeper meaning in a way that again recalls certain aspects of Adorno's own theorising, especially concerning the notion of the freedom of the individual and of change and spontaneity. Every organisation, structure or form – including the institutions of marriage and of family – is potentially a tyranny if it binds individuals without being the expression or realisation of their life process:

> Alberich and his Ring would have been powerless to harm the gods had they not themselves been susceptible to evil. Wherein then is the root of the matter to be sought? Examine the first scene between Wotan and Fricka, which leads up to the scene in the second act of *Die Walküre*. The necessity of prolonging beyond the point of change, the subjection of the tie that binds them – a tie resulting from an involuntary illusion of love, the duty of maintaining at all costs the relation into which they have entered, and so placing themselves in a hopeless opposition to the universal law of change and renewal, which governs the world of phenomena – these are the conditions which bring the pair of them to a state of torment and natural lovelessness.
>
> (A. Goldmann and E. Sprinchorn 1981: 290–1)

The development of the whole poem sets forth the necessity of recognising and yielding to the change, the many-sidedness, the multiplicity, the eternal renewing of reality and of life. Thus Wagner also locates the moral downfall of society in the principle of subjection, whereby individuals and particulars are subsumed within an abstract totality and lose the freedom to change and develop freely in relations with others. The threat posed by the development of the modern state to the freedom of the modern subject dominates Wagner's thinking in the construction of *The Ring* as it did that of Adorno and Horkheimer in *The Dialectic of Enlightenment*.

However, notwithstanding the apparent resonances between the two very different projects, Adorno was deeply ambivalent concerning the music of Richard Wagner. In his book on Wagner he sought to argue that, at a musicological as well as a philosophical level, Wagner's brilliant development of advanced musical techniques was integrally wedded to a reactionary and regressive musical praxis. When Wagner's commitment to change, to many-sidedness and multiplicity, is examined in the light of his music, its meaning places him in sharp contrast with Adorno's own idea of the principle of change.

Self-abandonment

Again, as with Beethoven, Adorno identifies the pathology of the age with the overwhelming disparity in power and force between individual and society. He identifies Wagner with the would-be free individual confronted by the repressive force of a monolithic bourgeois social order. The individual who seeks the illusion of completeness, self-sufficiency and self-fulfilment in such a world is merely self-deluded. The weakened subject can surrender to collective force, can cease to claim to be in possession of himself, can acknowledge his weakness and let himself go. Insofar as Adorno sees Wagner in a positive light, it is this interpretation upon which he draws. The artist implacably opposed to the suffocating power of bourgeois order, refusing identity with it or the pretence of fulfilment in it and abandoning himself to an all-consuming passion – even to the point of dying for love – is a stance with which Adorno at least feels able to sympathise. He acknowledges, too, the wealth of Wagnerian musical inventiveness and Wagner's influence on what he sees as progressive modern music.

> There is not one decadent element in Wagner's work from which a productive mind could not extract the forces of the future. The weakening of the monad, which is no longer equal to its situation as monad and which therefore sinks back passively beneath the pressure of totality, is not just a representative of a doomed society. It also releases the forces that had previously grown up within itself, thus turning the monad into a phenomenal being as conceived of by Schopenhauer . . . the monad is 'sick', it is too impotent to enable its principle, that of isolated singularity, to prevail and to endure. It

therefore surrenders itself. Its capitulation does more than just help an evil society to victory over its own protest. Ultimately it also smashes through the foundations of the evil isolation of the individual himself. To die in love means also to become conscious of the limits imposed on the power of the property system over man. It means also to discover that the claims of pleasure, where they were followed through, would burst asunder that concept of the person as an autonomous self-possessed being that degrades its own life to that of a thing, and deludes itself into believing that it will find pleasure in the full possession of itself, whereas in reality that pleasure is frustrated by the fact of self-possession.

(T. Adorno 1981: 153)

Identification with the aggressor

Running in tandem and ahead of this image of self-surrender, however, is a very different interpretation, one which played a considerable part in Adorno's ideas concerning pathology in modern society. For many individuals, the response to the confrontation with the suffocating power of modern society was to be complicit with it. Adorno drew upon Freudian theory here and equated the power disparity between individual and society with that between parent and child. Freud analysed this power disparity in terms of an 'Oedipal crisis'; a boy identifies with the father he fears – that is, 'identifies with the aggressor' – and thereby achieves relief from his psychological distress, no longer fearing the aggressor that he himself has vicariously become. This psychoanalytical mechanism informed Adorno and his colleagues in their later study of 'the authoritarian personality' (T. Adorno *et al.* 1950) and it surfaces, too, in Adorno's critique of jazz (see Chapter 9). In the study of the authoritarian personality, the authors argued that identification with authority – with the aggressor – masks the utmost hostility towards that same authority. This hostility, in itself a source of anxiety, is then safely displaced onto groups and individuals who are not a source of threat. Heinrich Mann's novel *The Man of Straw*, which was published as early as 1913, depicts just such a character.

In his book on Wagner, Adorno generalises the phenomenon by identifying it with the crisis of individuation which he sees to be endemic in late capitalist society. Wagner is an early example of the changing function of the bourgeois category of the individual. 'In his hopeless struggle with the power of society, the individual seeks to avert his own destruction by identifying with that power then rationalizing the change of direction as authentic individual fulfilment' (T. Adorno 1981: 17). Identification with the aggressor does not preserve the individual, however. The price that is paid for it is the de-sociation of the individual to the level of the 'isolated ego'. It is in and through relations with a variety of others that each individual is constituted as a distinctive being and as differentiated from others and distanced from the world. Sociality engenders difference, a gap between self and other to the extent that each individual's relational experience is distinctive; differential sociality constructs the non-identity of subject and object. The closing of this gap between the subject and society – that is, the achievement of a complete identification of the subject with the collective force of society – demands a process of de-sociation, of de-individuation. To identify with collective force as the aggressor is to abandon, at a stroke, the individuality that has been socially constructed and, as pure ego, to merge with the oppressor and gain access vicariously to its power.

Wagner's psychology, according to Adorno, confounds the sociality of the individual with the asocial condition of the isolated ego. His music and his art are filled with the gestural posturing of the ego, with the clamour of great deeds to be done and heroic feats to be performed. For Adorno, the de-sociated ego is marked by its emptiness, its lack of substance. The substantiality of the individual, by contrast, is constituted in and through social relationships. The emptiness of the ego, its character as 'façade', renders it comparable to the *commodity*. Just as the commodity presents itself to consciousness as a reified thing abstracted from the social relationships through which it is constituted, so the asocial ego similarly presents itself as 'in-itself'. The two are not merely comparable: egoism is the subjective state that corresponds to the commodity-form.

Wagner's admiring public

Wagner's relationship with his public is a key aspect of his entire development as a composer. He calculated the *effects* he wished to bring about in the consciousness of his audiences, and he planned carefully the construction of every technical means possible to bring about those effects. He sought to ensure, too, through the design of a special theatre for the presentation of his work, that his work would achieve a status which would set it apart from the work of others, and this has to be counted in as part of the calculated effects. The power of Wagner's music over its devotees has to be seen in the context of a growing disparity between the consciousness of the modern artist and the understanding of the general public. Ever since Beethoven's late style, there had been a growing disjunction between the aesthetic directions taken by composers and the consciousness of their audiences. Beethoven's middle-period compositions may have been aesthetic works in which a bourgeois public could participate enthusiastically, could see its aspirations and energies mirrored, but from the late style on this was no longer the case. Music was increasingly taking up a position more distanced and opposed to bourgeois society and, to that extent, it was becoming progressively distanced from ordinary bourgeois consciousness. This opposition was pressed further in Wagner's advanced musical experimentation. It may seem paradoxical, therefore, that Wagner had no difficulty in finding an admiring public.

Not so, according to Adorno; the gulf that had opened up between the aesthetic objectives of the composer and the bourgeois consciousness of the public was carefully masked by Wagner through a process of actively *commodifying* his works; that is, calculating, in advance, the 'effects' upon an audience and building that calculation into the composition itself as well as into the staging of the works. Adorno implicitly draws a distinction here between two types of appreciation. There is the appreciation of an audience whose sociation and life-world projects resonate with the aesthetic project of the artist, and who can achieve a degree of self-understanding through art; and there is the type of enthusiastic appreciation by an audience for whom no such connection exists between the artist's aesthetic projects and their own, and who surrender to the implosive effects of art upon a de-sociated (reified) consciousness. A public that rejected the music of a modern such as Arnold Schoenberg as incomprehensible and even as unpleasant, nevertheless had no difficulty in accepting such music when its *effects* were simulated by film music composers. Adorno saw the type of appreciation in which music is abstracted to the level of pure effects upon the individual as regressive. Unlike Schoenberg, however, Wagner actively connived at exploiting this reified consciousness in his audience and at developing an appreciation of his work as pure commodity. Adorno thus sees the degree of aesthetic estrangement experienced by the audience as a cultural and social impoverishment which fuels the commodification of art and the development of the culture industry. It is an impoverishment for which the historical conditions of late capitalism prepared both Wagner and his audience. It is an impoverishment that is directly correlated by Adorno with the very intensity of the effects and the enthusiasm and fascination experienced by an audience. Adorno argued that it was only high capitalism that produced an audience whose social and aesthetic assumptions were so far removed from those of the artist that the audience could become the reified object of calculation by the artist (T. Adorno 1981: 31). Thus Wagner's intense preoccupation with staging and with controlling the effects upon the audience is held by Adorno to be in itself an integral aspect of the reified and estranged condition of the audience in respect of the art work.

The transformation of the public into a reified object of calculation is at the very heart of Adorno's analysis of the culture industry, too (see Chapter 9). To the extent that it is accomplished in so-called serious or popular art, it implies a de-sociation of experience and, therefore, a 'de-individuation'. Commodities are not made to vivify or activate an integral sociality but to engender 'effects' upon the psyches of a mass of atomised and estranged individuals. The tendency of commodification is to create 'crowds' – identity of response among individuals – not 'communities'. The crowd is precisely that amorphous body in which the individual can be moved by a surge of emotion and yet, lacking adequate means of differentiation from others, is at his or her weakest. The crowd, as Zimbardo describes it, is a de-individuating phenomenon (P. Zimbardo 1969). Such a de-sociating/de-individuating process was all too visible in Germany and elsewhere during the Nazi period. Anyone seeing Lenie Riefenstahl's pre-war films, particularly, might be inclined to suppose that the entire purpose of the Nazi project was to turn the whole nation into a vast de-individuated crowd. For Adorno, at the time he wrote his book on Wagner, this was a lived nightmare. Commodification and the culture industry were not merely an incidental accompaniment to Fascism, something inherently different but called in aid as means; Adorno insisted on seeing them as aspects of the same phenomenon, the same reifying, de-sociating process. He drove his social and cultural critique to what he saw as the heart of the problem. Fascism in its political form was one aspect of modern pathology, but an understanding of both it and the modern condition had to probe the total system of social and cultural relations of which the political form was but a symptom. In music and in other cultural artefacts, he could see, actualised, a process of construction which was the very analogue of that 'total system'.

Beethoven's subject acknowledges the power of the external force of society but refuses to merge with it. Wagner's subject colludes with that collective force (the identification with the aggressor), turning it – through commodifying it – upon his public. This was, for Adorno – as it was for Marx and for Lukács – the true 'magic' of commodities; the exploitative and antagonistic system of social relations through which commodities are produced for exchange on the market is both concealed and congealed in them and manifests as the power of their appeal.

The *Gesamtkunstwerk*

We thus designate the most perfect unity of artistic thought as that in which a widest conjuncture of the phenomena of human life – as content – can impart itself to the feeling in so completely intelligible an expression that in all its moments this content shall completely stir, and also completely satisfy, the feeling. The content then has to be one that is ever present in the expression and therefore the expression one that ever presents the content in its fullest compass; for whereas the absent can be grasped only by thought, only the present can be grasped by feeling.

(R. Wagner 1995: 348–9)

Completely satisfying the feeling, for Wagner, involves producing a 'total' work of art, one in which the senses, sight and sound combine in a unity, in which words and music, dance and drama are all one integral totality, a *Gesamtkunstwerk*. This was part of Wagner's effort to construct the total experience for his audience. Again, the theory sounds progressive. The division of labour which is the product of bourgeois society has divided the production of works up into works by different specialists – visual, musical, poetic and so forth – and with it the senses themselves. Overcoming the division of labour in the production of the art work, and producing the total integrated work of art in which every sense is brought by a unified consciousness to enrich and express the feeling content, promises to repair at a stroke the ruptures brought into art by an antagonistic division of labour. Adorno is scornful of such a claim. He too acknowledges the negative consequences of the division of labour for culture and for art. However, only a reified and de-sociated consciousness can imagine itself capable of bringing about such a unity in the midst of a bourgeois society. An aesthetic totality cannot be simply willed by an artist alone and in the absence of the social conditions that would be necessary to sustain it. The basic idea of *The Ring*, that of encapsulating the world process as a whole, reflected Wagner's hostility towards everything isolated, limited, fragmentary or existing wholly for itself. It is a protest against the bourgeoisification of art:

> The Wagnerian totality is the enemy of genre art. . . . Like Nietzsche and subsequently Art Nouveau, which he anticipates in many respects, he would like, single-handed, to will an aesthetic totality into being, casting a magic spell and with defiant unconcern about the absence of the social conditions necessary for its survival.
>
> (T. Adorno 1981: 101)

Nothing is free from the determination of bourgeois reality, not even the senses, according to Adorno. An aesthetic totality, as the unification of all the senses, cannot be simply willed into being. Adorno argues that the senses all have a distant history and end up poles apart from each other as a consequence of the reification of reality and the division of labour. The latter divides each man and woman within himself or herself and does not just create division between people. The up-front process of integration serves as a cover for the underlying fragmentation. The different senses have become specialised; they apprehend different realities. Adorno notes the extent to which the eye which perceives reality as a world of solid and graspable objects is an instrument of bourgeois rationality; an organ of concentration, of effort, of work, it is adapted to an objectified and commodified world. The ear, by contrast, is archaic. It has something passive and unselfconscious about it. The desire to render all the senses equivalent and interchangeable in a social world governed by the division of labour could not survive exposure to ordinary cognitive consciousness. That is why, argues Adorno, Wagner's music has, at its heart, a hostility to consciousness. Intoxication, ecstasy and the heady brew of the unconscious become necessary to sustain the delusion of an aesthetic totality. This is the fare Wagner serves up in the music dramas.

The autonomy of the individual arts is not sacrosanct. It is simply a consequence of the division of labour. Wagner's attack on it may have been in the name of humanity but what he offered was not liberation but intoxication and delusion. The greater the degree of commodification and of reification, the more the bourgeois resorts to the unconscious mind to produce an intoxicating and magical world of sensuous events and relations. It is magic in the sense of the irrational and the unconscious which corresponds to the reified consciousness of a commodified society. It is at the level of a more or less primitive irrationality that an attempt can be made to unify the sensuous elements of bourgeois life. Consciousness, which is of the specialising and differentiating type – that is, ordinary rational-technical bourgeois consciousness – would prevent any such project from achieving fruition.

What is needed, Adorno argues, is for a spiritual regeneration of society to arise from genuine and rational co-operation in social production. (It is instructive, in this respect, to consider Adorno's rejection of the authenticity of the social co-operation in the composition and performance of jazz.) Wagner's world is but a reflection of the alienated and impoverished consciousness of bourgeois society which would seek to recover at a sensuous level what it has lost through instrumentality. But such a unification has no basis in social reality; there are no means to achieve it in anything but appearance. Genuine liberation would have demanded the rational control of the labour process in the cause of freedom, but this was not possible for Wagner: his totality was no real totality, but the fragmented world of the individual pretending to be totality. It was again the reified and de-sociated ego taking totality upon itself, a feat that would be quite impossible under modern conditions for the sociated individual. It is not possible for the individual to renounce the division of labour to which s/he owes everything, nor is it possible to conjure from within him/herself all the specialist skills necessary for the *Gesamtkunstwerk*.

Adorno cites Wagner's own critical insight into the necessary conditions for a *Gesamtkunstwerk*.

> No one can be better aware than myself, that the realization of this drama depends upon conditions which do not lie within the will, nay, not even within the capability of a single individual – were this capability infinitely greater than my own – but only in community, and in mutual cooperation made possible thereby: whereas, at the present time, what prevails is the direct antithesis of both these factors.
>
> (T. Adorno 1981: 112)

Phantasmagoria

Adorno explores this illusory world of Wagnerian music drama as a species of 'phantasmagoria'. While the world of Wagnerian heroes and heroines such as Siegfried and Brünnhilde, Tristan and so forth may seem to be a million miles away from the sober realities of European business culture, Adorno treats them as the very product and reflection of bourgeois life. In the first place the character of the operas themselves – as phantasmagoria – simply reflects their character as 'commodities'. The term 'phantasmagoria' was one used by Marx in his discussion of 'commodity fetishism'. The commodity is a phantasmagoria because it conceals the sinewy social relations that went into its production and presents itself to the consciousness of the subject as a 'reified' object belonging to a world of such objects. The real substructure of the commodified world consists in the social relations of production through which commodities are produced. These disappear from view in the process, and return in the guise of a more or less fantastic world of appearances. Because the commodity world appears to the mind of the subject as possessed of a purely external and independent existence, as though it were an autochthonous thing, the relationship of the subject to the externality of the commodity becomes fetishistic and the fetishised world of commodities appears possessed of mythic powers that are non-rational. The occultation of production by means of the outward appearance of the product is what Adorno claims to be the law that governs the works of Richard Wagner (T. Adorno 1981: 90).

Any such occultation of the relations of production through which the work is produced is, for Adorno, a flight from time and from 'nature'. Both time and nature are mediated by the structure of social relations. Eternity, a timeless and perfect totality, stands revealed, in Adorno's analysis, as nothing more than what Schopenhauer described as 'the outside of the worthless commodity'. Wagner could not have achieved such a totality had his subject-matter been genuinely historical, involving real change and development: that is, the all-important element of production. The device he resorts to is to invoke the memory of a pristine age, a phantasmagoria which represents the moment as the eternity which endures. Writing of the image of timelessness in which Brünnhilde sleeps in the phantasmagoria of the magic fire, Adorno observes of the music:

> While the manner of its production is completely concealed in its string sections, harmonically, its progression is most ingeniously that of a state of rest. Not only do the constant harmonic changes produce no new progressions; at the same time systematic modulation through the changing surfaces of different keys makes the music dance around the basic harmonies which remain constant at

any given moment, like a fire that perpetually flickers without ever moving from the spot.

(T. Adorno 1981: 89)

Adorno sees the phantasmagoria as the image of the impoverished imaginative world of the bourgeois. He cites Wagner's own claim, 'Thus, in the completion and production of *The Mastersingers*, which I at first desired in Nuremberg, I was governed by the idea of offering the German public an image of its own true nature, so botched for it before' (T. Adorno 1981: 96). Wagner's commitment to the production of a timeless eternity in the present is to be found in his own account of his aesthetic ideals. Wagner banishes all historical specificity from his works in his conviction that poetic depth is synonymous with the absence of historical specificity. In his effort to conceive of an unvarying human nature which lies beyond categories such as the natural, or even the supernatural or history, to a stratum where all is undifferentiated, Wagner resorts to myth. 'The pure human being turns out to be an ideal projection of the savage who finally emerges from the bourgeois, and he celebrates him as if, metaphysically, he really were the pure human being' (T. Adorno 1981: 116). This, for Adorno, is bourgeois force unmasked and the reason for the fascination of modern bourgeois culture with the idealisation of savagery and primitivism.

Wagnerian characters are representatives of ideas and as such are too empty, in themselves, to have anything to express. Music as accompaniment is essential to their dramatic effect. The characters are not required to be individuals. They are the mouthpiece for Wagner the poet, who speaks through them. The connection between bourgeois ideology and myth is stressed by Adorno throughout. Thus, he argues, in *Lohengrin* the links can be seen at their clearest; the establishment of a sacrosanct sphere inviolable by any profane tampering coincides directly with the transfiguration of bourgeois arrangements. Adorno deconstructs the bourgeois form of gender ideology that appears in the opera:

In line with the authentic spirit of ideology, the subjugation of women in marriage is dressed up as humility, as the achievement of a pure love. Male professional life, which must of necessity be incomprehensible to women by virtue of their strict exclusion from it, appears as a sacred mystery. The Knight of the Swan bestows glory, where the husband merely disburses money. . . . Female masochism generally transforms the brutality of the husband's 'That concerns you not' into the fervent 'My Lord, never shall this question come from me'. The Master's whims, his imperious commands and above all the division of labour which Wagner overtly criticizes, are all unconsciously affirmed. The man who 'fights' for his means of existence out in the world becomes a hero, and after Wagner there were doubtless countless women who thought of their husbands as Lohengrins.... Hence Wagner's mythology ends in conformism.... In Wagner's invocation of mythology, the cult of the past and of the individual are inextricably intertwined. To this the Ring of the Nibelung stands witness.

(T. Adorno 1981: 127)

Adorno rejects the romanticism, so strong in Wagner, which invests the dispossessed or the primitive with the power of liberation because they are supposed to stand outside the nexus of bourgeois social guilt, to be the uncontaminated ones. In Wagner, this romanticism is supplemented by the further romantic notion that the way in which society can liberate itself is to find its way back to its own unsullied origins. Ultimately, in *Parsifal* the regeneration of society is tied to the notion of a master caste. In these twin evocations of purity, that of the unsullied and uncorrupted *beginning* and that of the unsullied and uncontaminated *victim*, Adorno deconstructed the dark side of bourgeois ideology. He was aware of the frequency with which modernist art and culture resorted to representations and idealisations of the primitive and glorified primitivism. Not all such representations met with his disapproval, but Adorno set himself against what he thought of as representations of the primitive which were effectively allegories of bourgeois collective force. Frequently such representations included sacrifice and sacrificial victims, and he deconstructed them as identification with the aggressor, a collusion in the collective domination and 'savagery' of bourgeois society. Adorno's interpretation has a special ring to it in the context of the Nazi period during which he was writing. Not only did the Nazis revel in Wagnerian myth and romanticism, but Hitler himself, in his speeches, gloried in the accusation that he was a 'barbarian' and claimed that to be a barbarian was a superior estate. Not for nothing does Adorno describe Siegfried, the ultimate Wagnerian hero of *The Ring*, as 'a bully boy'. Moreover, the glorified brotherhood of *Parsifal* was seen by Adorno as the prototype of the sworn confraternities of the 'secret societies and Führer-orders of later years'. All relationships in the operas are distorted because they are integrated into a rigid system of master and servant which conceals itself behind the cloud of concepts such as reverence, loyalty and devotion. This is the case for distinctions of rank as well as gender.

Time

Music is intimately related to time. It is a process that takes place in time. Time unfolds in its internal relations. Events succeed each other in time. However, a sense of time passing requires more than the mere fact that one event follows another. It requires, too, some notion that the connection between antecedent and consequent is a necessary one. If events are merely interchangeable, if none have any necessary consequents or antecedents, then there is no development or change. But what makes the connection between antecedent and consequent a necessary one?

We experience change as relative to something unchanging. A ball that bounces changes its position with every instant but it remains recognisably a ball and its motion remains recognisably bouncing motion. The experience of change or development is inseparable from the experience of what remains unchanging, of what is conserved throughout all changes. Temporality, as Adorno understands it, is dependent upon two sources of invariance: one consists of the individual subject who undergoes change and development in relations with others; another consists of the society or totality in which individuals, in all their differences, participate in an overarching unity. Corresponding to the invariances of the individual there is thus the invariance of the totality or whole. There are therefore two poles or termini to the process. If the invariance of the element or part is the non-change conserved in the changing element, the invariance of the whole or totality is the non-change conserved in the whole which is changing. If we put this in terms of society, individuals interacting with each other are changed in the process while remaining essentially themselves (that is, while conserving their differences as individuals) and they merge with others at a higher level in the invariance of the social order, the society with which each is identified. Development is experienced as movement in relation to the poles of invariance in the subject and in society. It is such a transformation or process of change, defined by the invariances at either pole – subject and object – through which the individual experiences temporality, becomes an historical subject; that is, 'makes' history.

The Hegelian notion of dialectical progress exemplifies perfectly the bourgeois construction of the 'historical' and with it the identity between individual and society that is hypostatised in that historical becoming. For Adorno, such a claim concerning the overcoming of the difference between individual and society is a false one in a bourgeois society. However, Adorno remains committed to the notion of transcendence, and therefore of the need continuously to construct the historical. While he rejects any positive Hegelian notion of the historical, he substitutes for it a negative vision of transcendence as the non-identity of individual and society, of subject and object.

The subject that surrenders the power of expression in order to accommodate itself to the oppressive forces of society has engaged in an act of self-mutilation and immolation. Such a subject does not, through such an accommodation, gain power over those collective forces. Rather, the immolation of subjectivity as the sacrificial victim of such forces is reproduced in all the works of such a subject. The theme of sacrifice and of collective oppression is one that recurs in Adorno's treatment of musics he opposes: those of Stravinsky and of jazz, for example. Adorno draws a line between an art which acknowledges the oppressive force of society and the weakness of the individual but which is yet a vehicle for authentic – if negative – expression and is, therefore, a means of resistance, and an art which colludes in the extinguishing of the individual and of expression in order to embrace collective power as egoistic force. In the biblical phrase, 'What profiteth a man . . . ?'

The pathology of late capitalism is bound up with reification and commodification; the emergence of the asocial ego is an integral part of that pathology. Because both the commodity and the isolated ego lack sociality as their constitutive substance, they also lack a truly temporal existence, one in which change, organic growth and development can occur. Lacking a constitutive ground in social relations, the isolated ego knows no more of growth and change and development than does Narcissus. In self–self relations there is nothing to develop from or to develop towards. It is only in self–other relations that the subject can undergo real change, and such a change is the prerequisite for the construction of temporality in Adorno's analysis.

In his critique of modern music Adorno repeatedly points to the many forms of modern music which have 'turned their back on time', 'denied history'. They include, for example, the music of composers he admires (Schoenberg), the music of composers of whom he disapproves (Stravinsky) and music he hates (jazz). Again, for Adorno, this temporal unfolding in music is also intrinsic to his view of sociality and of the individuation that it constructs. The spontaneity and freedom of the individual is grounded in sociality and this is always a 'going out' from the self to the other. Such a going out from the self – an entering into mediated relations with others – is a 'development' in time. By contrast, if each element is independent and interchangeable with others and if there is no totality in which experience in one relationship emerges organically from experience in another, there can be no sense of development or of time.

Wagner's music cultivates stasis, according to Adorno. The principle of developing variation in Beethoven means that where motives are repeated, they are altered and developed, they become temporal. Developing variation constructs the historical in Beethoven's music. Motives in Wagner are not thematically developed so much as repeated and transposed. The expectation that something is about to happen is conveyed, but it is an expectation that is frustrated, since, Adorno claims, Wagner's music is music in which nothing new really does happen. It is music which revokes history; the impression of timelessness, of eternity, predominates in it. 'Eternal sameness presents itself as the eternally new, the static as the dynamic, or, conversely, intrinsically dynamic categories are projected onto unhistorical pre-subjective characters' (T. Adorno 1981: 62). Wagner's claims on behalf of the moral commitment of his music to continuous change and spontaneity in social relations are false, according to Adorno. The asocial ego is also atemporal. If Wagner's art is an art of continuous transition, such perpetual motion is not equivalent to temporality, change or development. Continuous motion is, on the contrary, the condition of the isolated ego captured in the ever-changing light of events. Its colours constantly change but it undergoes no real development from within itself. What appears to be development in such an egoistic state is merely a subject's faceting of its unchanging self; its construction of an interior monologue in different voices substitutes for an authentic dialogue – that is, for interaction or drama between different subjects. In the absence of this sociality, movement is endless passage through the unchanging ego.

Moreover, Adorno introduces a distinction here that he was to make more of in his later work on *The Philosophy of Modern Music* (1980), between the expressive-dynamic character of song and the rhythmic-spatial (atemporal) character of dance. Wagner's music is centred on song, but Adorno sees him as having reduced song to the atemporal character of dance, to an eternal 'act of static time, a turning in a circle' (T. Adorno 1981: 196). Adorno argues that Wagner's focus and understanding is centred upon motives and large-scale forms but not upon themes. The work lacks proper development, according to Adorno. Repetition of motives poses as development, and transposition of motives as thematic work. Wagner's music incessantly arouses the appearance, expectation and demand for novelty but it never fulfils it, argues Adorno, for it is music in which, strictly speaking, nothing new takes place.

Adorno attributes the enigmatic quality in Wagner's music to the fact that 'the inexorable progression [of the music] fails to create any new quality and constantly flows into the already known' – what Adorno calls 'the dynamics of permanent regression' (T. Adorno 1981: 43). The 'eternity' of Wagnerian music, like that of the poem of *The Ring*, is one which proclaims that nothing has happened; it is a state of immutability that refutes all history by confronting it with the silence of nature (T. Adorno 1981: 40). While no historical process is enacted in Wagner's music, there is a heightened intensity of expressive impulse which seeks release as *gesture* (T. Adorno 1981: 35) and it is this which, as Adorno puts it, gives the listener 'the embarrassing impression that someone is constantly tugging at his sleeve'.

Commodification and the leitmotiv

Adorno pursues the argument concerning the fundamental stasis of Wager's music by pointing to the rigidity of the basic building blocks of Wagnerian construction, for example the 'leitmotiv'. Wagner constructed miniature musical pictures which were intended to serve as 'holding forms' to encapsulate or represent significant ideas that were the subject-matter of the music drama. These musical pictures – the leitmotivs – are a particularly significant Wagnerian contribution to modern music. However, Adorno argues that the leitmotivs do not work as they were intended, 'to serve the meta-physical ends of the music dramas, as the finite sign of allegedly infinite ideas' (T. Adorno 1981: 45). In reality, he argues, these miniature 'sound pictures' never did merge, in the mind of the public, with the mental significations with which they were supposed to be identical. Rather, the public, even in Wagner's own day, easily made a crude link between the leitmotivs and the persons in the drama with which they were associated. Certainly they were a significant development, but in Adorno's critique they served what was, for him, the more or less degenerate function of announcing heroes, heroines and situations so as to enable an audience to orient itself in a drama with less effort or difficulty. It is for this reason, he argues, that the direct descendants of the leitmotiv technique are to be found in film music and in advertisements.

At the macrological level, Wagner's music rescinds temporal flow, revokes the historical. At the micrological level, in the atoms, the details of his music, rigidity and stasis are the law there too. In the leitmotiv, the 'gesture' becomes frozen into a picture of what it expresses, a kind of rigid allegory which never undergoes any kind of real development in the course of the music drama. Rather, change in respect of it occurs only in the sense of a 'change of lighting' (T. Adorno 1981: 45). However, Adorno sees this as progressive as well as regressive. The fragmentation introduced by the juxta-position of leitmotivs as discrete objects engenders a real resistance to their subsumption within a totalising musical form. Wagner's music does not constitute a logically consistent totality, an immanent ordering of parts and whole, as was the aim of Beethoven's middle-period compositions. It sets itself against the claims of bourgeois totality; indeed, according to Adorno, against the entire tradition of German idealism (T. Adorno 1981: 48). It is in this sense that Adorno argues that his music is progressive and regressive at the same time. It is modernist, in that it contributes to undermining the totality that bourgeois society has put together and moves against conven-tion and tradition.

> Wagner draws his productive forces from an irreducible contradic-tion, and wrests a progressive constructiveness from the regressive moment of gesture. . . . What this makes clear, however, is that progress and reaction in Wagner's music cannot be separated out like sheep and goats. The two are indissolubly intertwined.
>
> (T. Adorno 1981: 47)

Wagner's technique involves the atomisation of the musical material, breaking it down into the smallest possible motivic components with the aim of bringing about its subsequent integration. Adorno draws a direct parallel here with the development of micro-division of labour in industrial production:

This programme was fully implemented in *Tristan*. It is difficult to avoid the parallel with the quantification of the industrial labour process, its fragmentation into the smallest possible units, just as it was no accident that an act of material production was selected as the allegory of that principle. Broken down into the smallest units the totality is supposed to become controllable, and it must submit to the will of the subject who has liberated himself from all pre-existing forms. [citing Siegfried] 'Now I've made shreds of your shining sharpness, In the crucible I cook the splinters.'

(T. Adorno 1981: 49)

It is this totalitarian tendency in modern society that Adorno sees as projected in Wagner's music, what he calls 'the totalitarian and seigniorial aspect of atomization' (T. Adorno 1981: 50). It involves the devaluation of the individual vis-à-vis the totality, which excludes all authentic dialectical interaction. Pursuing the parallel with the atomised individual in the Fordist factory, it suggests an image of individuals as engaged in fragmented and repetitive operations that are rigidly prescribed and unmediated by any kind of genuinely interactive relationship with others. The path Adorno treads here is a narrow one. The reproduction of the process of fragmentation that occurs in the wider society through the division of labour is essential to what Adorno calls the 'truth-value' of modern music. It is strengthened and deepened in the atonal music of the Schoenberg school. In Schoenberg's *Die Glückliche Hand*, not only does this take place in the inner structure of the music but the industrial process is actually reflected upon in the text. The all-important difference concerns the purposes realised by the composer, his or her good faith, as it were. The test of this, for Adorno, is the extent to which the total organisation can be constructed within the music as a vehicle for manifesting the suffering of the subject – its resistance, absence, refusal of identity, making this its raison d'être. This is the case with Schoenberg, he argues, but not with Wagner.

Simmel had argued that the devaluation of the individual in the modern metropolis which resulted form his or her reduction to the status of a mere cog in a machine was accompanied by a tendency to develop an exaggerated personal style or gesture. The cult of personality, of fashion and distinction, grew rife in the leisure spaces of the modern metropolis; an individual consumer, as the fabricator of a life-style, could seek to convince himself that he was someone important and not the nothing that an atomised production system had made him (G. Simmel 1950). Adorno offers a similar point in relation to Wagner's treatment of the individual element – the atomised motive – in his music. Wagner's music, he argues offers a glimpse of late-bourgeois consciousness whereby the more specious and impotent the individual has become in reality, the more he insists on his own importance. This is reflected, Adorno argues, in the large rhetorical gesturing of

Wagnerian motives (T. Adorno 1981: 50). Adorno contrasts the nullity of Beethoven's motives with that of Wagner's. While the nothingness of the motive 'as a mere postulate' is common to both and both recognise the ephemeral nature of individuation,

> In Beethoven, the isolated occurrence, the creative idea, is artistically trivial wherever the idea of totality takes precedence; the motive is introduced as something quite abstract in itself, simply as the principle of pure becoming, and as the totality emerges from it, the isolated motive, which is submerged in the whole, is concretized and confirmed by it. In Wagner the over-inflated creative idea denies the triviality that inheres in it by virtue of its status as a pre-linguistic gesture. The penalty it must pay for this is that it itself is denied by the development it proves unable to generate, even though it unceasingly claims to sustain that development and provide it with a model.
>
> (T. Adorno 1981: 50–1)

The triumphalism of Wagner's music, its resounding cries of struggle and victory and its claims to have done heroic deeds are all 'mendacious', according to Adorno. In reality, the absence of any genuinely dialectical relations within the Wagnerian totality means that the music can find no real enemy within itself to subdue; it makes all such resounding cries and claims mere empty posturing (T. Adorno 1981: 51).

In addition to its aesthetic function, in the development of the new music Adorno also sees the leitmotiv as having a commodity-function, as anticipating the practice of advertising as a universal feature of mass culture. The leitmotiv is an aide-mémoire, it is music designed to be remembered. Like any other commodity, the music needs to plant itself in the memory, to remind one of what it has to offer.

Wagner's social and spiritual condition

There are other reasons why Adorno would be critical of Wagner, and although these are not the real basis of his critique, which remains determinedly musicological, they are nevertheless subsumed within it, as is the general critique of Fascist and totalitarian society. Adorno was Jewish, and Wagner was a virulent anti-Semite. Moreover, Wagner's music was greatly admired and promoted by Hitler and the Nazis at the very time in which Adorno was writing. So much of what surrounded the subject of Wagner was unsavoury, from the point of view of a Jewish 'exile' living at the time of the holocaust, that a mind less brilliant or insightful than Adorno's might have got itself tangled in ideological positions and have lost all perspective. His book on Wagner is a tribute to the power and consistency of his music critique. Adorno's analysis of the decadent and regressive aspects of Wagner's music is delicately counterposed with an appreciation of the progressive contribution that Wagner made to the development of modern music. Moreover, Adorno does not just treat this as the mere presence of gold among the dross. The regressive and progressive features of Wagner's music are seen as integral and inseparable from one another.

The question of what relationship an artist's personality or character has to his or her art is problematic. Some have argued that the quality of art, even its 'greatness', directly reflects the quality of the personality; others claim that the link between the two is tenuous and that great art can be made despite considerable flaws in the character of the artist. Adorno's claim is a different one. He insists that art frequently draws its very energy from the faults and weakness of the artist, that great art may often be achieved because of such faults and not despite them. In this way he prepares the ground for the argument he later develops, namely that the progressive aspect of the art of someone like Wagner often grows out of the most dubious personal foundations:

> It would be rewarding to examine the heaps of rubbish, detritus and filth upon which the works of major artists appear to be erected, and to which they still owe something of their character, even though they have just managed to escape by the skin of their teeth. Shadowing Schubert is the figure of the tavern gambler, with Chopin it is the frequenter of salons, a type very hard to pin down; with Schumann it is the chromolithograph and with Brahms, the music professor. Their productive energies have asserted themselves cheek by jowl with their parodies, and their greatness lies in the minute distance that separates them from these models from which at the same time they draw collective energies. It is not so easy to discover a model for Wagner but the chorus of indignation that greeted Thomas Mann when he let fall the word 'dilettante' in connection with Wagner suggests that he touched a raw nerve.
>
> (T. Adorno 1981: 28)

Adorno slips easily from a consideration of this regressive aspect of Wagner's music to an appreciation of its progressive aspect. This is not something different from the regressive aspect but is rather the result of Adorno's willingness either to reposition himself – that is, to move around his subject – or to remain where he is and to 'rotate' his subject, providing in either case a different perspective on it. The atomisation of the musical material, the revoking of temporal development, of history, in the music, are all responses to the crisis of individuation in modern society. It is this which fundamentally weakens the individual in modern society, and that same weakness is reflected in the fragmentation, for example the rigid stasis of the motives in Wagner's music. When Adorno performs his rotation, it is to observe that this weakened individual does not just benefit infinitely in terms of concrete richness, expressiveness and subtlety but, compared with the would-be sovereign individual in the age of bourgeois ascendancy, he exhibits positive features such as 'a willingness to let himself go and a refusal to harden out and keep himself to himself' (T. Adorno 1981: 61).

> For this reason the really productive element in Wagner is seen at the moment when the subject abdicates sovereignty and passively abandons itself to the archaic, the instinctual – the element which, precisely because it has been emancipated, renounces its now unattainable claim to give meaningful shape to the passage of time.
>
> (T. Adorno 1981: 63)

An Adorno reader might recall that Adorno has spoken of this resort to primitivism in another context in very different terms. In his critique of Stravinsky (Adorno 1980: 160–5), for example, archaism and the instinctual are certainly not seen as 'the really productive element' in the latter's music – quite the contrary. It is this kind of apparent inconsistency which gives the reader the impression that s/he can never quite pin this philosopher down, that each critical point or philosophical argument appears to lack solidity and, thus, 'melt into air'. However, when dealing with a true modernist such as Adorno, it is necessary to navigate carefully between examples and arguments that belong to different contexts. The context is key. There is, I would argue, an iron consistency in Adorno's arguments, but this is not visible if we look for it in the wrong place. When he discusses the resort to primitivism in Stravinsky, Adorno is pursuing a different 'rotation' from the one he performs in the passage referring to Wagner, quoted above. As I read that passage, it recalls Adorno's appreciation of a similar act of abdication of sovereignty in the music of late Beethoven: the subject's acknowledgement of its weakness in the face of an overwhelming external and irrational force. For Adorno, this lapse into timelessness, this embrace of archaism, which is the subject's acknowledgement of its weakness (the acknowledgement being the subject's strength) gives rise to some of the richest and most expressive developments in Wagner's music. If melody is really closely linked with time and temporality, harmony and colour – Adorno refers to them as sonority – are remote from the temporal and can therefore develop freely and unimpeded by the tendencies that paralyse temporal development in the music.

It is Wagner's expressiveness which Adorno sees as key to his musical genius and the great advances he made in the development of harmony, for example in inventions like the sleep-motive in *The Ring*, which Adorno describes as 'capable of enticing all subsequent harmonic discoveries from the twelve-tone continuum' (T. Adorno 1981: 63).

The increasing tendency towards chromaticism in Romantic music is advanced further by Wagner. As stated above, a pervasive chromaticism undermines the diatonism that is the basis of classical tonality. It opens music to a 'chaos of new sounds'; it liberates dissonances. Wagner's progressiveness is to be seen in the extent to which the dissonances in his music assume the character of sovereign subjectivity (another rotation) vis-à-vis the resolutions (of dissonance). What Wagner does is to introduce an important asymmetry between dissonance and resolution and to weigh it heavily in favour of the former. Adorno reads the individual (as subject) into the dissonances, and society (as object) into the resolutions. All the energy is on the side of the dissonances. They protest against the right of social authority to make the rules. By comparison with them the resolutions are described by Adorno as 'threadbare, as superfluous decor or conservative protestation'. In Adorno's analysis, the liberation of dissonance in Wagner is synonymous with the resistance of the subject to the alienating force of society and with the development of a radical disjunction between subject and society within the music. In this sense there is a continuity with the progressive developments introduced in Beethoven's late style. Adorno often unites two distinct modes of discussion concerning such matters. He offers his 'hearing' of the inner structural relations in the music, much as a critic might offer a 'reading' of a text. At the same time he frequently offers a technical analysis, a 'machinery' that might be said to account for his hearing.

> Tension is made into an absolute principle by ensuring that, as a giant credit system, the negation of the negation, the full settlement of debt, is indefinitely postponed. . . . In *The Mastersingers*, which is largely diatonic, the archaic stylisation, very close to Brahms's modality, permits that reinforcement of the secondary triads which limits the primacy of the dominant and simultaneously enriches tonality; the old-fashioned becomes the leaven of the modern. However, the weightiest consequence of this countertendency, the process by which the harmonic detail becomes autonomous, is precisely the emancipation of the dissonance from its various resolutions. . . . In the progressive harmonic sections, the accents fall consistently on the dissonances not the resolutions.
>
> (T. Adorno 1981: 65–6)

Wagner's development of dissonance is seen by Adorno as progressive in another sense. It enlarged the range of expressive values that dissonance could take on within music. In Beethoven these are more or less fixed, with dissonance standing for negation and suffering and consonance for the positive feeling and fulfilment. In Wagner's music, however, there is a greater subjective differentiation of the emotional values of harmony. Pleasure and pain mediate one another in the music, generating a rich expressive admixture – suffering can also be sweet. For Adorno, modern music learned a great deal from Wagner's experiments in harmony, and it is this which enabled dissonance, in the music of the Schoenberg circle, to extend its range of operation over the entire language of music and to complete the undermining of classical tonality (T. Adorno 1981: 67).

While Adorno does not hesitate to acknowledge the progressive character of Wagner's contribution to modern music, his deconstruction of the part played by those very same progressive and experimental discoveries within Wagner's own work – that is, within the compass of his own project – is deeply critical. Again, Adorno's rotation of his subject, his switching between contextual frames, frequently occurs in a flash. The critical opposition to society which is represented by the emancipation of dissonance and its refusal to be silenced by being resolved is, in Wagner, something of a sham resistance, an empty posturing. Adorno argues that Wagner does not truly deviate from the musical idiom of tonality; rather, the expressive values of all his dissonances continue to be determined by their implied distance from consonance, from triadic harmony, even when the consonance is omitted. Thus, argues Adorno, the system of tonal harmony stands behind Wagner's dissonances, as the master-system from which they are developed. In that way they become what one might term 'Her Majesty's loyal opposition', but not the revolutionary force they may claim to be. Because they are always in a sense bound to the tonal master-system, Wagner's dissonances and inventions are ultimately easily absorbed by its tradition. For this not to happen they would have to have developed an autonomy, a genuine independence from what they protested against. That they did not do so is not attributed by Adorno to some technical failing – progressive composers such as Mahler were extremely radical, making use of very traditional means to achieve just such a decisive autonomy – but is ultimately seen to have its origins in Wagner's character and social orientation at a particular historical stage in the development of the crisis of the individual. Wagner protests vehemently at the encroachment of a rational bourgeois order on the freedom of the individual but he does not, in his own life and relations, deviate significantly from the immanent reality of bourgeois society, and that fact in itself ensures that his music does not truly deviate from the dominant musical idiom of tonal harmony.

In his discussion of the other element of Wagner's 'sonority', namely colour, Adorno is equally appreciative of Wagner's progressive contribution to the development of a radical modernist music. He draws attention in particular to Wagner's development of the art of orchestration, through which 'colour itself becomes action', something which he claims did not really exist before Wagner. Wagner was the first, he argues, 'to make the most subtle compositional nuances tangible and to render the unity of compositional complexes by colouristic methods' (T. Adorno 1981: 71). In a discussion of a passage in *Lohengrin* where the composer uses clarinets to double both the flute melody in the top voice and the second soprano part, which is also played by the flute, Adorno insists that its function is not amplification or emphasis but a change in tone colour:

The unison combination of flute and clarinet gives rise to floating oscillating acoustic 'beats'. In it the specific sound of each instrument is lost; they can no longer be separated out, and the final sound gives no clue as to how it is created. In this it resembles the thing-like sound of the organ. But at the same time – and this is highly symptomatic of Wagner's orchestration – such a process of objectification has advantages in terms of a greater flexibility for the whole. Any loss in individual timbre sustained by the single instrument as a result of doubling is made up for by the possibility of smooth integration with the orchestra as a whole. No doubt it is less able to assert its own individual character, but if the partial, subjective performances of the players are absorbed into the overall effect, it is equally true that the latter, in turn, becomes the willing medium of the expression the composer wishes to exact. The more reification, the more subjectivity: the maxim holds good in orchestration as in epistemology.

(T. Adorno 1981: 74)

There is a theoretic density to passages such as this one. Moving beneath the surface is a constellation which ties together 'commodification', 'reification', 'subjectivisation' and 'objectification'. The central characteristic of the reified world of the commodity is that of concealing the sinewy relations by which it was produced. The commodity stands over and against the individual, as an absolute objectivity, promising to work its magical effects upon an equally abstracted subjectivity. Behind the commodity stands subjectivity in the guise of the producer of the commodity. Objectification in the commodity-form is thus associated with subjectification on both sides. In Wagner's complex construction of tone colour through his innovative orchestration, the unison sound loses the contribution that each individual sound makes to it – hence Adorno's reference to its objectification and his recognition of its reification. At the same time the power of the composer to shape the total effect is heightened, and with it the power of the effect to be worked upon the reified subject, the audience.

With the transformation of the unruly body of instruments into the 'docile palette' of the composer, orchestral sound is subjectivised. However, such a subjectivisation is also, according to Adorno, a de-subjectivisation, since it tends to render inaudible what goes into the production of a particular sound. The immensely subtle nuances of Wagner's orchestration thus represent the victory of reification in instrumental practice. The idea that governs Wagnerian orchestration, that of the production of sound from which all traces of production have been elided, renders it, for Adorno, as belonging, for all its brilliance, to the category of the commodity, as surely as the most banal products of the culture industry (T. Adorno 1981: 82).

By aiming at the production of a continuum of timbres, the Wagnerian orchestra inaugurated a tendency that was to be extensively appropriated in modern music, both serious and popular. Adorno points to the developments in the music of the Schoenberg school, where the instruments become interchangeable and where the melody or harmony may be shared among them in various ways, to the situation in jazz where 'muted trumpets sound like saxophones and vice versa, and even the singer, who sings in a whisper or through a megaphone, sounds not unlike them, too' (T. Adorno 1981: 78). Here Adorno performs a similar rotation to the one he has used in connection with harmony. The progressive significance of Wagner's contribution to modern music is acknowledged, as is the regressive character of his technique in the context of his own musical project. This time, however, Adorno has not shifted contexts in a sequential move but has doubled them so that both the progressive and the regressive appear integral – a technique not unlike the one he is describing in respect of Wagnerian colour. He takes it one step further, however, by raising the contradiction to the level of the work of art in general. Works of art owe their existence to the division of labour in society and especially to the separation of physical and mental labour. To the extent that they seek to sustain themselves as autonomous self-contained unities, they force us to forget that they have been made; that is, they conceal the efforts and labours that have gone into their production and are thus stamped with the hallmark that identifies them as commodities. This contradiction is true of all autonomous art and not just Wagner's. However, in Wagner's art the problematic concealment of all traces of the production of a work of art is made programmatic at the same time.

In this respect, suggests Adorno, Wagner's oeuvre comes close to the consumer goods of the nineteenth century which knew no greater ambition than to conceal every sign of the work that went into them, perhaps because any such traces reminded people too vehemently of the appropriation of the labour of others, of an injustice that could still be felt. A contradiction of all autonomous art is the concealment of the labour that went into it, but in high capitalism, with the complete hegemony of exchange value and with the contradictions arising out of that hegemony, autonomous art becomes problematic and programmatic at the same time. 'To make works of art into magical objects means that men worship their own labour because they are unable to recognise it as such' (T. Adorno 1981: 83). It is this, says Adorno, which gives Wagner's works the impression of a pure and absolutely immediate appearance, a purely spatial phenomenon.

Again, however, Adorno recovers the integral binding of regressive and progressive features. The abstraction of the work from its own production is achieved only in and through the growing mastery of its own artistic material. For Adorno, the paradoxical truth of modern art lies in the fact that it is only through its reification, its commodification – the perfection of its character as illusion – that it can speak of the human in the modern world.

5

BREAKING THE CODE

The developments that took place in all the arts during the first decade of the twentieth century were explosive; they shattered the codes that had governed the ordering of elements in art works since the time of the Renaissance (those discussed in Chapter 2). Nevertheless, the decisive break with the past had been well prepared in the art and music of the nineteenth century. In literature, the centre of gravity had shifted from an object-centred realism, quintessentially represented by the novels of Balzac, to a subject-centred naturalism that culminated in Zola and the modernists. Literature had thus moved from a concern with the coherence of the object world as an ordered reality – a coherence which presupposed the integral unity of the individual – to a concern with the intra-subjective conscious-ness of the subject as a locus for the ordering of experience.

The argument of this chapter is centred on theoretical issues concerning social structure, consciousness and art that have preoccupied me for some time. I seek to move out from them to consider Adorno's concerns about the development of modern music. My aim is to establish a means, however crude and tentative, for reading across from the development of sociological modes of analysis to the development of musical structures.

The unitary character of an outer objective reality and the coherent logic of the object world dissolves when the focus shifts from the scene of interac-tional relations and the outer reality to the domain of intra-subjective experience. At an intra-subjective level, the subject is constituted in the reflexive interplay of experiences deriving from the whole range of disparate situations and relationships that make up the life-world. Such a shift of centre from the 'inter-subjective' to the 'intra-subjective' means leaving behind the logic of the unitary objective situation and bringing the multiple facets of the subject's different relational worlds into play in the same experi-ential space. All the massive deformations, the twisting, wrenching and pulverising of conventional literary and aesthetic forms in the early decades of the century, registered the decisive stage reached in this shift in the locus of order to the intra-subjective. The term 'stream of consciousness' writing was coined to capture the movement from the logic of objective reality – an inter-subjective and inter-actional reality – to the interplay of disparate elements that made up the intra-subjective and intra-actional world of the experiencing subject. Narrative historical structure was challenged by writers such as Joyce, Proust and Virginia Woolf, not simply for the sake of experiment but because narrative form was centred on presenting the world as a 'functional' unity, as an objective (historical) reality; it was unsuited to depicting the present-centred and multi-faceted synchronicity that constitutes the 'substantial' unity of the subject.

In painting, the revolution of Picasso and Braque's Cubism with its flattening of space, its distortions and facetings in and through which different views of objects could be incorporated, reflected this vital shift in the locus order. This faceting of subject–object relations in a construction of fractured viewpoints undermined the entire logic of realist representation in painting and replaced it with a new treatment of spatial relations that could serve as a semiotic vehicle for depicting the intra-personal constitution of the subject (R. Witkin 1995, see Chapter 8). In ordinary perception, as it was simulated in painting since the Renaissance, an object was pictured as though seen from a single point of view. What we take for granted in viewing it is the total system of different points of view that is presupposed in making sense of the object from any one point of view. If this suspended reality (the other points of view) was not somehow present and active in shaping our perception, then the world we were looking at would be seen as very different. Each of those other suspended points of view reflects a definite and particular subject–object relationship. If we are able to take these other subject–object relationships for granted, to treat them as non-problematic, then it is because the variety of different contexts in which they have been formed are integrated with each other in constituting a unitary system of object relations. Each specific viewpoint, therefore, brings the total order instantly into play. As subjects, in relation to this object world, we would have no cause to doubt ourselves.

However, if we imagine object worlds which are no longer unitary but which have fragmented into discrete and disjunctive realities, there is no more any possibility that the subject can project a unified view of the world on the basis of a single viewpoint. Insofar as the variety of different viewpoints is constitutive of the subject in its relations with the object, the (intra-subjective) constitution of the subject has become problematical. The focus of attention and of order shifts decisively from the object and objective reality towards the subject and the intra-subjective ordering of experience. As Durkheim understood so well, when the structures of everyday life come apart, so, too, does the personality and sensuous coherence of the subject (E. Durkheim 1951). At an intra-subjective level, the synchronous and faceted co-existence of the subject's variegated experiences is key to the constitution of the subject.

In music, late Beethoven, Brahms and Wagner were among the most important precursors of the development of the atonal and twelve-tone music of Schoenberg and his followers. Classical tonality was first deformed, stretched and parodically deconstructed before it was more or less extinguished as an organising principle in the case of the latter composers. What is true of a Cubist canvas might also be claimed for an atonalist score. If we see its different elements or parts as reflecting different and disjunctive subject–object relations, then the co-presence of all these differentiated subject–object relations, as realised in a complex tonal 'faceting', can be seen as constitutive of the subject as a whole in its relations with the world – that is, as constituting an intra-subjective order.

In modern music, the progressive erosion of tonality and the key system, together with the principal forms in which it had developed (e.g. sonata-form), represented both a liberation of music and a crisis of order. The abandonment of the unified key system in the shift from diatonicism to chromaticism meant that the individual tones were liberated to enter into relations with each other in ways that would not have been permitted by the restrictions inherent in tonalism. Modern music was first and foremost characterised by what appeared to many to be a chaos of new sounds, most of which were dissonant to the hearing of most people. Of course, relations among the new sounds were ordered and not chaotic; remnants of the old tonal organising systems were still there, including vestiges of sonata-form. Moreover, other dimensions could be called upon to organise the sounds – rhythm, timbre and so forth. Composers resorted to literary texts and to formal or abstract schemes of various kinds (such as Berg's number systems) as well as to personal whim in producing a music in which relations were, if anything, more total and more dense than had formerly been the case. In Adorno's phrase, the new music was 'music in which nothing actually could be different' (T. Adorno 1980: 41); every note was somehow absolutely necessary and determined by its relations to all the others. Whereas, in classical tonal music, the parts are 'nothing' and fall away in their construction of a unitary whole, in modernist music the focus of attention shifts to the level of the parts which do not die away in some larger construction, but co-exist in a dense relational multiplicity. It is precisely this densely faceted manifold of elements that I am equating here with the semiotic realisation of the intra-subjective. It is that same dense faceting which is characteristic of Cubist paintings and of 'stream of consciousness' writing.

The radical reconstruction of music presaged in the chromaticism of Wagner, and especially in *Tristan*, proceeded in accordance with its own intrinsic logic. It was clearly related to the development of social relations in the wider society but it would be wrong to think of this connection as a crudely causal one. In his essay 'Image, Discourse and Power', Norman Bryson asks how it is possible to connect two sets of facts, those concerning changes in aesthetic codes and practices and those concerning changes in the wider society. He insists that representational practice has to be seen as evolving structure and as modifying according to laws in its own autonomous province. 'The problem is one of understanding the articulation of a technical process against the history of social formation, of charting one material evolution in the sphere of practice against its reflection and refraction in a further domain of practice' (N. Bryson 1983: 134).

Adorno, too, insisted on the autonomous logic of aesthetic construction, and he saw this logic unfolding in an effortful and reflexive resonance with the social formation which is, after all, the wider sphere of praxis of which aesthetic praxis is a part. Works of art can ultimately be judged in terms of their success or lack of success in speaking to the social formation, without there being any implication that they have been formed simply as copies or translations of some prior construction achieved in the wider social praxis. Nevertheless, because this dynamic resonance between the social formation and aesthetic form is a necessary one if works of art are to be perceived as meaningful, we need to consider more closely the structural parallels, obtaining at the level of part–whole relations, between social structure and aesthetic form.

It may have been the case in an earlier bourgeois society that the sensuous life of the subject and of the community could be experienced as more or less integral with the developing bourgeois modes of production, distribution and exchange. The acceleration of industrial development and of urbanisation in the nineteenth century, however, gave rise to an increasingly monolithic economic and political order centred on rational and instrumental means–end relations. The sensuous and personal life of the subject, the proliferation and expansion of the interpersonal sphere, the family and domestic life – all those relations making up the solidary structures of community and subject – became increasingly disjoined from the instrumental order. The former, as classical sociologists such as Tönnies saw, are governed by values. The elements or units of these structures are not means to an end but are valued ends in themselves. Instrumental structures, by contrast, are driven by motives. They are structured means in pursuit of empirical ends. The more completely the instrumental order was developed and expanded, the more were the sensuous subject and the community driven to the margins of that order. For Marx as well as for Adorno, this process was seen as fundamentally alienating and de-sociating. A world increasingly governed by 'exchange values' dealt with the subject and the sensuous life only at the level of individual 'motives' or 'drives'. The instrumental order exists both to stimulate and develop motives and to gratify them. In the process, it undermines the discourse of values and of community, assimilating it to a discourse of motives (Witkin 1997). The instrumentalisation of value – that is, the producing of effects upon the subject that are instrumentally oriented to satisfying desires and needs in the subject – becomes central to the reproduction of the *instrumental* order.

The more that the sensuous life is instrumentalised in this way, the more it is de-sociated.

For Adorno, as a Marxist, the modern subject was oppressed by the advance of rational capitalism, the commodification of life and the domination of exchange values and markets. The instrumental individualism of bourgeois life undermined both the cohesiveness of community and of the sensuous subject. It became increasingly difficult to sustain the *solidary* in the face of an ever encroaching and corrupting *instrumentalism*. The more that attention shifts to the intra-personal constitution of the subject, the more is it the case that the subject's responses in disparate systems are brought together in the construction of agency and of sensibility.

In solidary systems, the manifold of irreducible elements constitutes the substance, the 'stuff' or the 'material' from which the subject is made, that is, through which a sensibility and agency is constituted. Development consists in the figuration of this material in a variety of different forms or realisations. Just as the material – as substance – antedates the things which are made from it, so the relations which constitute that material are fixed prior to the construction of forms. We might liken this to the situation in which a building may be formed from bricks which are themselves pre-constituted material, used for the construction of different buildings. There is no longer any change, development or history in this pre-constituted material; change and development belong to the process of construction through which this material is figured. At the level of intra-personal experience, the subject is constituted of a range of different subject–object relations. These are brought together in a given action context to realise the necessary sensibility and agency – a specific sensibility for a given action context. While the relations among the elements that constitute the material are fixed, the process is driven by the action context of the subject and when that changes so, too, do the capacities demanded of the subject – its sensibility and agency – and therefore its substantial 'material'.

The unity constituted by a group of related objects is a *functional* one if the objects in question are related in terms of purpose or end to be achieved. On the other hand, a group of objects that are disparate and unrelated in any functioning sense may yet form a *substantial* unity if they are all made of the same substance or stuff – if they are all made of wood, for example. The property of being wooden may unify objects that belong in different functioning systems, while a single functioning system may bring together objects that are substantially different – objects made of metal and of plastic as well as wood, for example.

Analogously, we can liken the social being represented by the *solidary* community and by shared values and common fate as a substantial unity, and we can contrast it with the social functioning of the *instrumental* organisation governed by a division of labour and oriented to the attainment of some end or purpose. Instrumental structures are governed by a *discourse of motives* and desire, while solidary structures belong to a *discourse of values*. In an instrumental structure, the constitutive elements are valued and selected in terms of the contribution they make to the pursuit of certain goals or ends; we can speak of such elements as being motivated. Such an idea is conveyed by Weber's notion of the dominance in the modern world of legal-rational action oriented to the use of the most technically efficient means in the pursuit of ends or goals. The organisation of means is rational, functional and historical. In the substantial unity of communities, or Weber's 'status groups', relations are more or less fixed and constitute a value-order (M. Weber 1946). Such solidary social structures are not constructed in themselves as 'historical', although histories may be made from them.

The advance of modern societies is associated in the minds of many observers with the disintegration of community and of communitas and a crisis of identity for the sensuous subject. The growing effectiveness of the instrumental order was seen in the sociological record to be inversely related to that of both the community and the sensuous subject. The proliferation of exchange values, of the market and of the economy, of formal organisation, of calculative and instrumental practice and so forth, was set against a sphere of subjective, non-rational relations which was seen as being increasingly eroded and uprooted by a voracious instrumentalism. If the sensuous subject had found it possible in an earlier society to experience community and identity as non-problematical, the very conditions of life in the modern metropolis were making this increasingly difficult.

The Chicago sociologists studying the city in the late 1920s and 1930s saw the growth of cities as correlated with the social disorganisation of traditional communities (R. Park 1952). The image of the metropolis as disrupting the solidary ties that bind communities and as producing a variety of relational and life-world conditions, even for a single subject, meant that the identity of the subject as a coherent subject – his or her substantial unity, that is – could no longer be presupposed.

The single most obvious change in the culturescape from the middle of the nineteenth century was the advent of the large metropolis. In a small rural community, social relations are high in density, in that the different persons with whom one has relationships also tend to have relationships with each other. In the metropolis, the individual is involved in a relatively larger number of contacts and relations with others who are often unrelated to each other. This lack of relationship among one's role partners is a measure of density. The density of social relations in the metropolis therefore tends to be relatively low. High density relations have always been associated in sociological thinking with strong solidary relations and a strong sense of community, whereas low density social relations are associated with more fractured and problematic intra-personal as well as intra-communal structures (J. Mitchell 1969; J. Boissevain 1974). From a structural point of view it is easy enough to see the process of fragmentation and problematic order as having direct parallels in the structure of modern art and of modern music. There, too, the dissolution into more or less disjunctive elements could be described in terms of a loss of density that demanded new principles of ordering.

Although Adorno subscribed to large parts of the Marxist analysis of modern social life, it is also true that he did not accept the positive view of the historical mission of a working class that would liberate modern society, nor did he identify with the so-called communist societies; they practised the kind of state oppression which he abhorred. The enemies are always clear in Adorno: commodification, instrumentalism and all the alienating conditions which threaten the freedom, sociality and spontaneity of the (oppressed) modern subject. Modernity is thus inextricably bound up with a crisis of the instrumentally oppressed subject. Art and the aesthetic remains, for Adorno, the last cultural stronghold in which the oppression of an instrumental order – one dominated by mean–end rationality and exchange values – can be resisted. The construction of works of art, of aesthetic form, then becomes a mode of spiritual resistance, in which the values governing the solidary structures of community and of subjectivity can be asserted in the teeth of the instrumental oppression that would overwhelm and extinguish them.

Three models of structuration in sociology and music

We can identify two major divisions in Adorno's account of the transition from tonal to atonal music. The first emerges in Beethoven's late style and culminates in Mahler's music. It involves a transition from classical tonality to a music in which the language of tonality is deployed in a second-order and distanced way; that is, in an ironising manner. Mahler's symphonies appear to use the familiar language of tonal music but they do not use it innocently; rather they make the language of tonal music itself – its forms, conventions and functions – the very content of the work. This is a process that Beethoven had begun in his last quartets. The distance between the subject and the world is registered in the tense contradiction between the expression of the subject and the outworn tonal material deployed as means. I shall label this second mode *tonal irony* as distinct from the *classical tonality* of the first mode.

The third stage begins with Schoenberg's *atonal* revolution in modern music, and culminates in the dissolution and abandonment of tonal structures as an organising system in favour of the radical constructivism that emerged with *twelve-tone* serial music. With the progressive fragmentation of musical material – its decomposition into its smallest elements – the hierarchically ordered tonal structures, together with the restrictions they placed upon possible relations and combinations among tones, were dissolved. Expressed as an ideal, instead of each tone being hierarchically ordered in

100

terms of its distance from a tonal centre, every tone became 'equidistant from the centre' and no tone (theoretically) had greater importance or precedence than any other. In reality, this theoretical ideal does not hold. Certain notes take precedence – through octave doubling, for example, or through being repeated more often than other notes and so forth. Moreover, the structure of a freely atonal composition, the binding or ordering of the elements, may be a matter of arbitrary or subjective choice. One way of resolving the problem of the too early repetition of notes is to fix the ordering of the whole composition at the level of its parts. Schoenberg's practice of composing with a 'row', comprising all the notes of the full chromatic, arranged in advance in a definite and invariant order – the twelve-tone method – is just such a solution. The row becomes the 'building block' which is substantially invariant and which is yet figured in myriad juxtapositions.

A parallel can be drawn between these stages in the structural development of modern music and 'stages' in the *individuation* of modern society that describe the structural development of social relations in the modern world. Adorno himself did not draw the parallel that I draw below between modes of musical construction and modes of individuation. Nevertheless, establishing such a parallel is useful for reflecting upon the correspondence between structural relations in music and in society. Corresponding to the three types of music discussed by Adorno – classical tonality, tonal irony, atonality and twelve-tone serialism – we can identify three modes of individuation which I shall label 'classical individuation', 'divided selves' and 'individuated agency', respectively. Each of these modes of individuation can in turn be identified with a major school of sociological analysis.

Classical individuation

The transition from classical tonal music to modern atonal music – a transition prefigured in the middle and late styles of Beethoven – corresponds to the transition from middle to late bourgeois society. It is consistent with Adorno's perspective, as I argued in Chapter 2, to view the structural relations of art works and society as isomorphic. In Durkheim's model of organic solidarity, individuation and individuality arise from social differentiation in the division of labour (E. Durkheim 1933). Viewed abstractly, individuals who are differentiated from one another are nevertheless interdependent. Above all, they must *interact* co-operatively in ways that reproduce the social system in and through which each individual plays his or her differentiated part. Interaction is thus constrained by the need of the participants to take care of the system of relations upon which each depends and to formulate their relationships and interactions with these constraints in mind. It is a feat achieved through socialisation, through the pressure of one generation upon the next.

The values that describe social order are conceived of as internalised in personalities and as institutionalised in social systems (T. Parsons 1951: 3–23). Each individual is identified with and corresponds to the social order which has been internalised in his or her personality through socialisation. Action in a division of labour society comes to assume a teleological character. Through social interaction with others – interaction through which society is constituted and reconstituted – the individual undergoes a personal development. Personal biography is thus identified with the wider historical development. The most developed social psychological formulation of what I have called the 'interactional model' of sociality (Witkin 1995) is George Herbert Mead's idea of the development of the self-concept through the 'taking of the attitude of the other towards oneself'. The self is then constructed at the intersection of all the significant attitudes taken towards the subject by all the differentiated others to whom the subject relates (G.H. Mead 1967). Again the form is teleological and again there is an identity between society and individual.

Both models locate the problem of ordering at the level of social *interaction* between individuals. The subject's individuality develops as the counterpart of the subject's sociality; individual identity thus corresponds to society. The stability of the system of social relations as a whole is reflected in the stability of the intra-personal relations that constitute the identity of the subject. Durkheim clearly acknowledged this in his theory of anomie (Durkheim 1951). When social order breaks down it has consequences for the intra-personal coherence of the subject. Where the system is fully integrated and unified, its integrity is reflected in the intra-subjective coherence of the individual. Such a society is historical. Each individual develops through interaction with others, while remaining recognisably the same individual and contributing to the development of a society to which that underlying identity and its development correspond.

Classical tonality, as it was perfected in the late eighteenth century in the music of Beethoven, constituted a system of part–whole relations corresponding to those of the classical model of the bourgeois society. This is, in effect, the basis of Adorno's argument concerning the sonata-symphonies of Beethoven's middle-period compositions. The composition develops organically from its basic motives, which enter into relations with each other and which, through developing variation, construct the musical totality. Whole and part correspond to one another in a way that is directly analogous to the correspondence between society and the individual. The mode of construction is also 'historical'. Development is the process by which motive and form become what they are.

Divided selves

In the transition to modern music it is possible to discern two distinct 'approaches'. In late Beethoven, as was observed in Chapter 3, the subject as a spiritual centre withdraws from forms which had formerly been its realisation. These forms – the conventions and clichés of tonal music, mere form as such – are used in the composition to express the condition of the subject in and through the subject's non-identity with them. Adorno brings them under the category of the 'banal', which he identifies with the appearance of 'commodity'.

Working with such forms enables the artist to oppose the false reconciliation of subject and world, while preserving the subject's identity negatively through establishing a distanced and ironising relationship between the subject and the banal forms in which its presence can be glimpsed. Preserving the subject through its negative relationship to society also preserves the temporal or historical mode of construction in music, and this was key to Adorno's philosophy of music.

Within modern sociology, the concern with the preservation of the identity of the subject in a negative sense – that is, through the subject's non-identity with the forms it inhabits – can be exemplified by the sociology of Erving Goffman (E. Goffman 1959, 1961a, 1961b, 1963). In Goffman's sociology, the self is not a unitary structure corresponding to the social order, as in the model of a classical bourgeois society; the modernist subject is a 'holding company' for multiple selves corresponding to the divided worlds in which the individual participates. The identity of the Goffmanian subject, the self-as-player, can only be glimpsed in its partial disjunction with the forms it inhabits, the forms of social life from which it is always distanced. Goffman's classic concept of 'role-distance' expresses this well (E. Goffman 1961a, 1961b). The modernist subject is an anxious and divided subject. The construction of self and the conservation of a sense of personal identity is increasingly problematical. This is reflected in the development of Goffman's sociology around critical and liminal life-worlds: those of mental patients, nuns, prisoners and the terribly disfigured or disabled. In his account of the struggles for selfhood in a late modern society, Goffman is drawn, like modernist artists and musicians, to critical social contexts to obtain his material. The rituals, routines and performances of a Goffmanian subject can be subsumed under the category of the banal.

Two characteristics that are central to the treatment of forms in a modernist art or music are, therefore, the lack of depth or interiority in the form – a condition that is met in the 'flatness' and 'conventionality' of forms (a literal flatness in the case of paintings) – and the lack of transcendence which demands the cultivation of ordinary and prosaic content. Together, these characteristics go to make up the category of the banal. When Manet exhibited his painting *Christ insulted by the soldiers* in 1864, what was no doubt deeply offensive to its many detractors was the banality of the treatment of Christ and the events of the story, the lack of precisely that kind of transcendental significance which viewers would be accustomed to expect of such a work. The central figure is bereft of any of the signs of those higher qualities that one expects to be conveyed in the depiction of the person of Christ. He might just as well be any common criminal or prisoner. If Christ's form is no longer infused with the transcendental spirit, if it is empty and banal, it does the job in painting that Adorno expects of the forms of a truthful music; it realises the non-identity of the subject with the forms it inhabits. There is something profoundly Christian realised in the ignobility and ordinariness of Manet's Christ figure, but not for a viewer who is looking for the inner spiritual centre to manifest itself in the outer form; the very power of Manet's vision lies in the opposite direction, in the conflict of the spiritual centre with the 'vulgar' forms in which its presence is glimpsed. 'Banality' is the phrase that best captures that sense of the poverty of forms in relation to the enormity of spiritual catastrophes.

The tension between subject and form can be realised in a number of ways. It can be a matter of language: that is, of using language designed for one purpose to express ideas that would normally conflict with such a purpose. When Damon Runyon uses the linguistic forms and prose of polite and genteel society to speak the world of gangsters, racketeers and criminals, the conflict between expression and form can seem hilarious and even familiar and reassuring. One finds a similar conflict between expression and forms in Beckett and Kafka, but to engender the opposite, a sense of profound discomfort, of alienation, isolation or despair. A similar use of disjunction between expression and form can be observed in the music of Kurt Weill. Evanescence can also be realised through producing complex and ambiguous forms such as Magritte's deeply paradoxical paintings: the evanescence of the subject in such works is realised in and through the mutually deconstructive clash of counter-forms that define the ambiguity. I have argued elsewhere that this deconstructive interplay within the construction of a modernist form plays an important part in another of Manet's paintings, *Olympia*, which was exhibited together with his *Christ* in 1864 (R. Witkin 1997).

In Adorno's treatment of modernism, Mahler is a composer who excels at the creation of this tension between expression and form, especially the art of using the musical language inherited from Viennese classicism against its own inherent intentions. The grand symphonic style, the elaborate programmatic content, the evocations of nature, are all there but are deployed in ways that deconstruct the very model from which they are drawn. Irony and deconstruction are central to Mahler's modernism.

Such a commitment to a continuous process of becoming, to the ever-new, to creation and decreation, demands the most thoroughgoing mediation of subject and object, of individual and society. Such music must grow from its elements, which means that the direction taken by the music in its journey cannot be known in advance. New 'characters' can emerge in the music at any moment and take over its course.

The fragmentation of the subject into multiple selves is a weakening of the self-identity of the subject and, conversely, a strengthening of the subject as a constructive centre. Increasingly the subject is identified with this constructive activity. When this constructive process is strengthened to the point where it becomes predominant then even the 'candidate-selves' dissolve, and the elements making them up are liberated to enter into new relations with other elements in response to the demands of an omnipresent constructivism. The problem of order is then shifted from the macro-structure of inter-actional relations to the micro-structure of intra-actional relations. The drama of part–whole relations moves from the level of the totality to that of the part. The problem of social action thus becomes the problem of constructing the *agency* and *sensibility* with which action gets done. Agency and sensibility displace self. The intelligibility of action, the meaning-conferring practices through which skilful performance is brought off, then becomes a central focus of sociological interest.

Individuated agency

This ever-strengthening constructivism is a feature of Goffmanian sociology but Goffman remains committed to the construction of the self and the defence of its territories. Ethnomethodology represents a more radical constructivism in which the problems of the construction of self are displaced by the micrological sphere of the construction of social agency (Garfinkel 1967). If social action is inter-actional, social agency is intra-actional. By intra-action is meant the micrological processes in which subjects draw on local materials, on members' understandings, practises, routines, topics, resources, on variegated experiences in different contexts, in putting together the agency and sensibility – the *under*standing – with which action gets done. In Durkheim's model there is a unitary and coherent society – a transcendental system – which gets into individuals through socialisation and generates a unitary selfhood that corresponds to it. In Goffman's model, society is made up of multiple systems that are only partially continuous with one another and which give rise to multiple selves corresponding to the variety of role contexts, a multiplicity for which each individual is a 'holding company'. In the 'individuated agency' model, by contrast, attention shifts from the macro-structure to its constitutive elements, each element identified by its functional character, as an action being brought off – an 'opening', a 'closing', a 'diminishing' or whatever – that is, each action or event-element is identified by what it 'does' or what it 'affords', and each structure or organisation is constituted by actors as integral to the business of bringing off actions and making sense.

These functions become the building blocks with which the sociologist (re)constructs the 'social agency' and sensibility that might account for the subject's actions and choices in a given context. The subject, here, can no longer be identified with the individual as a unitary structure or even the individual as a multiplicity of selves. Rather, the focus is upon the activity of the subject together with the subject's local understandings and account-ings – accountings which are integral to the bringing off of that activity. Typically, the analyst might focus upon an event of some kind, a doing or an account, and seek to disclose the sense-making activities of the subject through which the event or doing is brought off or its meaning constituted. Each event-element can be referred to the functional ordering which is brought about by its activities and in and through which it makes sense. But that construction will not do for the next event-element; the process must begin again.

For my purposes I will offer the following somewhat idiosyncratic conceptualisation: a complex structure or sequence of action is broken down into what are seen to be significant event-elements. Beginning with an event – for example, a question asked – an attempt is made to construct a 'social machinery' through which the subject hearing the question might consti-tute its meaning. The process can then begin again with the next element. It is a continuous process of structuration and de-structuration, beginning and ending with the event-elements.

Consider the following situation, described by Wootton (A.Wootton 1975) in which a woman patient apologises to the psychiatrist for being late, commenting that her husband does not like her to come to therapy. In an extensive interview the analyst confines his interest and focus to just one element in the exchange. The psychiatrist asks the woman how old she is. She replies that she is 35. The researcher *hears* the question not as a question about the woman's chronological age but as a *diminishing* of a complaint. The total interaction between patient and client comprises a very complex sequence and each significant element in it requires its own machinery to account for it. The researcher is interested in this particular element and, having heard this question as 'diminishing a complaint' that the patient had made earlier about her husband's dislike of her coming to therapy, he goes on to construct a machinery from the ordinary knowledge, understandings and practises available in the local situation from which the actor hearing that question might generate such meaning.

And how is the question heard? It is heard in its functionality, as the *diminishing* of a complaint that the patient had made concerning another person delaying her appearance at the clinic. The social machinery constructed to recover this hearing is also seen in functional terms; that is, in terms of the kinds of sense-making activities, knowledge, practices and understandings through which a member could generate the meaning the question is heard to carry.

We can draw a parallel between this model of structuration and the atonal revolution in music. Tonalism, with its hierarchical relations among notes determined by the gravitational pull of the tonic, was dissolved in favour of atonalism, in which all notes are equidistant from the centre. Construction, here, too, can be a matter of proceeding from each element to generate the form in and through which that element acquires its value and then going on to repeat the process with other elements.

The problem of achieving a coherent sense of identity is made greater with every increase in fragmentation. Without there being a coherent structure through which the subject can move, the distance between subject and context dissolves. The forms of existence of the subject and the transformations of context become one. At this level the locus of ordering shifts from the inter-actional to the intra-actional, from the inter-subjective to the intra-subjective.

What we normally experience as linear historical time is associated with the 'classical individuation' model. This is temporality which concerns only the macro-structure, the development of the whole from interactions among the elements or parts. Change does not penetrate the micro-structure; that is, the constitutive elements of the intra-subjective. However, in the radical constructivist model, change – and therefore time – penetrates the micro-structure, and the laminate of elements which constitutes the intra-subjective develops its own temporality. The drive in modernist art is not perhaps towards an atemporal and ahistorical reality but towards a poly-temporal laminating of the elements that constitute the intra-subjective.

6

MAHLER AND BERG

The musical material that a composer works with consists not simply in the sensuous substratum – the elementary sounds – but all the accumulated conventions, habits and styles of music-making; the material instruments of music-making and the historical accumulation of composed forms; the standard expressions – musical utterances – with their meanings and intentionality. The composer does not construct music by combining elementary sounds freely; the compositional process is grounded in the language of music which, like natural language, is a culturally inherited structure – learned and shared – and in which the history of past utterance – of subjectivity and expression – is congealed in its innermost cells. In speaking or in composing music, the subject is being historical. Speech is made in the tension between the historical constitution of the subject, as reflected in the forms of the language, and the immediate demands of the life-world. Its character, as speech or expression, is conditioned by this tension.

Language, whether natural or musical, is shot through with intentionality, with subjectivity. Intentions congeal in the forms of utterance. However, at the level of the whole – the work of art, the composition, the drama or the novel – the intentionality of the constitutive elements is negated and transcended in the intentionless objectivity of the art work. The notion that the true work of art is an objective construction, transcending any and all of the subjective and intentional 'moments' it brings into play, is deep in aesthetic theory as well as in Hegelian philosophy, and Adorno was steeped in both. Thus, in appreciating a tragedy such as *King Lear*, we can easily hold in a single frame both the subjectivity and intentionality of each of the characters and also the transcendent character of the work as an intentionless and objective totality. Put in a different way, we might say that in summoning the 'intentionlessness' from the manifold of intentions, the work of art realises the 'spiritual'.

Adorno was insistent upon this dialectical relationship between parts and whole in a work of art. He opposed as futile the project of attempting to construct a work of art as a kind of pure, intentionless language. The intentionless work of art, as object, is seen by him as inseparable from the manifold intentions which give rise to it and which, in the context of the total work, 'summon the intentionless' (T. Adorno 1993: 404). To conceive of either the intentional or the intentionless as an absolute, as an 'in-itself', would be equivalent to the dream of a pure 'in-itself' subject or a pure 'in-itself' object. Adorno was rigorous in his rejection of all such dreams of purity; the intentionless aesthetic object emerges from and is constructed by the manifold of intentions.

The desire, however, to construct works of art that would somehow be purely objective, devoid of intentionality – the desire to construct a pure music, purged of all subjective intentions and expression, for example – was a very real project for many modern artists, and Adorno saw it as a mark of pathology. He detected the signs of this pathology in music ranging from the neo-classical works of Hindemith and Stravinsky to the works of modern serialist composers building upon Schoenberg's twelve-tone technique. The path he trod in his championing of modernist art was always a very careful and selective one, and the art of which he approved, whether modernist or pre-modernist, was art which preserved, as integral, both terms of the dialectic – the intentionality of the elements and the work of art as an intentionless whole. Two composers who appeared, to Adorno, to meet this ideal more fully than most were Gustav Mahler and Adorno's own teacher, Alban Berg.

Adorno's treatment of this dialectic at the level of structure can easily be assimilated (in a manner consistent with his thinking) to the analysis of structural relations in language generally. The isomorphism between society, language and art at the level of part–whole relations is key to his sociological perspective, and especially to his claims for the 'function' of works of art as modes of knowing or understanding. Not only do works of art participate in and derive from social praxis generally, but they can serve as a means of understanding social reality – of knowing and perceiving society – because in their structural relations they inscribe its likeness.

The crisis of modernity, for Adorno, is bound up with the withdrawal of the subject as the spiritual centre, from forms which have ceased to express him and with which the subject is no longer identified. However, such 'empty' forms or conventions do not thereby cease to be intentional simply because a present subjectivity cannot be realised or expressed in them. Past subjectivity is congealed in such forms, and this embedded or sedimented intentionality can be deployed by the subject, negatively, as a vehicle through which to express its condition. What is key here, for Adorno, is what a subject does with such 'empty' forms, what use is made of them. By establishing its non-identity in and through its distancing of itself in relation to such forms (and in its presence as an absence from such forms) the subject takes up the stance of irony. The practice of irony thus becomes central to modernist art. This is essentially what Adorno held to be the source of the expressive power in late Beethoven, and he invoked a similar explanation in the case of Mahler's music. In both cases, the traditional language of tonal music is used by these composers, but in a way that is no longer innocent but knowing. For Adorno, the use of the outworn materials of tonality by composers such as Mahler could not be compared with the commitment to diatonic means in the music of late Romantic composers such as Elgar or Sibelius.

Modernist music, however, is popularly associated with the radical shift from tonality to atonalism. With this shift, even the husks, the empty forms and conventions of a tonal music that has been vivified by the musical inventiveness and compositional power of a composer like Mahler, begin to dissolve. The very power of composition that is unleashed in order to bring off a genuine expressivity through the use of out-worn conventions ultimately becomes decisive and bursts through the form-husks, shattering them into fragments and subjecting the fragments to an omnipresent constructivism. The atonal music of the Schoenberg school was the major modernist revolution. From within that school, Adorno remained committed to the belief that 'free atonality' had the potential for developing a genuine 'musique informelle' in which the dialectic of the intentional and the intentionless would be realised. That is why Mahler, who used tonal rather than atonal means, could remain such a potent ideal for Adorno; even more than many of those who came after, he met this fundamental objective of summoning the intentionless from the manifold of intentions.

Music's similarity to language

For Adorno, music's similarity to language is fundamental:

> It is not only as an organised coherence of sounds that music is analogous to speech, similar to language, but also in the manner of its concrete structure. The traditional doctrine of musical forms has its sentence, phrase, period and punctuation. Questions, exclamations, subordinate clauses are everywhere, voices rise and fall and, in all of this, the gesture of music is borrowed from the speaking voice. When Beethoven, referring to the performance of a Bagatelle from opus 33, asks for 'a certain speaking expression' he only emphasises, in his reflection, an ever-present aspect of music. . . . If not concepts, tonality has, in any case, generated vocables: first the chords which are always used in identical functions, even worn out combinations like the steps of a cadence.
>
> (T. Adorno 1993: 401)

Adorno acknowledges the existence of two types of similarity to language. There is first the approximation of music to a signifying language, music as a repository of established figures and forms shot through with intentions. Then there is music which approximates to being an intention-less language, to being a pure language which transcends signification, intention and expression. Adorno dismisses the notion that signification in music could ever be absolute; in that case it would cease to be music and would pass, falsely, into language. At the same time he rejects the notion of music without any signification, a pure objective music; the mere phenomenological coherence of tones would resemble a kind of acoustic kaleidoscope. The dialectical mediation of the two – signifying language and (pure) intentionless language – conditions music's similarity to language:

> The whole is realised against the intentions; it integrates them by means of the negation of each individual, indeterminate intention. Music as a whole rescues the intentions, not by diluting them into a more abstract higher intention, but by readying itself in the instant in which it crystallises, to summon the intentionless. Thus it is almost the antithesis of the kind of coherence that makes sense, even though it may appear as such in comparison to sensuous immediacy. . . . But in truth, the musical content is the wealth of all those things underlying the musical syntax and grammar. . . . If musical structures or forms, then, are to be considered more than didactic schemas, they do not enclose the content in an external way, but are its very destiny, as that of something spiritual. . . . Just as those musics in which the existence of the whole most consis-tently absorbs and moves beyond its particular intentions, seem to be the most eloquent, so music's objectivity, as the essence of its logic, is inseparable from the element in it which is similar to language, from which it derives everything of a logical nature.
>
> (T. Adorno 1993: 404)

In stating his position in this paper concerning the nature of music as similarity to language, Adorno discloses some of the conflicts that condition his critique of modern music, philosophy and society. He recognises a powerful tendency in modern music to construct a pure musical language free of all intentionality. Such an ideal is met with in modern philosophy in the tendencies of phenomenological and existentialist philosophies to hypo-statise a radical disjunction of subject and object, and in modern society in the atomising and totalitarian tendencies of the modern political and indus-trial order. Adorno sees it as an ever-present threat in modern music. He identifies two approaches in modern music to the destruction of intention-ality and the pursuit of music as a pure language. The first is the path taken by Stravinsky (see Chapter 8), whose neo-classical style constituted, for Adorno, a reversion to musical models which, because of their remoteness from modern expressivity, seemed architectonic and far removed from signifying language. By further eliminating from such models every vestige of the intentionality of signifying language, pure music, purified of all intentions was supposed to result.

Adorno also acknowledges a second, later form in which the rebellion against the subjective, expressive aspect of music – its similarity to language – is advanced. It is a development of the very musical tradition of which Adorno himself is a part, the music of the second Viennese school of composition but particularly the twelve-tone music of Schoenberg. In the extreme form in which twelve-tone technique – especially in the models provided by Webern – became the inspiration of the musical avant-garde composers of the 1950s and 1960s, Adorno saw only a capitulation to the most totalitarian tendencies:

> In its second, later form, the rebellion against musical similarity to language desires nothing less than to catapult itself out of history altogether . . . the young composers jump to the conclusion of a tabula rasa. They want to liquidate the element of musical language in music, to end subjectively mediated musical coherence itself and create tonal relations dominated by exclusively objective, that is, mathematical relationships. Consideration of any reproducible musical sense, indeed the possibility of musical imagination itself, is irrelevant. The remainder is supposed to be the cosmically superhuman essence of music. Finally, the process of composition itself is rendered physical: diagrams replace the notes; formulas for the generation of electronic sound replace the act of composition, which itself is ultimately seen as an arbitrarily subjective act.
>
> (T. Adorno 1993: 409)

However, musical objectivism turns into its opposite. The force that imagines that it is overcoming the arbitrary rule of the subject and of subjectivity is identical, according to Adorno, with complete reification. In the desire to be pure nature, music is reduced to the status of the manufactured thing.

> Nothing can sound more accidental than music that ostracises the ultimate act of discrimination; the electronic production of sound, which thinks of itself as the voiceless voice of being itself, sometimes sounds like the droning of machinery. . . . But with the proscription of everything that is even remotely similar to language, and thus of every musical sense, the absolutely objective product becomes truly senseless: objectively absolutely irrelevant. The dream of a wholly spiritualised music removed from the sullying

influences of the animalistic nature of human beings awakens among rough, prehuman material and deadly monotony.

(T. Adorno 1993: 410)

Even the pretence of pure intentionless music is a sham, because the onto-logical region that lies beyond subjective accident is exposed as being in reality a subjective mastery over nature that has been absolutised as mere technique. The dominating subject has merely divested itself of its own humanity and simultaneously failed to recognise itself.

What Adorno advocates is a music which reconciles these opposed tendencies as represented by the musical signification inherited from tonal material and the musical-linguistic structures that result from a radical disqualification of such material. Both are somehow necessary. On the one hand, the technical rationalisation of tonal material which resulted in the twelve-tone technique presses for a new reorganisation of musical structure according to the immanent laws of the material as it unfolds – that is, a new musical language *sui generis*. In the opposite case, musical linguistic forms – themes, transitions, questions and answers, contrasts, continuations – abstracted from the musical material that was previously provided by tonality, can be followed in their development and 'constructed out'. Adorno sees this technique as characteristic of Berg's music and also film music:

> But the attempts to wring its own separate language from the mate-rial, in the first case, and to treat language itself as material and make it self-reliant, in the second, converge in the free disposition over the means of composition. This is attained by the individual who abandons himself, in a kind of active receptivity, to that towards which the materials are striving on their own. This, however, would be nothing less than the mediation of subject and object. As one hears within the mere material the language that is enclosed within it, one becomes aware of the subject that lies concealed in that mate-rial and as one breaks the linguistic elements, which without exception represent sedimented subjective feelings, out of their blind quasi-primitive natural coherence and constructs them out oneself, purely, one does justice to the idea of objectivity that charac-terises all language in the midst of its subjective signification.
>
> (T. Adorno 1993: 413)

Gustav Mahler

Mahler's progressiveness did not reside in tangible innovations and advanced material. He was, argues Adorno, opposed to formalism and followed no straight historical path. In his symphonies he rejected any idea of reconcilia-tion between subject and object, individual and society, of the kind sought

113

in the Viennese classical tradition which developed the musical language he actually worked with. At the same time his music opposed the inexorable advance of chromaticism in modern music, an advance which tends to the removal of all individual qualities from the musical material with which the composer works and which, when developed completely, strips the material down to the level of the individual tones. Thus Mahler insists on the diatonic – on tonalism – as a sure foundation even at the very historical moment when it has been shaken and undermined by the beginnings of a new music (T. Adorno 1992).

However, Mahler's use of traditional musical language was not innocent. He drew on its standard forms in order to ironise them and establish their distance from the subject. That he chose to work with those forms rather than to destroy them altogether in the manner of later composers is linked by Adorno to the fundamental attitude of Mahler's music. Adorno implies that a superior wisdom guides Mahler's choice to mobilise traditional musical language; the rationalising domination which destroyed traditional musical language was identified with the same force that crushed the victims of modern society. In a subtle passage, Adorno links the compassion of Mahler as an artist for the weak and defeated and his opposition to the strong with Mahler's insistence on binding himself as a composer to traditional material. Adorno thus reveals the extent to which he sees the very musical revolution of the second Viennese school, with which he himself identified so strongly, as itself part of the disease.

> The instinct of the peddler's grandson does not make common cause with those forming the battalions of the stronger but, in however despairing and illusory a manner, with the margins of society. The undomesticated element in which Mahler's music collusively immerses itself is also archaic, outdated. This is why a music inimical to compromise bound itself to traditional material. It was thereby reminded of the victims of progress, even musical victims: those elements of language ejected by the process of rationalisation and material control. It was not the peace disturbed by the world's course that Mahler sought in language; rather, he endowed it with power in order to resist power.
>
> (T. Adorno 1992: 17)

Mahler's music gives the impression of being in perpetual motion, of 'aimlessly circling'. According to Adorno, it is music which reproduces images of what Hegel called 'the world's course', images of empty activity devoid of autonomy, images of the blind functioning of the individual who finds herself yoked into the world's course without finding herself reflected in it. The flow of movement in Beethoven's second-period compositions is one which accords with the idea of purposive goal-oriented activity; the actions of a vigorous subject, reflecting socially useful work, inspired the classical symphony. Mahler's music, by contrast, imitates the world's course – its bleak banality – in order to resist and oppose it.

The image of the automaton as the symbol of empty activity devoid of autonomy reflects the condition of labour and of the subject in the modern world. In the art of painters such as Giorgio de Chirico or Marcel Duchamp or Ferdinand Leger, the mannequin and the machine replaced the organic figures of perceptual-realist art (figures moving under their own volition and expressing, in their outer forms, their inner spiritual and emotional dispositions). The emptiness of the automaton, of meaningless activity, of outworn language and cliché forms, this is the stuff of the banal. It is Adorno's argument that art must imitate the alienating force of modern society as it manifests itself in the banality of a world abandoned by the spiritual, but only in order to force that banality to express the spiritual negatively.

In his appropriation of the outworn material of tonal language, Mahler deliberately produces estrangement from that language. This is clearly to be seen in the treatment of nature within his music. Where his music arouses images of nature and of landscape, these are not so much stated as absolutes as inferred from the contrast to that from which they deviate in the music. The richness of his expressive means is bound up with the variety of ways in which he produces deviation and therefore distance within his music. In this statement attributed to Mahler by Natalie Bauer-Lechner, the composer indicates the deliberate way in which he goes about such estrangement and distancing effects:

> If I want to produce a soft, subdued sound, I don't give it to an instrument which produces it easily but rather to one which can get it only with effort and under pressure – often only by forcing itself and exceeding its natural range. I often make the basses and bassoons squeak on the highest notes, while my flute huffs and puffs down below. There's a passage like this in the fourth movement – you remember the entry of the violas?. . . . I always enjoy this effect; I could never have produced that powerful forced tone if I had given the passage to the cellos (the most obvious choice here).
>
> (T. Adorno 1992: 16)

Someone listening to Mahler's Third Symphony for the first time after being told of the centrality of the images of nature might be a little puzzled. But Mahler's approach negates the high musical language in which natural beauty is simply 'taste', in a second man-made nature. His music can be seen as registering the presence of nature in its 'exacerbated deviations from high musical language'. Nature is not directly depicted but is glimpsed in and through the de-naturing of 'second nature'. Mahler's music robs music of its innocence:

Through the contrast between the disruptive intention and the musical language, the latter is transformed unobserved from an a priori convention into an expressive means: in a similar way, Kafka's pointedly conservative, objectively epic prose, schooled in Kleist, accentuates its content by contrasting with it.

(T. Adorno 1992: 16)

In Kafka and elsewhere in modern art and literature this antagonism between art and its language reflects the rift within society, the transcendental homelessness of a subject who can no longer find any reconciliation or harmonisation of the spiritual and material life, of the inner and the outer realm of existence, a point which is central to the sociology of the novel advanced by Lukács and also Lucien Goldmann. The 'outer', in this case, might be thought of as society and the 'inner' the sensuous life of the individual subject. The disjunction between music and its language appears in Mahler, as in late Beethoven, as the antinomy of the individual and society.

Adorno invokes the opposition he repeatedly draws between the mimetic or spontaneous and expressive moment in music and the constructive or rational moment through which the musical material is controlled. The more developed the rational constructive principle in modern music, the more is the mimetic moment repressed and the less the music accords expression its place. However, for a composer seeking, as Mahler did, to make use of tonal language in late bourgeois society, the problem of expression becomes problematic in another sense. For the subject to be heard at all within tonality, as an outmoded language,

it must seize on an individual means, heighten it to an overvalued idea, harden it to a bearer of expression as the surrounding system is hardened. Mannerism is the scar left behind by expression in a language no longer capable of expression. Mahler's deviations are closely related to gestures of language; his peculiarities are clenched as in jargon.

(T. Adorno 1992: 22)

It is the refusal of synthesis, of reconciliation between subject and object, which produces mannerism. This lack of reconciliation – Mahler's mannerism – is seen, in one of its formal aspects, in terms of the play of major and minor modes in his music. 'As a deviation from the major, the minor defines itself as the not-integrated, the unassimilated, the not yet established' (T. Adorno 1992: 26).

Adorno argues that the contrast between the major and minor modes, in Mahler, reflects the divergence between the particular and the general. Minor is the particular, major the general. As the deviant, the minor mode in Mahler is equated by Adorno with the suffering and with truth. With the

116

loss of an organic identity between whole and part, which had been the aesthetic ideal of Viennese classicism, modern music generated an expanding profusion of musical elements and so faced, as a consequence, the need to find new constructive principles of ordering. There was a need for the clearest articulation of part–whole relations in order to achieve the maximum degree of order given this proliferation of musical details. But details that were no longer anchored in their organic relationship to a large whole were emptied of their substantive content. For Mahler and for Berg, who followed him in this, to realise this degree of tight organisation meant replacing the lost substantive and organic links among the parts with functional ones. From the largest movement to the tiniest motive, the 'function' of an element announces itself clearly, that it is an 'opening', a 'closing', an 'elaboration', a 'continuation' and so forth.

> Elaborations seem to say: this is an elaboration; interruptions occur with unmistakable abruptness; if the music opens up one hears colons; if it is fulfilled, the line noticeably exceeds the preceding intensity and does not depart from the level now attained. Resolutions clearly blur the contours and the sound. Marcato underlines the essential, announces: 'Here I am'; a following passage is demonstrated by fragments of earlier motives, a picking up by harmonic continuation; what is to be entirely different and to appear new is really that. Such precision makes the characters emerge clearly: they coincide with their emphatic formal function, the *characteristica universalis* of Mahler's music. The rule of clarity to which he rigorously subjected the instrumentation in particular resulted from his reflection as a composer: the less the music is articulated by tonal language, the more strictly it must ensure its own articulation. For this reason it calls its forms, as it were, by their names, composes their types as Schoenberg's wind quartets did paradigmatically, later. . . . What characterises is, for that very reason, no longer simply what is, but, as the word 'character' intends, a sign. Mahler drew his functional characters – what each individual part contributes to the form – from the stock of traditional music. But they are used autonomously without regard to their place in the established pattern. He can therefore invent melodies that clearly have the character of sequels, essences of the closing themes of sonata form; of such kind, for example, is the *Abgesang* figure in the Adagietto of the Fifth Symphony.
>
> (T. Adorno 1992: 47–8)

Clearly, this coming apart of form and substance in music draws attention to the detail, makes the detail stand out in all its distinctiveness and unassimilated character. However, the less the form is substantially prescribed, the more insistently it is sought by composition that begins with the unprotected individual figure. For Adorno, it is still vital that music seeks to go out from the details to the whole, that the elements or parts seek to transcend their limits:

> Even when the young Mahler writes genre-like pieces in the manner of the time, they vibrate with the whole; even what takes delight in limitation seeks to be rid of its own limits. In the well-ordered groups of the first movement of the Fifth, dynamic passages are inserted, as in the section leading back after the first trio. The fanfare, on its first return in the exposition of the March, plunges seething into a mass that hisses with a clash of cymbals. So a lament opposed to discipline is set at liberty amid the somewhat static planes of a stylised military march. In Mahler the lyrical subject is plainly divested, by the formal sequence that it initiates, of its mere individuality. The part and the whole do not harmonise as in Viennese classicism. Their relationship is aporetic.
>
> (T. Adorno 1992: 49)

For all their particularity, Mahler's sensuous details remain, in relation to the idea of totality, essentially incomplete. Either Mahler experiments with the particular until it finally becomes a whole, or he studiously avoids rounded completeness, thereby invoking the whole implicitly through its imparting of a sense of incompleteness to the particular and also of stamping it in such a way that it strains beyond itself, beyond its limitation; always, Adorno maintains, Mahler avoids the academic formalism which reconciles particulars in the whole as fiercely as he does the tendencies in German music to culminate in the flat organisation of particulars no longer mediating one another that characterises twelve-tone technique and serialism.

Mahler was unable to rely for his particulars on the stock of figures available to him in Viennese classicism because the unqualified primacy of the whole over the parts meant that the figures in that music frequently resembled one another and converged. Mahler's musical world depends upon a rich contrast of figures of the kind that was shunned in Viennese classicism. He sought his figures from late Romanticism and, above all, from so-called vulgar music. Because of his need to achieve this separation between the expressive content of the music and its formal structure, he must necessarily work with material in which the intentions are already formed.

> Mahler's themes each bear their own names in themselves, without nomenclature. But such characterisation has a prospect of validity only insofar as the musical imagination does not produce intentions at will, does not, therefore, think out motives that express this or

that according to a plan, but works with a musical linguistic material in which intentions are already objectively present. As preconceived entities they are quoted as it were by the musical imagination and dedicated to the whole. The materials that achieve this are those called banal, in which meaning has generally sedimented, before the advent of the individual composer, and has been punished by forfeiting the spontaneity of living execution. Such meanings stir anew under the staff of composition and feel their strength. They are reduced to elements of composition and at the same time freed from their thing-like rigidity.

(T. Adorno 1992: 58)

Adorno characterises Mahler's symphonies as novel-symphonies. He contrasts Mahler here with what he sees as the drama-symphonies of Viennese classicism. The distinction he is making presupposes that the drama, unlike the novel, is one in which the whole has primacy over the parts and in which its idea is developed in a manner that is analogous to discursive logic. Such a form resists the introduction of new material that has not been prepared for or is not logically to be deduced from what has preceded it. Adorno saw it as characteristic of the novel that new characters could emerge at any time, and the novel was simply borne along from the force of the movement of its particulars and whatever came into it. Mahler's symphonies are full of these surprising elements, brought in without warning or without being capable of being simply deduced in the manner of a Beethoven symphony, whose entire construction can sometimes be seen as an elaboration of its opening measures. Mahler's relation to the novel as a form can be demonstrated, for example, by his Fifth Symphony, where

after one of the slow interpolations, a somewhat secondary figure from the exposition is taken up and reformulated, as if, unexpectedly, a previously unregarded person now entered the scene to assist development, as in Balzac. . . . Proust is said to have pointed out that new themes sometimes take over the centre in the same way as previously unnoticed minor characters in novels.

(T. Adorno 1992: 68)

Adorno insists that the whole movement and progression of Mahler's music begins from below, from the elements, 'the facts', each of which emerges in succession like the characters and details in a novel. The composer somehow strikes from the whole movement that spark which goes beyond the details. He does not begin from above, with an ontology of forms, from which he deduces his elements; rather, he meets the demands of the musical novel form, that it should avoid knowing in advance how it is to continue, and this abolition of tradition is achieved using traditional means, a strategy with which Adorno himself sympathised deeply.

Adorno's contrast between Mahlerian novel-symphony and dramatic-classical symphony raises a crucial point about the relationship of music to time. The classical symphony 'beguiles time' by converting into spirit the integral development, the unfolding idea and unity. In Mahler's symphonies thematic figures do not remain indifferent to or unchanged by the flow of the symphony, any more than the characters in a novel remain indifferent to the dimension of time in which they act. Even as the same beings they become different through time, shrinking, expanding, ageing. Adorno sees this modification of fixed elements as profoundly unclassical.

> As soon as traditional great music ceased 'working out' through a development, it was content with a conserved architectonic identity; if an element recurred identically, it was, aside from the key, identical and nothing else. Mahler's symphonic writing, however, sabotages these alternatives. Nothing in them is ever entirely consumed by the dynamic but nothing ever remains what it was. Time passes into the characters and changes them as empirical time alters faces.
>
> (T. Adorno 1992: 73)

In his discussion of Mahler's use of variation, Adorno points to some important differences with both traditional and modern uses. The Mahler variant is the technical means for the development of the novelistic or epic figures that appear in his music as the 'identical but ever-changing'. In effect Mahler's compositional technique can be contrasted with that of Beethoven. In the latter, it is the smallest motivic cells of the music that determine their elaboration into qualitatively different theme complexes. The thematic macro-structure of the music is thus simply the technical outcome of this elaboration. But in Mahler's music the 'musical micro-organisms' are incessantly modified within the more or less fixed outlines of the main figures.

Mahler's music acknowledges what is already figured in late Beethoven, namely that the individual is not the grand and powerful entity on whom the fate of the world depends but a weakened, impotent and fragmented being. Music, however, must remain true to this defeated figure, must take on its fractured form as the very script of truth. If modern music has turned its back on the symphony, it is because, at the level of both social structure and the materials of aesthetic form, the grand design of bourgeois individuation has collapsed and music that has recourse to it in anything other than an ironising sense is necessarily false.

Alban Berg

Quite apart from his particular closeness to Berg because the latter had been his teacher, Adorno was clearly drawn to Berg's music because it somehow combined what were, for him, two essentials: that music must be uncompromisingly modern and yet must retain its expressive power. The price of progress in modern music, to which he alluded when he praised Mahler's music for having avoided it, was the progressive destruction of the expressive power of music, its mathematising and spatialising of musical relations and its elimination of all autonomy and subjective choice, not to mention all history and genuine temporality. As in the case of jazz, Adorno hit out hard at the mid-century serialist composers (T. Adorno 1956) and again, as with jazz, critics complained that he did so from a standpoint of lack of adequate knowledge of the music he was criticising (H.-K. Metzger 1960). Whatever the truth of the argument – and there is certainly justice in some of the accusations of Adorno's critics – Adorno's arguments and judgements are, as always, broadly based in his wider conception of music's project.

In his analysis of Berg's music, Douglas Jarman attributes its expressive power to the fact that, for long sections, it encourages tonal interpretation while at the same time refusing to confirm this interpretation.

> Although the handling of the tonal implications and the manipulation of degrees of tension and relaxation in Berg's music articulate the musical design in a way comparable to that of the tensions and relaxations in traditional diatonic music, the tonal areas to which the music occasionally resolves do not have the unifying function of tonic keys in eighteenth and nineteenth century music. The tonal areas do not usually give rise to an ordered hierarchy of functional relationships.
>
> (D. Jarman 1979: 17)

It is difficult to escape the impression that, in Adorno's judgements of modern music, this continued and integral involvement of the music of such composers as Berg and Mahler with tonal language is key to his hopes for a music that successfully avoids the price of progress while being, in the most advanced sense, progressive. Berg was not a composer in the tradition of diatonic music but a radical atonal composer who formed part of the Schoenberg revolution in modern music and belonged to atonalism as much as Leger or Gris belonged to Cubism. In his commitment to what Adorno saw as 'free atonality', Berg more nearly met Adorno's own ideals than other members of that school. With the destruction of key centres as a means of organisation, the technical problems of establishing cohesion and organisation in the music were dramatically increased. One possible solution was to replace tonality with a set of theoretical propositions of the kind represented by Schoenberg's twelve-tone system. However, as Jarman points out, in free atonal music each work creates afresh the compositional context, and therefore the basis of order, within which it operates.

> Any aspect of the music – from a traditionally shaped melodic pattern to a tiny intervallic cell, a rhythmic figure of harmonic formation, a timbre or a single pitch – may act as a cohesive element if the composer chooses to assert it in a way that enables it to operate as such.
>
> (D. Jarman 1979: 22)

It is this ideal of a free 'musique informelle', in which order is realised spontaneously and expressively from below in response to the living context, which Adorno sets up as one pole of an antimony, the other being that of an absolute subject-alien totalitarian administrative order. Adorno's castigation of all theoretical systems that appeared to threaten the autonomy of the subject is always and ever the real basis of his criticisms of modern music, from Schoenberg and Webern through to Boulez and Stockhausen. It is his apparent certainty on this point which determined many of his critical polemics and may have led him to be less than diligent in developing a critical appraisal of actual musical scores in the case of both his attacks on serialist music and on jazz.

The developmental process which penetrates the micro-structure of the music, transforming its smallest elements, is made central to Adorno's analysis of Berg's music. In my terms, the taking of the developmental process into the innermost cells of the music is a reflection of the movement from an inter-actional to an intra-actional order. In an intra-actional order, time passes into the elements as material, as stuff; they are in a continuous process of becoming, of change, of flux; they age, 'like faces'. Whereas, in Mahler's music, this means that within themes that remain constant in broad outline a continuous reshaping of elements occurs (in contradistinction to classical Viennese construction in which the elements remain more or less hard in outline and are elaborated into qualitatively distinct themes), in Adorno's account of Berg's music themes are dissolved into their tiniest components in the very process of being developed. Development is spread throughout the music, and this endless process of dissolution is endless becoming. Adorno describes this aspect of Berg's compositional technique:

> Berg possesses a special technique for taking defined thematic shapes and, in the course of developing them, calling them back to nothingness.... His music cultivates a favourite technique... from each theme a remnant is retained, ever smaller until, finally, only a vanishing small vestige remains; not only does the theme establish its own insubstantiality, but the formal interrelationships

between successive sections are woven together with infinitesimal care. . . . One can illustrate this Bergian manner – manner in the larger sense of Mannerism – with the children's game in which the word 'Kapuziner' is disassembled and put back together again: Kapuziner – Apuziner – Puziner – Uziner – Ziner – Iner – Ner – Er – R; R – Er – Ner – Iner – Ziner – Uziner – Puziner – Apuziner – Kaputziner. That is how he composed, that is how all of his music plays in a Capuchin tomb of whimsy, and his development was essentially a development towards the spiritualisation of that manner.

(T. Adorno 1994a: 3)

Berg was a chromaticist through and through. His music develops something which Adorno holds to be a truly distinctive contribution in modern music. Because his themes are in a state of continuous dissolution and the tiny fragments into which they decompose border on an amorphous nothingness, his music offers itself as a radically continuous process in which none of its structures are consolidated but all is in perpetual dissolution. In this, however, it can be argued that Berg realises the ideal so characteristic of modernity, the ideal of evanescence. Adorno returns repeatedly to this characteristic of Berg's music, its reliance on the smallest link, its perpetual dissolution into its tiniest elements. Traditional analysis, with its emphasis on the articulation of part–whole relations, misses the mark in the case of Berg's music, suggests Adorno. Structurally, Berg's music does not consist of elements in any commensurably traditional sense. It strives towards the individual element as its goal, towards a threshold value bordering on nothingness.

On the one hand Berg's technical inclinations suggest that his music as an unrelenting and permanent process of becoming, continually fragments itself into the smallest entities. On the other hand, because of its infinitesimal nature, this smallest entity can really no longer be regarded as an element, as is usually the case in analyses. That implies nothing less than that, in terms of the structural aspect of becoming *per se* (a becoming that resists all consolidation and thereby revokes its own structure), Berg's music, in relation to all other new music, offers something radically new.

(T. Adorno 1994a: 39)

From his teacher Schoenberg, Berg had assimilated the technique of 'developing variation' through which the composer seeks to generate, from a minimum of basic elements, a maximum of shapes. In Schoenberg this is the culmination of a principle that is very much at the heart of Viennese classicism. Adorno points out that the Bergian compositional technique adds an important dimension to the technique which he holds to be deeper. By continuously dissolving the developed whole into its tiniest elements, by ending in the minimum 'virtually in a single note', Berg steers the Schoenberg principle in the opposite direction. The components of the music grow to resemble one another in retrograde, thus satisfying the principle of economy in reverse (T. Adorno 1994a: 38). The basically analytical technique of the music threatens it with the undifferentiated sameness of that into which it dissolves. That the music avoids this fate is due, according to Adorno, to its 'heightened constructive plasticity'. This again establishes a link to Mahler. Lacking the substantive unity provided by tonality, the composer resorts to articulation of the music based upon constructing its functions into a new whole, using them in terms of their functional characters as opening phrases, continuations or concluding phrases, for example. Thus Adorno makes an identical claim for Berg's music to the one he later made in the essays on Mahler.

> In Berg's mature works, ultimately every phrase or partial entity not only divulges with complete clarity to cognitive understanding its formal function, but also makes that formal function so emphatic a part of the directly perceived phenomenon that a concluding phrase declares: I am a concluding phrase; and a continuation declares: I am a continuation. . . . His music is without force, tangible and fatal like a vine; that comprises its true modernity.
>
> (T. Adorno 1994a: 39)

This functional articulation was bound up with another aspect of Berg's music which defined its modernism: that is, the importance of 'the banal'. The dissolution of the form into its tiniest elements and the loss of the substantive spiritual centre provided by tonalism gave rise to the development of a second formal construction from which that substantive or spiritual centre was banished. This second formal structure could be subsumed under the category of *the banal*. Adorno draws on a striking image from Walter Benjamin:

> Benjamin drew attention to those trays in bourgeois parlours on which stamps are mounted under glass in an irregular tableau; one is familiar with the terror emanating from them; how the stamps, glued painfully into place, seem to be twitching *en masse* for all eternity, divorced from their function and therefore banned as a dreadful allegory of that function. In Berg's pieces that sort of montage, allegory and terror is intensified to express the very embodiment of the dream. Under the glass plates of form, large as a house, in the wild distorted motley array of orchestral planes, those fragments awaken to a second and catastrophic significance. It is the

significance of banality. Banality is commodity as appearance. If the young Berg's development, like a recapitulation of romantic development, seems like a flight from banality leading to the atom, to the pure moment, then the realisation immanent to form marks a turning point: that in the world of commodities there is no escaping the commodity – each [commodity] only more deeply entangled in the world – that the musical atom once achieved, indeed ultimately the single pitch, is revealed to be just as banal as the deceptively uniform surface itself had been. Berg obeys this law in two ways; through its shape he unreservedly acknowledges the banality of the smallest particle and he nullifies that particle in the equilibrium of a second whole.

(T. Adorno 1994a: 75)

The loss of the binding force of tonalism, and with it the bourgeois spiritualisation of social objects, was met with at more than one level in the music of modern composers. Their music was very much a dialectical process which took as its raw material the musical forms it was in the process of demolishing. These forms were often an essential and integral part of such music. The most important of these forms, for Adorno, was that of the sonata-allegro. He saw its destruction, its annihilation, as being internal to the project of a great deal of modern music.

In the analysis of Beethoven's Sonata Opus 111 offered in Thomas Mann's *Doctor Faustus*, Beethoven is said to bid farewell to the sonata-form itself. It is even offered as an explanation for the fact that there was no third movement to Opus 111. Berg's First String Quartet is said to be in itself a 'loyal critique of the architecture that had until then been the requisite for chamber music' (that is, the sonata-form). The traditional sonata-form is subjected to a process which takes its false claims seriously and seeks to realise them fully; Berg subjects the sonata to an unrelenting and all-persuasive constructive unity in which absolutely every element derives its rationale from its relationship to the formal whole, and yet – insists Adorno – in which every force and form in the music is legitimised by the requirements and impulse of the individual elements.

What results from the conflict is nothing less than the liquidation of the sonata. The essence of sonata form is at the heart of the quartet; it disintegrates under the assault of unfettered, subjectively musical creativity; its disintegration, however, liberates the objective forces within it, permitting the creation of a new symphonic form in free atonality. . . . The Quartet no longer has any 'themes' in the old static sense, at least not in the second movement. Permanent transition softens every consolidated shape, opening it to what precedes and follows, holding it in a never-ending flow of variants, subordinating it to the primacy of the whole. Thematic paradigms shrivel: they are reduced to minimal motivic units. . . . The listener's task is not therefore one of noting themes and following their fate but that of becoming involved in a musical process in which every bar, indeed every note, is equidistant to the centre.

(T. Adorno 1994a :54–5)

Time

Because the radical constructivism of Berg's music dissolves all structures emerging in the music in a continuous process of becoming, there ceases to be anything in the music which is not in transition, in flux. Consequently there is no invariant structure against which to measure becoming or development. In such a situation there is the appearance of stasis.

> The Clarinet Pieces were created out of that sudden transformation of dynamism into stasis, out of stilled time itself. Each of them lasts only an instant, like Schoenberg's Opus 19, or Webern's Opus 11; but this instant which knows no development and no time, nevertheless unfolds in time; the principle of differentiation being implemented so radically that the time in which it governs – which in absolute terms is longer than in the corresponding Schoenberg or Webern pieces – is, so to speak, contracted and made to seem like an instant, whereas by contrast, Webern, as Schoenberg said, compresses a novel into a sigh.
>
> (T. Adorno 1994a: 68)

Adorno returns repeatedly to this characteristic of many compositions in the 'new music', the production of stasis through the spread of variation and development into every element. Development loses its meaning if everything is development and nothing remains behind against which it can be measured. In the Clarinet Pieces, Adorno argues, Berg liquidates the sonata by extending the developmental process over the entire musical structure. Musical time can only constitute itself through change relative to something independent. When it flows on without independent points of reference, it comes to rest.

While Adorno is always concerned to draw attention to those characteristics of Berg's music which draw it away from the rigidities of abstract schemes such as twelve-tone method (even when Berg uses the method), he is less attentive to those aspects of Berg's compositional technique which indicated a need to develop abstract theoretical schemes – arbitrary and extra-musical rather than musically necessary – and to impose upon himself precisely the kinds of formulaic disciplines of which Adorno so disapproved. Indeed, it might be argued that Berg's reliance on numerical schemes might well have been extreme in comparison to many others. Jarman offers the following account of the main structural features of Berg's *Lyric Suite*:

> The main structural features of the *Lyric Suite* are determined by the numbers 23 and 50. The first movement has 69 bars (3×23) and a tempo marking of {crotchet} = 100 (2×50); the second movement has 150 bars (3×50) . . . the third has 138 bars (6×23) . . . the sixth has 46 bars (2×23). . . . These numbers also determine the length of many of the smaller structural units in the work and the points at which events appear within these units. Thus the second section of the first movement of the *Lyric Suite* begins at bar 23, the central section of the third movement begins at bar 69 and ends at bar 92 and the last quaver of bar 23 of the final movement marks the turning point of an important palindromic figure.
>
> (D. Jarman 1979: 226)

Although Berg did not mention the important part played by the number 23 in his analytical notes on the *Lyric Suite*, the final pages of the manuscript are covered with mathematical computations based on this number and the comment 'followed by a retrograde to end at bar 138 (i.e. 46 bars) N.B. 138 = 6×23!'

Jarman points to the paradox resulting from the fact that such apparently mathematical, extra-musical, organisational procedures are involved in creating so emotionally charged and expressive a work. Artificial techniques, rigorous formal symmetries, ciphers, cryptograms and so forth are so thoroughly Bergian that Jarman insists that they were based upon deeply personal associations as well as acting as a stimulus for his creative imagination. In his book on Berg, Reich (1965: 26) claims that 23 was the day of the month on which Berg had his first asthma attack. Some years after this first attack, he was called into the army under regulation 23. While acknowledging their deeply personal significance, Jarman argues that the function of such abstract schemes for Berg was to transform subjective elements into objective restraints which, paradoxically, both embody and curb the subjectivity from which they sprang. Certainly in an art which, I would argue, is shifting to the intra-subjective and which is realising as its content the intra-subjective sensibility of the subject, the use of such devices may well provide the distancing necessary to make sensibility itself an object of special perceptual attention.

Suffering and compassion for the weak

The moral judgement that Adorno makes concerning music is nowhere better stated than in the passages where he writes of suffering in relation to modern music. An acceptance of weakness, an acknowledgement of smallness, of pain and defeat is characteristic of the music of Berg and of Schoenberg. Adorno sees such music as deeply compassionate, as inscribing, even in fragmentary dissolutions, a deep compassion with all suffering victims.

> This concept of health, inherently as ineradicable a part of prevailing musical criteria as it is of Philistinism, is in league with conformism; health is allied with what in life is stronger, with the victors. Berg abstained from such assent, as had the mature Schubert before him, as had Schumann, and perhaps also Mahler, whose music came down on the side of the deserter. While it may be true that, on the surface, his patiently and lovingly polished music has fewer sharp edges for the listener than has Schoenberg's, it is radical and shocking in its partiality for the weaker, the defeated: the figure of Berg's humanity. No music of our time was as humane as his; that distances it from humankind.
>
> (T. Adorno 1994a: 5)

7

SCHOENBERG

The subject

Music may be centrally concerned with the truth of the human condition at the level of the subject and of subjectivity, but Adorno conceives of this in a very particular way. He does not identify the subjectivity in art with the empirical persona of the artist, with the psychological individual. He does not see art or music as a painting of the individual's emotions – 'I feel anger, let me paint it.' Rather, Adorno sees subjectivity as a social process, as the development of those same technical forces of production inherent in society and in the musical material. All social relations terminate in the intra-personal confluence of experiences that constitute the subject. However, as an intra-personal subjectivity, as a socially constructed capacity, a sensibility and agency – that is as a subject-apparatus – the subject is 'objectified'. In contrast, the interpersonal subject – subjectivity as feeling-towards – is subjective. It is the artist's self-forgetting in obedience to these technical forces, in following where they lead, which ensures not only that s/he produces an objective work of art but also one in which subjectivity as a social process achieves the most advanced development possible. In the previous chapter, I argued that even Berg's resort to numerical and extra-musical schemes as a compositional device was among the means for achieving just such a level of objectification.

> The subjectivity at work in art is not the adventitious empirical individual, not the composer. His technical forces of production are the immanent function of the material; only by following the latter's lead does he gain any power over it. By means of such a process of exteriorisation, however, it [subjectivity] receives back a universality which goes back beyond the individuation of the particular producer. Valid labour on the work of art is always social labour. It is this that legitimates the talk of artistic rationality . . . such reason tends rather to be obscured by the psychological subject that leaves its imprint on the music.
>
> (T. Adorno 1994a: 300–1)

The composer is heir to the accumulated means of musical construction developed in the past – its 'grammars' its 'lexicons', its tonality, tempered tuning, principles of harmonic progression and all its formal means. These inscribe the (hi)story of subjectivity. They are the congealed residues of past subjectivity. From this point of view, to compose, no less than to speak, involves keeping an appointment with history. In Viennese Classicism, for example, the material comprises not just tonality, the tempered tuning system, the possibility of modulation through the complete circle of fifths; it also comprises countless idiomatic components which add up to the musical language of the age. Even typical forms such as the sonata, the rondo, the character variation, or syntactic forms like those of the antecedent and consequent, were largely *a priori* givens rather than forms actively chosen. As the sum total of all that the composer works with, the musical material is nothing less than 'the critically reflected objective state of the technical productive forces of an age in which any given composer is inevitably confronted' (Adorno 1994d: 281).

There is thus an identity between the development of technically productive forces in the society and the musical material which, as a social praxis, reflects that level of development. Any change at the level of social production, for example as between the socio-technical development of early and late capitalist societies, is reflected in the productive possibilities available to the composer in developing the musical material. That material is of the same origin as the social process and continually registers its traces. As a previous subjectivity – now forgetful of itself – such an objectified impulse of the material has its own kinetic laws. That which seems to be the mere self-loco-motion of the material is profoundly reflective of the social process and thoroughly permeated by its historical development (T. Adorno 1980: 33).

The self-conception of artist and musicians, the way that they conceive of the creative process or their own part in it, is also a function of the development of the technical forces of production, as these manifest themselves in the material. Thus, in the late eighteenth century it made sense to think of art as synonymous with the creative expression of individual geniuses. In the twentieth century, the artist may think of his own contribution in a decidedly more humble way, even to the extent of denying any role for individual self-expression. It may matter little with respect to the nature of the artistic process, since in both cases the artist would be diligently obeying the demands of the material. It is this focused obedience to those demands which is shared by artists of different epochs and with widely different conceptions of the art process. The material thus conditions both the creative work of artists, their conceptions of the art process and their self-conceptions as artists.

Adorno's concept of the subject and of subjectivity in modern art also stands opposed to what we ordinarily understand to be positive 'communication' and to all the residues of tradition and convention which support it. It is communication which Adorno sees as central to the culture industry, to the mass-produced and popular construction of aesthetic media. No matter how subtle or sophisticated the intentions of a composer like Stravinsky, his music becomes, in Adorno's analysis, part of the culture industry or, at the very least, one of its fellow travellers.

> The structure of musical creativity through the subject and not towards the subject sets it off sharply from communication. This latter concept properly belongs to the culture industry, which calculates questions of artistic effects, as well as in applied market research, which tells us what intellectual products must be like if they are to find purchasers. To this informal music is intransigently opposed. It is concerned instead with the representation of a truth content and with a true consciousness, not with adapting to a false one. Within the all-embracing blindness and delusion the only things which inhabit their rightful place in society are those which have broken with communication, instead of seeking to discover its genuine or supposed laws.
>
> (T. Adorno 1994d: 320)

Loneliness

Adorno's exploration of the likeness of music to social life is nowhere better exemplified than in his exploration of the theme of loneliness in the new music of the Schoenberg circle. In this respect, Schoenberg's monodrama *Erwartung* is an obvious reference. It has as its heroine a woman looking for her lover at night. Subjected to all the terrors of darkness she finally comes upon his murdered corpse – a murder for which she may herself have been responsible. In the very construction of the music, in the dissonances, abrupt and discontinuous juxtapositions of musical segments, the composer presents what Adorno describes as a 'case study' in anxiety and loneliness. Adorno is actually identifying, here, certain structural imperatives which inscribe 'gestures' he believes to be general in the modern music he writes about, such as the experience of 'bodily convulsions' and of what might be described as the experience of being transfixed or 'petrified' – what Adorno refers to as 'crystalline standstill'.

> The seismographic registration of traumatic shock becomes, at the same time, the technical structural law of music. It forbids continuity and development. Musical language is polarised according to its extremes: towards gestures of shock resembling bodily convulsions on the one hand, and on the other towards the crystalline standstill of a human being whom anxiety causes to freeze in her tracks. It is this polarisation upon which the total world of form of

the mature Schoenberg – and of Webern as well – depends. . . .
There is not one of Schoenberg's technical innovations that cannot
be traced back to that polarisation of expression.

(T. Adorno 1980: 42)

Adorno saw Schoenberg as having developed this lonely discourse in his
music to its 'ultimate extreme'. The anxiety of the lonely becomes the law of
aesthetic formal language (T. Adorno 1980: 42–3) and, as such, discloses the
social character of loneliness. It is a common loneliness, that of the city
dwellers who are totally unaware of each other. The gesture of the lonely
person offers a basis for comparison with others; it is a gesture that can be
quoted and loneliness is thereby revealed as universal (Adorno 1980: 47).
Adorno's pursuit of the semblance between music and society is characteris-
tically fixed at the level of form – but form viewed as content. Adorno
insists that the 'forms of art' reflect the history of man more truthfully than
do documents.

The treatment of loneliness as a structural law, 'the law of aesthetic
formal language' (T. Adorno 1980: 43), underpins his distinction between
art which communicates or expresses emotions and art which somehow
registers, in its very constitution, what Adorno calls the 'genuine emotions
of the unconscious'. But what can be meant by such a distinction? The
atmosphere of *Erwartung* is charged with emotion. It would seem that we
have to distinguish here between emotions as the sensuous responses an
individual may have to situations, persons or events, and which, through
their connection to those objects, can be imaged and communicated, and
emotion or feeling, as actually constitutive – in *Erwartung* as the 'bodily
convulsions' and 'crystalline standstill' (T. Adorno 1980: 42) – of the
subject. To depict the individual's feelings towards an object or person is
somehow to describe that person's 'being-subjective' in relation to others; to
depict the sensuous and intra-personal constitution of the subject is to
render 'subjective-being' as an objective state.

Society is reflected in the isolation of the Expressionist
movement. . . . 'Deny that you also belong to this – you are not
alone.' Such a bond, however, reveals itself in that pure expressions
in their state of isolation liberate those elements of the intra-subjective and therewith the elements of aesthetic objectivity.

(T. Adorno 1980: 48)

Adorno saw this as fundamental in expressionism, its commitment to the
objectification of the subject and the subjective life. It is also what distinguished modern European art from the art of the previous five centuries.
Whereas Alberti could speak of painting the emotions, art, in the twentieth
century, had turned away from such an idea; it did so at precisely the

moment when movements in art came to conceive of feeling as the sensuous process through which subjectivity is constituted. In other words, the distinction drawn here is between emotion as the nexus between the subject and its objects and emotion as intra-subjective, as the constitutive sensuous relations of subjectivity itself. It is this which accounts for Adorno's insistence on the 'case-study' character of modern music.

> If the drive towards well-integrated construction is to be called objectivity, then objectivity is not simply a counter-movement to Expressionism. It is the other side of the Expressionistic coin. Expressionistic music had interpreted so literally the principle of expression contained in traditionally Romantic music that it assumed the character of a case study. In so doing, a sudden change takes place. Music, as a case study in expression, is no longer 'expressive'.
>
> (T. Adorno 1980: 49)

I would argue, too, that it is this same focus on the intra-personal constitution of the subject which accounts for the importance of interior monologue in the dramas of Ibsen and Chekhov, or in literary works such as the monologue of the idiot in the opening pages of Faulkner's *The Sound and the Fury* or Molly Bloom's soliloquy in James Joyce's *Ulysses*, which also might be said to be instances of case-study construction.

Music has the power not simply to depict the alienating conditions of modern social life but to inscribe, in its inner construction, the loneliness and anxiety, the suffering engendered in this society's subjects, and can make that suffering the inner law of its constitution – music as weeping. Utopia is to be glimpsed in the sense of what life is not. Utopia is thus inscribed negatively in suffering, in pain and loneliness – in suffering as resistance, as longing. Art does not simply describe modern society; it inscribes the technical relations of social production as the inner process constructing the sensuous life of the subject.

Twelve-tone technique – serial disaster?

The avant-garde 'free atonality' of the years around 1910, the period of *Erwartung*, remained the mode of musical construction to which Adorno himself was musically committed throughout his life. In one of his late essays, where he explores the possibilities of 'une musique informelle', he declares that it was in this period that there was truly the possibility of creating a genuinely free and spontaneous music, one unconstrained by the formulaic technicising that had, in his view, bedevilled mid-twentieth century music since Schoenberg's 'discovery' of twelve-tone technique. Alban Berg, who did develop his own distinctive use of twelve-tone technique, nevertheless shared many of Adorno's doubts about it. Schoenberg himself acknowledged the doubts of both Berg and Adorno at the time of the controversy over Thomas Mann's novel *Doctor Faustus*.

The story of twelve-tone technique that is usually told is one that attributes its development to a *rappel à l'ordre* made necessary by the development of free atonality. With the undermining of tonality and the consequent liberation of a 'chaos' of new sounds, new means of ordering were improvised to make up for the absence of constraints. Composers often bound the music to a literary text or poem which could provide a basis for ordering, and music greatly developed its reliance on dimensions other than tonality – colour, timbre, rhythm and so forth. A variety of means were available to do the ordering. Nevertheless, it was reasoned that if music was to generate large forms without the binding force of tonality, then some new principle of centricity to replace tonality had to be found. It was not a concern expressed only in music. It has its counterpart in all the arts. For Adorno, truth and not order is the primary category. The only order that is important is order necessitated by true perception, and this he sees as mobile, mediated and dialectical. The development of twelve-tone and serial music is ultimately anathema to Adorno because it subordinates all expression, all inventiveness, to the domination of a rigid prefigured ordering.

Notwithstanding his ultimate rejection of twelve-tone technique as the future of music, Adorno recognised it as grounded in the historical development of music and as a solution called forth by the problematic condition of modern music. The very achievements of atonalism in undermining the outworn hold of tonal structures resulted in the emergence of a music in which the notes were no longer hierarchically differentiated on the basis of the relationship of each to a tonal centre. Nevertheless, it was not easy to remove all vestiges of the old centricity. It was still possible to establish hierarchical distinctions. Certain notes – and certain sequences of notes – might achieve a more prominent position among other notes or sequences simply because they were repeated more frequently. Octave doubling also contributed to such prioritising. Schoenberg's development of twelve-tone technique can be seen as an attempt to realise the most thoroughgoing submission to the drive in atonal music to eliminate all such hierarchical means in ordering the new music. In the terms which I have developed here, which are not those in which Schoenberg or Adorno thought about the matter, it represented an attempt to realise an uncompromisingly intra-actional and intra-subjective level of aesthetic experience.

> That the row uses no more than twelve tones is a result of the endeavour to give none of the tones, by means of greater frequency, any emphasis which might render it a 'fundamental tone' and thereby evoke tonal relationships. . . . With every new pitch the

choice of remaining pitches diminishes, and when the last one is reached there is no longer any choice at all. The force exerted by the process is unmistakable.

(T. Adorno 1980: 72–3)

By establishing, as the basic building block of a composition, a 'row' consisting of all twelve notes of the full chromatic in a prefigured order, the composer can avoid the too early repetition of any given tone in his composition:

> The row rationalises what is instinctive in every conscientious composer; sensitivity towards the too early recurrence of the same pitch, except for cases in which it is immediately repeated. . . . Static twelve-tone technique actualises the sensitivity of musical dynamics in the face of the unconscious recurrence of the same. The technique makes such a sensitivity sacrosanct. The tone which occurs too early, as well as the tone which is 'free' or coincidental in the face of the totality, becomes taboo.
>
> (T. Adorno 1980: 64)

The simple rule is that no note may be repeated before all twelve notes of the row have been played and that note's turn has come round again in another presentation of the row. The basic postulates of the twelve-note system, as given by Rufer (J. Rufer 1961: 84) are:

1 A twelve-note series consists of all twelve notes of the chromatic scale arranged in a specific order.
2 No note is repeated within the series.
3 Each series can be used in four forms: the original form, its inversion, retrograde and retrograde inversion.
4 The series or segments of the series can be stated horizontally or vertically.
5 Each of the four forms may be transposed to begin on any note of the chromatic scale.
6 It is usual (conventional) that only one series should be used in a work.

The composition is thus made up of the same row (or lawful derivatives of that row), serially presented both horizontally in the melody line and vertically in the harmonic line. In the case of the different forms of the row used, each is derived by an operation performed on the whole row and therefore the fundamental principle concerning too early repetition is not violated, since each note retains its relative position in the row. The fact that the row is the integral building block of both the horizontal and the vertical dimensions pursues another drive in the development of modern music, the total integration – and musical 'indifference' – of the vertical and horizontal dimensions.

Of course, the hierarchical relations of pitch in tonal music were only one organising factor, albeit the most important. Other aspects of music have the capacity to organise musical relations and musical experience. Rhythm plays an important organisational role in music, as does orchestral colour and timbre. As tonality decayed these came to assume a growing importance in binding the expanding universe of sounds in music. Timbre, for example, was developed to a remarkable degree by these composers. Schoenberg coined the term *Klangfarbenmelodie* to refer to the possibilities of working with variations in timbre to replace pitch intervals in the construction of melody – a further instance of the indifference of musical dimensions. The later serialist composers took twelve-tone technique further than Schoenberg, subjecting not just tonal relations but rhythmic and other relations, too, to serial presentation.

It is easy to see why a spirit such as Adorno could not accept any such dream of total integration in music. In the first place he viewed truth in music as a matter of being true to the real condition of social relations in society. Music that sought this kind of total integration – the product of a purified musical language – in an age of antagonistic and alienating social relations dealt in dreams and illusions, not in truth. Music could not successfully reflect the social process when its elements had been prefigured as a closed system. Also, the type of reconciliation was rejected by Adorno. The only true compositional process would be one which proceeded spontaneously from the free movement of the parts or elements towards each other and towards the whole. In twelve-tone technique and serial music the elements are completely determined by the prefigured material, and all organic relations and continuities among the elements are (ideally) destroyed. The destruction of the organic possibilities of music is something that Adorno identifies with social pathology. The *rappel à l'ordre* is seen by Adorno as part of the disease, and not the cure.

The abolition of time and the submission to fate

The static prefigured material undermines development, variation and progress in the music. It condemns music to becoming a collection of isolated juxtaposed moments with no organic development or spontaneity in them. Adorno consistently resists what he sees as the undermining of temporal relationships in modern music and the reduction of music to 'coincidence'; from this standpoint, modern music is seen as in danger of spatialising time, of becoming a pseudomorphism of painting.

> The true quality of a melody is always to be measured by whether
> or not it succeeds in transforming the spatial relations of intervals

into time. Twelve-tone technique destroys this relationship at its very roots. Time and interval diverge. All intervallic relationships are absolutely determined by the basic row and its derivatives. No new material is introduced into the progression of intervals, and the omnipresence of the row makes it unfit in itself for the construction of temporal relationships, for this type of relationship is based upon differentiation and not simply upon identity.

(T. Adorno 1980: 71)

With the disappearance of all 'inessential' moments in music, the principle of variation is extended over the entire surface of the work which becomes subject to an omnipresent construction. As soon as everything in the work becomes variation we might as easily claim that there is no longer variation or development. For there to be variation or development presupposes the existence of something which undergoes change. As soon as everything is absorbed to the same degree into variation not one theme remains behind, and all musical phenomena define themselves without distinction as permutations of the row.

The tool of compositional dynamics – the procedure of variation – becomes absolute. In assuming this position, variation frees itself from any dependence upon dynamics. The musical phenomenon no longer presents itself involved in its own self-development. The working out of thematic materials is reduced to a preliminary study by the composer. Variation as such no longer appears. Everything, yet nothing, is variation; the procedure of variation is again relegated to the material, preforming it before the actual composition begins. Music becomes the result of processes to which the materials of music have been subjected and the perception of which is in themselves blocked by the music. Thus music becomes static.

(T. Adorno 1980: 61)

Adorno identifies this state of affairs with the submission of music to the domination of 'fate', which he identifies clearly with the domination of nature. He sees the concept of fate as patterned after the experience of domination, as proceeding directly from the superiority of nature over man. Mankind has therefore learned to become stronger and to master nature, and in the process fate has reproduced itself.

Fate is domination reduced to its pure abstraction, and the measure of its distraction is equal to that of its domination; fate is disaster. . . . Twelve-tone technique is truly the fate of music. It enchains music by liberating it. The subject dominates music through the rationality of the system, only in order to succumb to the rational system itself.

(T. Adorno 1980: 67–8)

What is threatened in the development of this music is nothing less than the musical extinguishing of the subject. The parallels with the modern condition inscribed in the imagery of totalitarian domination, of loneliness and isolation, of fragmentation in the labour process, are always clear, however implicit. The subject denies its own spontaneity. Having liberated music from the blind domination of tonal material, the subject immediately submits to a 'second blind nature' in the form of the regulatory system of serial technique.

While Adorno remained sympathetic to Schoenberg and his music – even to his twelve-tone music – he never changed his view of twelve-tone technique as the musical embodiment of what he claimed was, from the point of view of the life process of the subject, 'disaster'. If it seems paradoxical that Adorno was able to appreciate this music as deeply as he did and to offer the most sensitive analyses of it, the explanation is probably quite simple. Adorno understood the tradition very much from the inside. Twelve-tone technique was not something grafted onto his own musical tradition as an alien entity. He himself had composed music making use of it, albeit without compromising his commitment to free atonality; it was a natural development of the very 'kinetic laws' which drove him in his own music. If, in his sensitivity to these composers as well as to their music, he perceived the dangers sufficiently to resist adopting the musical solutions to which Schoenberg had committed himself, he nevertheless believed that Schoenberg himself had managed to survive those dangers and to side-step the consequences of those musical solutions.

Twelve-tone technique was not equivalent to composition. The prefiguring of the material in the construction of the row was merely to construct the building blocks with which the composer would work in building the composition. Schoenberg's 'elements' were 'rows', and their derivatives and his composing involved moving these rows around and juxtaposing them in various ways. Adorno claimed to detect, in Schoenberg's late music, a subversive process at work which undermined the strict consequences of twelve-tone technique, and it is to this that Adorno attributes the spark of greatness in the music of Schoenberg's later period:

The new ordering of twelve-tone technique virtually extinguishes the subject. The truly great moments in late Schoenberg have been attained despite the twelve-tone technique as well as by means of it – by means of it because music becomes capable of restraining itself coldly and inexorably, and this is the only fitting position for music following its decline; and despite twelve-tone technique because the spirit which thought it out remains sufficiently in self-control to penetrate repeatedly the structure of its technical components and to cause them to come to life, as though the spirit were ready, in the end, to destroy, catastrophically, the technical work of art.

(T. Adorno 1980: 69)

Moreover, this is not seen as merely a capricious decision on Schoenberg's part. Adorno argues that there is a certain sense in which twelve-tone technique actually incorporates tendencies which invite resemblance to traditional tonal music. Certainly, in his own music, especially in the earliest of his compositions as I hear them, Adorno himself made use of twelve-tone technique in a much freer way, suggesting more resemblance to traditional tonal music. It is possibly this that provoked Frank Zappa's comment that Adorno's music sounded like 'enjoyable Schoenberg' (F. Volpacchio 1991). Adorno argues that the contrast inherent in all twelve-tone music, according to precise row exposition, divides the music into primary and secondary events as was the case in traditional music. The formation of this division closely resembles, according to Adorno, the relationship between theme and 'working-out'. In his late music, Adorno claims that Schoenberg succeeds in 'forgetting to observe the strict constraints of the use of his technique' in what were then his recent works, and in practice, renounces his fidelity to the sole domination of the material – 'that very fidelity which he had once designed' (T. Adorno 1980: 123).

Nevertheless, in his opposition to twelve-tone technique, in his castigation of it as 'extinguishing the subject', Adorno is unrelenting in his attack upon the lack of freedom of the elements, their absolute obedience to a prefigured formula. He senses in this – and especially in the serialist compositions of the mid-century – the old dream of creating a pure music free of anything arbitrary or subjective. Notwithstanding his great admiration for Schoenberg's achievements – even, as stated above, many of his twelve-tone compositions – Adorno's analysis leads to the same conclusions that he draws in the case of other movements of modern music and modern art which he believes to have extinguished the subject and expression and to have turned their back on history; they belong in the constellation that includes political totalitarianism (of either the left or the right) and are a capitulation to the oppressive forces of a total 'rationality'.

The collaboration with Thomas Mann over *Doctor Faustus*, in which Adorno acted as musical adviser, was a union between two minds steeped in German culture and in a consciousness of the parallelism between the unfolding of modern German history and the development of modern German music. The parallelism is explored through the life and work of the central character, a composer called Leverkuhn, who (much to the fury of Schoenberg himself) is credited in the novel with the invention of the twelve-tone technique. The inexorable slide into authoritarianism and

Fascism is paralleled in the novel with the development of the totalitarian element in music that culminates in the invention of the twelve-tone technique, in the composer's pact with the Devil, and in his deliberate contracting of a fatal and sexually transmitted disease.

Of course, Schoenberg was well aware of the reasoning that equated twelve-tone method with political structures. In a piece written in 1947 entitled *Is It Fair?* (L. Stein 1975) Schoenberg considers such efforts. After noting that some people had described his method as 'bolshevik' because every tone in the series was considered by them as independent and exerting equal functions since there was no tonic or dominant, he dismisses such arguments as wrong in all respects; for example, the structural independence of each 'individual' tone is somewhat limited since each tone is bound unchangeably to a definite place in the series. Schoenberg also notes that the German composer, Paul von Klenau, had composed, during Hitler's time, a whole opera in twelve-tone style, and had published an essay in which he argued that the method was a true embodiment of National Socialist principles. In a tone that appears almost to mock Adorno's own position, Schoenberg concedes that the Fascist analogy is probably the more likely of the two:

> In a 'fascist' interpretation, the basic set accordingly would represent the leader, the Duce, the Fuehrer, on whom all depends, who distributes power and function to every tone, who is also the originator of all the three mirror forms, and who is responsible for the subsequent transpositions of the basic set and its derivatives – to function as sub-Fuehrer in minor affairs. Whether this concept is an advantage or a handicap to the composer or to the listener, certainly it has nothing in common with 'Liberty, Equality and Fraternity', neither with the bolshevik, the fascist or any other totalitarian brand. Most important: is it an evaluation?
>
> (L. Stein 1975: 249–50)

Adorno's belief that the serialism, so popular during the mid-century, was sterile, might or might not prove to be a prophetic insight. Certainly, many composers in the last twenty years have returned to the inspiration of the early atonal revolution around 1910, to precisely the music that Adorno valued so highly. Moreover, there is one modern composer, Nicholas Maw, whose own rejection of post-Webernian serialism in modern music is a testimony, on the part of a professional composer, to the power of Adorno's insight. Maw objected to serialist music because it had a completely different relationship with time. It had forsaken all sense of narrative and had become 'more like scintillating pieces of sculpture that you walk around rather than travel through'. Because the new music obliterated the past, it extinguished both the individual and history.

That seemed to me to be the road to catastrophe. A lot of what has gone wrong with this century socially and politically has been the attempts by monsters like Hitler and Stalin to destroy whole peoples. Without being too apocalyptic, this music seemed to me to be a metaphor for the destruction of the memory of the individual and for the destruction of the imagination, for the only way the imagination can work is through memory.

(M. Hall 1997: 236)

I would argue, however, that we need to keep distinct the necessary technical realisation of a new basis of ordering, a new and substantial unity at the level of an aesthetic presentational code, and the type of explorations and discoveries that such a realisation makes possible. The hostility to extinguishing the historical, subjective and expressive element is not inconsistent with recognising a basis of ordering – of intra-subjective 'substance' which, in itself, is non-historical and yet which may underpin the very construction of all historical projects, even to provide an atemporal binding for multiple temporalities. The profound insight into visual order provided by Cubism has been a necessary basis for most twentieth-century visual art, hardly any of which is Cubist. Not even Picasso painted in a Cubist manner for most of his life. Perhaps twelve-tone and serialist experimentation has to be seen in a similar way as realising a new insight into the possibilities for ordering in musical experience. Perhaps even music which appears to have turned away from this direction has merely absorbed its insights into the compositional process and made them a constitutive part of its understanding. The issue is one to which I return (Chapter 10).

Schoenberg and Stravinsky

In contrasting the music of Stravinsky with that of Schoenberg, Adorno identified two different poles of modernist music. He was always concerned to emphasise the historical character of musical material and to see the historical in a dynamic sense as a process with its own 'kinetic laws'. In this view, the material, as the sedimentation of past subjectivity, has a latent project and development within it. To seek to bring forth this project, to engage authentically with the material and to develop its latent project, is to keep faith with history. As a member of the same society from which this material has been inherited, the composer is heir, too, to the condition of the subject and of subjectivity generated by the same historical process that has produced the musical material with which s/he works. In seeking objectively to develop the possibilities inherent in the musical material – to fulfil music from out of itself – the composer can *express* or realise his own life process as a subject, not through conveying his personal feelings-towards but in the most objective service to the motive force of the material. Adorno saw the music of Schoenberg and the Viennese composers as progressive in precisely this sense; it was music that attempted to express the subject through fulfilling the latent project – the kinetic laws – of the musical material inherited by these composers. Their music was progressive in Adorno's philosophy because its thoroughgoing objectivity was pressed into the aim of realising the subject.

At the other pole of modernist music, he identified a quite different approach to music and to musical material. The individual may be affected by music, made to feel in response to it, to register its effects without engaging in any expression of his or her life process. Insofar as being a subject and expressing one's life process are integral, an individual void of the power of expression is not truly a subject, in Adorno's philosophy. Musical material may be constructed as a pure medium of effects. The musical ideal of Stravinsky or of Hindemith – to develop a pure music as an objective language through which calculated effects can be generated – does away with the notion of music as the expression of the subject or the development of the musical material. In Adorno's view, it transforms the relationship of the individual to music. It does not fulfil or express the individual; rather it (manipulatively) constructs emotion and excitement for the individual, offering not serious music, which demands concentration and responsibility, but entertainment and distraction and the abdication of responsibility. Such music is a flight from entanglement with history. It is a version of the same dream of purity which Adorno ceaselessly attacked. At the heart of such a music was the ideal of a pure objectivity and an equally pure subjectivity. The attempt to break the indissoluble ties that bind subject to object was a response to the unhappy state of that union. In Adorno's view, any such attempt contributed to a fatal weakening of the subject. He saw it not only as characteristic of so-called art music, such as that of Stravinsky, but also as characteristic of jazz and of all entertainment music, and even of many modern performances of classical music. In each case a similar relationship between the music and the individual is realised: a relationship in which music comes to represent external and manipulative force and to stand in for the manipulative force of the collectivity. This identity between music as manipulation and the power and domination of the collectivity is key to Adorno's critiques of all modern culture, as well as modern music. Late capitalist society and commodification, together with its totalitarian political tendencies, appeared in modern music both in the forms of a capitulation to it and in the forms of resistance to it. Stravinsky represented the former in Adorno's philosophy, and Schoenberg the latter. However, as argued above, even Schoenberg's music (the twelve-tone technique and serialist experimentation) is not free of the charge of having betrayed both expression and the subject and of having capitulated to totalitarian tendencies.

In this second approach to modernist music, the composer eschews any struggle with historical development and appropriates the music of the past (in Adorno's formulation, the music of a pre-dialectical – classical – past), constructing out of it a second-order music, a music of quotation, a 'music about music'. The technique of the composer, in constructing this second-order music, is to adapt the raw material of his borrowings to the point where they meet the demands of effective communication under modern conditions. Modernity appears here, not as the self-development of subjectivity or as the historical development of the productive forces of music but as the crafting of communicative acts. Such an appropriation abstracts musical utterance from its generative (historical) context and constructs a pure medium of (objective) 'effects'. Music of this type is seen by Adorno as fatally impoverished no matter how well crafted, as being as sterile as the outworn material and cliché forms from which it has been derived. Adorno sees Schoenberg and his circle as exemplifying the first approach to musical material, and the inheritance from the past and Stravinsky and the neo-classical composers as exemplifying the second. It is in this sense that Adorno attaches the term 'progress' to the former music and 'restoration' to the latter (T. Adorno 1980).

The opposition which Adorno sets up between these two musics is fundamental in his thinking about modernity and modernism. They do not simply represent contrasting types of early modern music: they define the poles of modernism itself. Both the approaches that Adorno describes in respect of the musics of Schoenberg and Stravinsky can be seen in modernist painting, literature, dance and theatre. This is clearly recognised in the many references in Adorno's writings to the other arts and to artists and writers, and it gives rise to the judgements he makes there, for example, in associating Stravinsky's neo-classicism with Picasso's neo-classicism; in upholding as progressive the plays of Beckett, while seeing the plays of Brecht as (artistically) reactionary.

The relative popularity of Stravinsky's music and the lack of popular appreciation of Schoenberg was, for Adorno, a further sign, if one was needed, of the workings of the culture industry in the music of the former and its absence from the music of the latter. The two modes of engaging with musical material are (in Adorno's way of thinking) reflections of the wider opposition between a culturally and historically grounded revolutionary praxis – bringing the new music out of a struggle with the material bequeathed by the old – and a culturally reactionary praxis founded upon commodification and upon a fetishising of commodities.

8

STRAVINSKY

There were two sides to the classical normative model of an individuated society. If its functional integration was based, as Durkheim argued, upon individuation in the division of labour, its 'substantial unity' was provided by its 'mass' character, by its homogeneity. Individuation is reversed in mass society. The amorphous mass or crowd is de-individuated. These two aspects of modern society, individuation in the division of labour and de-individuation in mass society, are integral, two sides of the same coin. The mass character of modern society could be seen everywhere, in the mass-produced commodity, the mass-assembly factory, the mass consumer, the mobilisation of political masses and so forth. The term 'mass' suggests an asocial collectivity. It suggests force, too, and an overwhelming disparity in power between the individual subject and the totality, mass or collectivity. In the crowd, en masse as it were, the individual is thoroughly de-sociated and at his or her weakest, with no independent source of identity and swept along by the force of the collectivity.

De-sociation, in Adorno's sociology, was at the heart of the economic construction of modern society, manifesting itself in the advancing commodification which reached into every aspect of modern life. Commodities, reified and abstracted from the sinewy social relations through which they were produced and turned towards the isolated ego, continued the work of de-individuation and massification. This weakened de-individuated individual could fancy s/he amounted to something, that s/he counted, if s/he could at least share vicariously in the mass-ive power of the collectivity, the alienated power of each individual. The political life of the twentieth century has seen the repeated mobilisation of the masses, of crowd phenomena, of mass assemblies. In all of this there was the identification with the aggressor, the capitulation of the individual before the might of an alienated and reified collectivity, a condition that reached its terminal development in the construction of Auschwitz.

Commodification as human agency alienated from itself appears, too, in the inner cells of the modern art work. The subject endures intact only in the composer who expresses suffering and weakness in the face of the overwhelming forces of an asocial collectivity. Adorno saw Stravinsky and the neo-classical composers as capitulating to the power of the collective. Such composers, he claimed, identified in their music with the (collective) aggressor, imagining that somehow they preserved the subject by this act of capitulation, that through their identification with the collective they gained an objective means of control over the outer reality, together with the power to construct the subject from the outside, as it were. The sensuous loss suffered by a weakened subjectivity is then 'compensated' for by the substitution of 'style' for substance and sensation for feeling.

An art or music which colludes in this process, which reinforces the disempowering of the subject and surrenders to the collective and externalised force of realised forms, was judged by Adorno to be morally culpable. If Schoenberg's music is good, it is because Schoenberg makes, at a musical level, what Adorno sees as the 'proper' response to the powerful 'collective' forces that threaten to overwhelm the individual in modern society. Similarly, if Stravinsky's music is bad, it is because, in Adorno's view, it regresses into infantilism, primitivism and traditionalism; growing ever more complicit in the death of the subject and of expression, it is music which he sees as celebrating the triumph of oppressive collective forces.

Modern societies are those in which it is possible to imagine that the members 'write' culture, societies in which a culture can be conceived of as an artefact, even as a commodity, as something made to produce specific effects or 'benefits'. The relationship of culture to individuals and to bodies becomes instrumental. The products of culture are decontextualised and appropriated for their effects. Cultural forms thus expropriated can be used to work their effects upon the body of subjectivity from the outside. So far is the instrumentalisation of culture advanced that the leaders of corporate business can now talk of designing cultures for their organisations and of engineering them, in a way that recalls B.F. Skinner's dream of 'designing a culture' (B.F. Skinner 1953). Experts in corporate culture can now refer to culture as the 'software of the mind' (G. Hofstede 1994), with the obvious implication that new software packages can be designed, slotted in and slotted out.

Two modes of reflexivity

Reflexivity is probably characteristic of all human societies, including so-called 'simple' or 'primitive' societies. In the latter, however, the alienation of culture would not have proceeded to the point where it would be possible for a member to conceive of the society's culture as an exchangeable software. There is little reason to suppose, on the basis of anthropological accounts, that the members of a 'primitive' tribal society think of their culture in this way. They might well inform an anthropologist about their own culture and even about its differences from the cultures of neighbouring societies; it is unlikely, however, that they would conceive of themselves as constructing their cultures or as choosing among available alternative cultures.

In a modern society, everything is viewed as the outcome of a process of construction, including the subject, which becomes an object of construction to itself. 'Enchantment' evaporates, to the extent that we see the world and the subject in terms of the 'machineries of their making'. The instrumentalisation of culture has proceeded to the point where the subject can conceive of self-mastery as developing objective means for transforming itself; it can conceive of itself as material to be formed from the outside, as it were, to be acted upon, affected and shaped. What is outside is collective force and agency, capital. Adorno denied that, by surrendering the power of expressivity, the subject could thereby gain access to a superior power of self-mastery; in that way lay only self-annihilation. Living, breathing subjects develop through self-expression, through 'a going out from the self to the other'.

Cultural forms thus have a dual relationship to the subject. They are either dynamically configured through the expressivity of the subject or they are alienated from the expressive life of the subject and used to manipulate subjectivity from without. It is not the capacity of such forms to shape subjectivity from the outside that constitutes them as alienating; it is, rather, the disjunction – the alienation – of this shaping process from any grounding in the dynamic expression of the subject. I read the notion of cultural pathology in Adorno's works as referring to this fundamental disjunction. I have some doubts about this formulation of cultural pathology, which will be discussed in Chapter 10. In this chapter, my principal concern is with exposition.

Adorno *contra* Stravinsky

Adorno's opposition to Stravinsky might at first sight appear to centre around the identification of atonalism in modern music with progress, and tonalism with reaction. However, such an appearance is misleading. If this was all there was to the matter, Adorno's critique would lack the significance and serious purpose that it undoubtedly has. It would mean, for example, that he could have selected any twentieth-century composer who composes tonal music and substituted him for Stravinsky. This is clearly not the case. Adorno did not confound Stravinsky's music with the attempt, on the part of a number of composers, to 'revive' the past or to go on composing as if the world had not changed. Adorno was critical of all such composers but not in the same way that he was critical of Stravinsky. A composer who, like Sibelius, composed music that might truly have belonged to an earlier time was dismissed by Adorno as anachronistic. Such music must be false because truth was to be found only in sounds that answered to the demands of life in a modern society. Traditional tonality offered only empty clichés and could not suffice to comprehend modernity:

> It is not simply that these sounds are antiquated and untimely but that they are false. They no longer fulfil their function. The most progressive level of technical procedures designs tasks before which traditional sounds reveal themselves as impotent clichés. . . . If a contemporary composer restricts himself exclusively to tonal sounds – in the manner of Sibelius – these sounds are just as false as if they were enclaves within the tonal field.
>
> (T. Adorno 1980: 34)

But in his attack on Stravinsky he does not accuse the latter of anachronism; on the contrary, he opposes Stravinsky precisely because he recognises the latter's claim to be a modern composer and his music to be a response to the crisis of modernity. As Eric Salzman observed, the essence of Stravinsky's neo-classical style lies not in a revival of classical forms but in a thorough-going modernist renovation of classical forms, achieved through a rebuilding of tonal practice independent of the traditional functions which had first established those forms (E. Salzman 1974).

Adorno's critique of Stravinsky is articulated as an exposition of what he claims to be the pathology of modern society, a pathology carried in the very inner structure of its music. Stravinsky's music is accused of being anti-individual (which in Adorno is identified with being anti-subject). The liberation sought by Stravinsky is from the intentionality of the subject.

> The engraved precision of musical language – the permeation of each of its formulae by intentions – struck him not as a guarantee of authenticity, but as the erosion thereof. If its principle is to be effective, slackened authenticity should be eradicated. This is brought about by the demolition of intentions. From this – and from the direct contemplation of primeval musical matter as well – he expects to find the binding responsibility.
>
> (T. Adorno 1980: 138)

Adorno went further. He saw Stravinsky's neo-classicism as a response to modernity that had close kinship with modern philosophical movements such as phenomenology and existentialism, thus extending his critique of modern philosophy into modern music. Stravinsky's attempt to construct music as a pure objectivity (that is, object-reflexive music), impinging upon the body of the subject and unmediated by the subject and expression, had its parallel in the attempts of phenomenologists to realise an absolute contrast between subject and object, a contrast in which there was no trace of their mutual mediation:

The relationship [of Stravinsky's music] to concurrent philosophical phenomenology is unmistakable. The renunciation of all psychologism – the reduction to the pure phenomenon, as the process reveals itself – opens up a region of 'authentic' being which is beyond all doubt. In both cases mistrust of the unoriginal (at its utmost the depth of the suspicion of the contradiction between actual society and its ideology) results in the misleading hypostatisation of the 'remains', or what is left over after the removal of that which has allegedly been superimposed as truth. In both cases the mind is caught up in the deception that within its own circle – the realm of thought and art – it might be able to escape the curse of being only mind and reflection, but by no means essence itself. In both cases the unmediated contrast between the 'thing' and mental reflection is absolutized, and for this reason the product arising from the subject is invested with the dignity of the natural.

(T. Adorno 1980: 138)

Rhythmic-spatial versus expressive-dynamic forms

Many of Stravinsky's most striking scores were written for ballet. The alliance of music with dance drama is itself significant. Adorno believes that the possibilities of music as a vehicle for expression and for progress are linked to the fundamental choice of form. He sees dance-form as essentially static, 'rhythmic-spatial', as movement without progress. In contrast he sees the song-form and the sonata-form – the chosen forms of the Viennese composers – as 'expressive-dynamic' music and the natural vehicle for the development of the subject. 'True dance – in contrast to mature music – is an art of static time, a turning in a circle, movement without progress. It was in this consciousness that sonata form came to replace dance form' (T. Adorno 1980: 196).

Nineteenth-century tonal music was of the expressive-dynamic type, Beethoven being its quintessential exponent. Adorno, like Schoenberg, applies to it a traditional analytic technique, seeing such music in terms of its elementary 'particles' – its motives – and its thematic development through manipulations of these motives through repetition, variation, extension, fragmentation or dissolution. Adorno labelled music which lent itself easily to such an analysis 'expressive-dynamic'. The individual, complete with a biographical development, is identified, in Adorno's philosophy of music, with the germ of the musical idea, with its motive and with the course of the motive's development – its thematic evolution in the context of the composition as a whole. Classical tonality exemplified such a structure, as was argued above (Chapter 2). With the decline and exhaustion of classical tonality – its insufficiency and depletion before the tasks of modernity – music faced a crisis.

Stravinsky's natural affinity was with the expressive-dynamic type, according to Adorno, but he now abandoned it in favour of what Adorno holds to be the other principal type in Western music, the rhythmic-spatial. In this type of music, for which Debussy was an acknowledged source, thematic process largely avoids substantial motivic development or any such evolutionary principle as the binding force of the composition. The music relies more for its variation upon changing harmonic and orchestral backgrounds and through a tendency to savour the individual sound moment and the colouristic qualities of the individual harmony (J. Samson 1993). Samson points to this more spatial aspect of Debussy's technique:

> Debussy did suggest in some works a fundamentally different and prophetic approach to musical form *in which the ongoing movement of the music is generated by the gentle collision of differentiated materials* [emphasis mine]. Contrasting harmonic types are an important element in the constitution of these materials, but often their characterisation depends as much on non-pitched aspects of sound. The rejection of classical tonality made possible, indeed required, a rethinking of other parameters of music, rhythmic stress and articulation, texture and timbre – and these assumed in Debussy's music an unprecedented responsibility for the shaping and characterisation of the musical idea.
>
> (J. Samson 1993: 40)

The achievement of movement in the music, through the 'collision of differentiated materials' rather than through any intensive motivic development, is recognised by Samson to be close to procedures in Stravinsky's music as well as that of Bartók, and both composers acknowledged Debussy as a major source and influence.

> Multi-layered textures . . . are associated in Stravinsky's music with an attitude to form and progression which rejects evolutionary procedures in favour of a juxtaposition and superimposition of sharply differentiated and strongly characterised materials in a manner which is often analogous to cinematic intercutting techniques.
>
> (J. Samson 1993: 46)

It is this aspect of Stravinsky's music which defines its spatial and non-progressive character for Adorno. It is music in which succession merely unpacks and strings together (in sequence) those elements of subjective perception and experience which are simultaneous, as is the case in much modern painting, such as Picasso's Cubism, or in 'stream of consciousness' writing, such as the novels of James Joyce or Virginia Woolf. The spatialisation of time – which corresponds to the simultaneity of experience – is actually achieved through a suspension of an expressive subjectivity. It is the product of the kind of 'bracketing' that is associated with the phenomenological epoch and which assigns to consciousness the task of attaining to a pure unmediated knowledge of things. A consciousness that does not differentiate among its impressions does not select or abstract, but is completely open, non-intentional, is in the receptive state that Hegel described as 'sensuous certainty' in the opening pages of *The Phenomenology of Mind* (G. Hegel 1931). Such a consciousness – if it were possible – would be one of pure simultaneity. There could be no here or now, there or then, this or that. There could be no continuity or thread linking the contents, because the contents would not be subject to a differentiating awareness. To present such primary 'de-differentiated' contents as a picture would be to juxtapose them as in a montage of 'primary process' dream imagery. These images would be the antithesis of subjective expression – a rigid, narcissistic exter-nalisation of psychic contents. They would be lifeless, alienated, the elements of a second-order mechanical construction. The style appropriate to such a presentation would be what Adorno calls 'infantilism'.

> Infantilism is the style of the worn-out and ruined. Its sound resem-bles the appearance of pictures pasted together out of postage stamps – disjunct – but on the other hand a montage which has been constructed with labyrinthine density. It is as threatening as the worst nightmares. Its pathogenic arrangement, which is at the same time hoveringly hermetic and disintegrated, leaves the listener breathless. . . . Music must give up the attempt to design itself as the picture of the good and virtuous, even if the picture is tragic. Instead it is to embody the idea that there is no longer any life.
>
> (T. Adorno 1980: 180–1)

He would no doubt agree with Samson's reference to cinematic intercut-ting techniques. He frequently emphasised this aspect himself in drawing attention to modernistic and surrealist techniques of juxtaposition in montage, techniques which he opposed on similar grounds that they opposed development and progress and replaced them with a spatialisation of time. In discussing the technical aspects of *Le Sacre du Printemps*, he comments on the resemblance of the Impressionistic model of polytonality to the interlaced sounds of varying and spatially separated musics, as at a fair. This concept is common to Stravinsky and Debussy; in his discussion of *Petrouchka*, Adorno points to the juxtaposition (montage) of artistic frag-ments:

> *Petrouchka* – neo-Impressionistic in style – is pieced together from innumerable artistic fragments, from the minutely detailed

whirring of the fairground down to the mocking imitation of all music rejected by official culture. *Petrouchka* has its origins in the atmosphere of the cabaret, embodying a mixture of literature and commercial art.

(T. Adorno 1980: 141)

It is the rhythmic-spatial type of music which Adorno sees as 'sprouting forth everywhere in modern society as if it was rooted in nature'. There is clearly a link, here, to Adorno's preoccupation with modern popular music and those forms of jazz with which he was familiar. His analysis of the reactionary character of all forms of music emanating from what he calls the culture industry involves claims that are essentially similar to those he makes in the case of Stravinsky's music. He did, of course, recognise the difference between jazz and Stravinsky; he even acknowledged the differences between Stravinsky and his followers. But in what he saw as their anti-individualistic celebration of the domination of the collective, in their static and rhythmic-spatial emphases, their projects appeared to him to converge.

Stravinsky is distinguished from the subjectively dynamic principle of the variation of an element unequivocally determined, by a technique of permanent beginnings which reach out in vain, as it were, for what in truth they can neither reach nor retain. His music is devoid of recollection and consequently lacking in any time continuum of permanence. Its course lies in reflexes. The fateful error of his apologists is their interpretation of the absence of anything firmly defined in his music as the guarantee of life. This lack in Stravinsky's music is, in the narrower sense, a lack of thematic material, a lack which actually excludes the breath of form, the continuity of the process – indeed it excludes life itself from his music.

(T. Adorno 1980: 164)

Adorno attaches imagery of ruins and death to such objects and to the music which juxtaposes them spatially and accents them rhythmically. His language here recalls Benjamin's analysis of baroque allegory. Torn from any organic germinal process, the elements of such forms are merely 'sensational'. They have a capacity to 'impress' upon the subject from the outside, but they are already dead as expressive subjects and the mechanical and violent juxtaposition of these forms squeezes from them only their potential to arouse sensation, to move bodies. Images of puppets or of primitive and mechanised movement, the motions of fairgrounds and of circuses, are appropriate because such movement appears to be movement imposed upon bodies from the outside, to be the dance of the already lifeless.

His [Stravinsky's] music continually directs its gaze towards other materials which it then 'consumes' through the over-exposure of its rigid and mechanical characteristics. Out of the externalized language of music which has been reduced to rubble, *L'Histoire* constructs a second language of dream-like regression; this it does by means of consequent manipulation. This new language would be comparable to the dream montages which the surrealists constructed out of the residue of the wakeful day. . . . Stravinsky's attempt to achieve such a language recalls that of Joyce: nowhere does he come closer to the basic drive to construct what Benjamin called the primitive history of the modern.

(T. Adorno 1980: 183)

In his critical opposition to Stravinsky's 'music about music', with its spatialising of time and anti-progressive tendencies, Adorno argues that it is but the expression of the fundamental bankruptcy of bourgeois culture which, seeing nothing before it, takes refuge in the variegated synchronicity of the spatial. Parody and quotation are the natural means of such music, and Adorno sees such parodic techniques as degrading their objects.

Music about music insists that it is not a microcosm fulfilled within itself, but rather the reflection of shattered depletion. Its calculated errors are related to the open contours of legitimate contemporary painting – such as that of Picasso; such painting dismantles every hermetic aspect of the depicted figure. Parody, the basic form of music about music, implies the imitation of something and its resulting degradation through this imitation. . . . Infantile music treats its model in a manner much like that of the child who takes apart his toys and puts them together again incorrectly.

(T. Adorno 1980: 186)

Music against the subject

Music, in Stravinsky's project, is endowed with an objectivity which alienates it from the subject. In social terms Adorno interprets that anti-subject objectivity with the embrace of and identification with the 'collective'. This is the dark pessimism of Adorno, his conception of a totalitarian world in which the individual is enfeebled, 'sick unto death', incapable of expression and of self-development and subject to the oppressive impress of collective forces.

The decay of the subject – which the Schoenberg school bitterly defends itself against – is directly interpreted by Stravinsky's music as the higher form in which the subject is to be preserved. Thus he arrives at the aesthetic transfiguration of the reflective character of present-day man.

(T. Adorno 1980: 215)

It is not only the form itself – that of the dance – which lends itself to the project of eliminating temporal and progressive development and annihilating the expressive subject; it is also the dance drama itself. Stravinsky's ballets, according to Adorno, enact the barbarism of collective oppression and the destruction of the subject. He see this in *Le Sacre du Printemps*, for example, in the centrality of the sacrifice of a young girl. Music, dance and drama conspire together in a celebration of collective power which sides not with the victim but with the collectivity, and with the destruction of the victim. The subject in *Le Sacre* vanishes. Its destruction is symbolised in the business of sacrifice. What is key for Adorno here is that the music develops no aesthetic antithesis between the sacrificial victims and the tribe. Their dance completes the identification of the sacrificial victims with the tribe which is to destroy them.

> The chosen girl dances herself to death . . . her solo dance – like all the others, in its inner organization, a collective dance, a round dance – is void of any dialectics of the general and the specific. Authenticity is gained surreptitiously through the denial of the subjective pole. The collective standpoint is suddenly seized as though by attack; this results in a renunciation of a comfortable conformity with individualistic society. But at the very point where this is achieved, a secondary and, to be sure, highly uncomfortable conformity results: the conformity of a blind and integral society – a society, as it were, of eunuchs and headless men.
>
> (T. Adorno 1980: 158)

One of the important devices for bringing off this annihilation of the subject and of the expressive-dynamic aspect of music concerns the resort to 'primitivism'. This is something which has had deep roots in modernist art and literature. The visual artists at the turn of the century were fascinated by examples of primitive art, and they appropriated both primitive and archaic models in order to bring about a modernist revolution. In music, the resort to primitivism was just as marked. Adorno associates this resort to primitivism in Stravinsky with a deliberate attempt to invoke the pre-individual, pre-dialectical condition through constructing an ethnological model of the totem clan. Adorno observes that as the resort to the mythological representation of the pre-individual developed from the early nineteenth century to the twentieth, there was a regression to earlier and earlier ages. The early Romantics looked to the Middle Ages, Wagner to German polytheism and Stravinsky to the totemic clan (T. Adorno 1980: 167).

Primitivism was associated with a number of related but distinct impulses. It served the romantic urge to return to 'nature' and the 'natural', to assert the claims of the sensuous in a world increasingly dominated by reason; it served, too, the negative urge of bourgeois society to disclose the true nature of its system of domination as barbarism – Adorno claims that Fascism under Hitler could never have allowed the aesthetic acknowledgement of its true nature – an acknowledgement which Adorno saw as manifest in works such as *Le Sacre du Printemps*; finally, the embrace of primitivism in art was associated with the attempt to strike down what history and biography have put together as the 'ego': that is, primitivism is associated with anti-individualism. It is the breaking through into consciousness of archaic impulses which cannot be reconciled with civilisation and which, when admitted, annihilate the integral individual being. Of this last aspect, Adorno comments:

> The belief that the archaic simply lies at the aesthetic disposal of the ego – in order that the ego might regenerate itself through it – is superficial; it is nothing more than a wish fantasy. The force of the historical process, which has crystallized the firm contours of the ego, has objectified itself in the individual, holding him together and separating him from the primeval world contained within him. Obvious archaic impulses cannot be reconciled with civilization. The painful operation of psychoanalysis – as it was originally conceived – had, among its primary tasks and difficulties, the break-through of this wall. The archaic can be revealed without censorship only through the explosion to which the ego has succumbed: this takes place in the disintegration of the integral individual being.
>
> (T. Adorno 1980: 168)

Music and schizophrenia

Writing of *L'Histoire du Soldat*, Adorno argues that there is hardly a schizophrenic mechanism which does not find an equivalent in that work (T. Adorno 1980: 175). The alienation of the music from the subject, its negative objectivity, recalls the phenomenon of depersonalisation as observed by psychoanalysts. This alienated music has an analogue in the illusory physical sensations of those who experience their bodies as an alien object. The disjunction between the dance dramas enacted on stage and the music accompanying them is extreme. Adorno argues that the dancers inhabit a sphere 'unique to the ego' and totally dominated by it, but the music remains alienated, standing apart from the subject as an 'in-itself'. While Adorno denies that the music can simply be dismissed as what a German Fascist once called 'the sculpting of the mentally ill', he argues that

Stravinsky's music aims to dominate schizophrenic traits through the aesthetic consciousness. By aestheticising it in this way, he turns the tables and vindicates insanity as true health. Attempts to represent the schizophrenic as hero or to valorise schizophrenic traits are not uncommon in modernist art and literature. Indeed, they even achieve a kind of official formulation in the anti-psychiatry of the 1960s, most notably in the writings of R.D. Laing. Laing's terminology is closely tied to the phenomenal experience of the subject, the experience of ontological insecurity, the dread of the world imploding, the 'petrifaction' of the subject and so forth. Adorno's discussion of schizophrenia is influenced by the work of a contemporary writer, namely Otto Fenichel (O. Fenichel 1946).

For Adorno, the rejection of expression is a key feature of Stravinsky's music. He finds its clinical counterpart in hebephrenia, in the indifference of the sick individual towards the external – frigidity of feeling, emotional shallowness, but above all, a lack of libidinal possession of the objective world. It is a state of alienation in which the subject cannot develop inner resources through a healthy interaction with its objects, but simply externalises its psyche in a rigid immobility.

> Hebephrenia is finally revealed from a musical perspective to be what the psychiatrists claim it to be. The 'indifference towards the world' results in the removal of all emotional affect from the non-ego and, further, in narcissistic indifference towards the lot of man. This indifference is celebrated aesthetically as the meaning of this lot.
>
> (T. Adorno 1980: 177)

Adorno focuses here upon the tendency in some forms of schizophrenia for the motor apparatus to become independent and for the ill person to repeat words and phrases endlessly, or to perform certain stereotypical movements without expression or choice or subjective involvement. This is the condition that psychiatrists have labelled catatonia, a trance-like state in which the motor system seems to be running on independently of any kind of directive ego, the latter having been burned out (T. Adorno 1980: 178).

Adorno likens Stravinsky's rhythmic procedures to the schema of catatonia. He sees this music as recalling the condition of patients who have been overwhelmed by shock. The concentration of the music upon accents and time relationships produces an illusion of bodily movement which consists in nothing more than a varied recurrence of the same melodic, harmonic and rhythmic forms. Adorno denies that the motility suggested by Stravinsky's music is actually capable of any kind of forward movement. He insists that, as movement, it resembles the empty, repetitive, gesticulatory schemata associated with schizophrenia (T. Adorno 1980: 180).

Adorno sees the concept of shock as a unifying principle of the epoch, as belonging to the fundamental level of all modern music. He finds the social origins of this shock in the disproportionate and overpowering disparity in modern industrialism between the body of the individual and the things and forces in technical civilisation. Through such shocks the individual becomes conscious of his nothingness in the face of the gigantic 'machinery' of modern society. In Stravinsky, however, the music does not manifest as resistance in the face of shock, but as non-resistance. There is no sense of anticipation, anxiety and dread of the resisting ego. There are blows that the yielding musical subject receives but never appropriates for himself as an expression of his own feelings. Adorno likens Stravinsky's musical subject to the critically injured victim of an accident so terrible that he cannot absorb it and must continuously relive the shock in dreams (T. Adorno 1980: 156–7).

Stravinsky's compositions construct a second-order structure out of quotations – they are music about music. Adorno sees such a process in terms of pathology, because he views the project as the doomed attempt of the artist whose material has become exhausted, in respect of its possibilities for expression, to take hold of this 'shattered depletion' – the inherited forms – and through constructing a second-order structure out of them, to alienate them completely from the subject. Adorno's rejection of this use of the depleted language of classical tonality has to be contrasted with his unstinting praise for Mahler's use of the exhausted forms of tonal music. In Mahler's case, Adorno reasons, the means are deployed in actually realising the expressive powers of the subject, whereas in Stravinsky such means are employed in quite a different way and are designed to extinguish both the subject and expression. Thus, in Adorno's critique, the tonal materials of classicism are the 'shattered depletion' with which Stravinsky works, in his neo-classical compositions, to produce music about music. The composer deliberately works with ego-alien materials, with what has already been isolated or separated from the expressive life process of the subject; he works with the precipitates of past expression and, in so doing, raises alienation to a higher power. It is in this sense that Adorno tends to treat this whole current in modernist art, music and literature as exemplifying the pathological at the level of social praxis.

By linking Adorno's musical polarisation to a theory of abstraction and agency, it is possible to see the necessity for both poles of modernist music. The objects we make may express us as subjects. However, as made objects they also affect us; they constitute what Armstrong termed 'an affecting presence' (R. Armstrong 1971) which works upon us rather than proceeding from us. When confronted with African masks or sculptures, many modern artists were excited by the aesthetic impression made upon them by these objects. It is difficult to imagine that this can have had much to do with empathically identifying with the constitutive process through which African subjectivity achieved expression, with feeling that one was participating in a subjectivity to which the object in question answered. It is more likely that the affecting presence of such objects lies in their 'objective' stimulus properties, in their capacity to impinge upon and organise the body of the observer from the outside, as it were. Moreover, these objects were probably constructed to have such an external affecting presence even within their originating culture. Indeed, Picasso and Matisse clearly did respond to the expressive possibilities of such objects, but they did so within the context of what these primitive artefacts afforded in the way of *expressive* possibilities in a modern European context.

Adorno's aesthetic sociology has a relatively short time horizon – he makes very little reference to anything earlier than the seventeenth century – and his perspective is entirely Eurocentric. He does, of course, refer to archaic art as pre-individualistic, which it undoubtedly was, but there is, in Adorno's sociology, neither a theory of reception nor a theory of aesthetic agency that would enable him to assimilate such art to his sociology. For this reason, his entire sociology of music, as well as his aesthetic theory, remains bound to the crisis of individuation that develops over a period of little more than a century of European history.

As Hauser and others have argued, the expressive and the individualistic tradition in art is associated with the growth of urban cultures with developed middle classes. The post-Renaissance societies of Europe are perhaps the most developed examples of this tradition. However, in most of the world's aesthetic production, and particularly that of archaic civilisations, art objects are constructed to be objective, in Panofsky's sense of the term; that is, to be self-contained and possessed of an affecting presence, they come complete with their own authority and minimise the need for the imaginative projection of the observer to make sense of the presentation. In many cultures that is the highest ideal of art; and any attempt to involve the observer in a more subjective and expressive way would be strongly resisted on moral grounds, even if such a possibility could be contemplated at all.

An important question for Adorno to have asked – but which he is prevented from asking within the compass of his aesthetic theory – is: what relationship do Stravinsky's aesthetic objects have to the aesthetic objects made in an archaic or primitive society? As most critics acknowledge, Stravinsky's primitivism is modern rather than primitive. It is an attempt to develop an appropriate means for constructing an objective music by identifying with this aspect of earlier (pre-individualistic) cultures. However, its modernity, which lies in the treatment these so-called primitive images receive in the artist's work – the second-order construction they are subjected to – is also a clue as to how one might go about theorising what differentiates objectivity in Stravinsky from objectivity in archaic or primitive art. I would argue that the self-contained objectivity of the archaic art object does not negate the expressivity of the subject (conceived of as a collective and not a 'mass' subject). On the contrary, the self-contained art object is designed to embody the expressivity of the subject in its 'generalised otherness'. The subject's own expressivity appears to it as an affecting presence in which s/he participates. It is possible to view such a process as a vivification and reinforcing of the expressivity of the subject.

A collective subject that represents a society in all its complex differentiations must be distinguished from the concept of a subject as a homogenous mass, such as a crowd. It was a weakness of much nineteenth-century sociology – for example, that of Durkheim – that it tended to assimilate so-called primitive societies to the category of the homogeneous crowd, the uniform mass or collectivity, counterposing them to the complex social differentiations of a modern industrial society. There is little evidence in the writings of modern anthropologists that would support such a view – quite the contrary. The art objects of so-called primitive societies – the masks, figures and cult objects that figure in complex rituals – are powerful symbols that answer to complex and variegated systems of social relations. A collective subject that is fully social is one in which differential and variegated social relations constitute its expressivity.

Mass society, on the other hand, is a dimension of modernity, the homogeneous complement of the highly differentiated and mechanically reductive division of labour society. To be mass is to be de-individuated and de-sociated. In a mass society, collective expression is (ideal-typically) uniform. If we place Stravinsky on the negative side, as Adorno does, then his music has to be identified not with the collective subject of archaic or primitive societies but with the mass subject of modernity. In effect, Adorno claims that Stravinsky's subject is a 'mass' subject. According to this view, the heightened sensuous power of Stravinsky's musical 'objects' has its origins in the movement of the crowd, of the mass as concretised in *Le Sacre du Printemps* in the imagery of the tribe. The mass collective subject, unlike the differentiated collective subject, does not strengthen the individual subject in his or her social identity but destroys that individuation. It appears to be in this sense that Adorno identifies Stravinsky's music with the dark face of the mass societies of the first half of the twentieth century, accusing it of siding with the de-individuation and de-sociation of the individual subject. In opposing this, one might argue that Stravinsky's subject has more in common with the archaic collective that is not mass in the modern sense. Adorno, however, does not make the type of conceptual distinction I have introduced here.

Adorno does not accuse Stravinsky of being personally sympathetic to the oppression of modernity. He repeatedly acknowledges Stravinsky's own negativism in the face of modernity. It is the strategy for survival that Stravinsky has chosen that he rejected. Such was the crisis of modernity that many avant-garde artists felt that the new could not come into being until the old had been destroyed. The 'old' in this sense can be identified with the individual as an ego, a social agent put together by history. Remaking the world and the subject appeared to demand nothing less than the annihilation of the bourgeois subject, the annihilation of the individual. The artist could take this work and seek to realise this annihilation at the level of the aesthetic.

Although Adorno develops a theory of culture which allows him to conceive of music as participating in a social praxis through which subjects as agents are configured, he limits his notion of 'participating', here, to the level of consciousness removed from the praxis of everyday life. The consciousness of the subject becomes a sheltered realm – 'free from empirical entanglements' – into which the individual can withdraw to order genuine experiences of modernity. Adorno does not develop a theory of culture which would allow him to conceptualise the role of the arts and of aesthetic communication as actually shaping praxis in everyday life – where it is not free of empirical entanglements. Nor does he develop a theory of culture which explores the complex mediations among different aesthetic projects – for example, between jazz and classical music, between different popular musics, functional musics and so forth. Equally absent from his theorising is a concern with how these different musics, in their mediations, enter into the configuration of agency in everyday life. The audience for Picasso and Braque may have been small, but their discoveries have passed in altered form into everything in twentieth-century society from the design of buildings and furniture to the design of wallpapers and curtain fabrics, not to mention into the graphic arts, film, etc. We can make out a similar case for the fate of Schoenberg's music or that of Stravinsky. Different types of listening are associated with different types of music and different conditions of consciousness, good or bad; but while Adorno always allows of the moral force of music in respect of the consciousness of the subject – in his theory, music always has serious moral charge, either positive or negative – he denies to music a constructive role in the development of empirical social action; he lacks a theory of music and social agency in the context of everyday life; such a theory would appear to be ruled out by his commitment to a Kantian view of works of art as 'purposeless'.

9

THE CULTURE INDUSTRY
AND ALL THAT JAZZ

To many people the most distinctively modern music of the first half of the twentieth century was jazz. Instrumental, dance and song styles proliferated at a rapid rate from the time of the earliest recordings of jazz music, which appeared during the First World War. The journey to mass popularity was impressively fast, and by the late 1920s jazz had permeated the entire field of popular music and entertainment. In the era of dance crazes and dance bands, the jazz idiom made itself felt both in its presence and sometimes in its absence in all the leisure space of bourgeois society. The term became a metaphor and cipher for an entire epoch, the label 'jazz age' gaining as much currency in some circles as had the 'machine age' at the time of the Futurists. Even the modernity of certain figures in American literature – Scott Fitzgerald, for example – was identified with a style of interpersonal relationships and social life that was summed up with the label 'jazz age'. Jazz was a music that seemed to be part and parcel of the modern city and its leisure spaces, a music that was accessible, in its various forms, to city people everywhere; a genuinely popular modern music, sounding the dreamscape of the metropolis and reflecting the colour and pulse of life and relations in the city.

The discourse surrounding jazz went further than this. Jazz was praised for its inventiveness. Its devotees invested its best examples with the kind of serious respect due to an avant-garde music which they saw as opposing the stuffy conventionality of the bourgeois order. The 'mantle of primitivism', eagerly donned by many so-called serious modern artists and composers, seemed to be the very birthright of jazz musicians; what modern Western music could stake a greater claim to genuinely 'primitive' origins? In the context of modernist art, the primitive has often been invoked as the hallmark of all that is progressive. Also, in its more advanced forms, jazz could claim to be a music that was developed in live *performance* by the people who played it. Unlike classical music, it did not turn its performers into mere executants of something created by a composer; even when playing 'standards', the best jazz musicians developed their own variants or improvised their own versions.

The claims concerning jazz went much further, however. Jazz in its more 'advanced' forms was seen by the cognoscenti to have a right to be taken seriously as art music, the audience for which was more select, less 'mass'. Such jazz – 'cool' or 'modern' as distinct from 'traditional' – was perceived by its 'afficionados' to be creative and experimental. A quality of 'liveness' and spontaneity had always been prized among jazz musicians and their audiences. Indeed, many would argue that spontaneity, improvisation and the uniqueness of every live performance of a piece is the sine qua non of true jazz of any kind. It was in the musical culture of improvisation – the 'tuning in' to the moment and the occasion – that jazz could stake a claim to being the 'sound-track' of its age. This emphasis on the improvisatory possibilities in jazz and upon the primacy of the living performance over the abstracted act of composition could also be seen as progressive in the modernist context.

Finally, jazz could lay claim to developing a musical language more capable of inscribing the sensuous life of the modern city, the feelings of ordinary people, their hopes, affections, fears and griefs; it could lay claim to being an authentic voice of the subject in the modern metropolis, of being a vehicle for the spirit and a reservoir of subjective energies. While its devotees recognised a spectrum of seriousness in jazz ranging from the most popular banalities of the mass entertainment industry to the most avant-garde performances of 'advanced' modern jazz, the shimmer and vitality of the 'contemporary' was to be seen throughout.

What this amounts to saying is that jazz was not simply perceived as just another contemporary artistic musical form. To its devotees it was the archetypal modern music, and the claims concerning its achievements and its possibilities for the future could easily be taken as implicitly questioning the relevance of European art music in the modern world. Modernity (and modernism), when applied to the classical tradition, was associated with a narrowing of audience, with an increase in exclusivity, a lack of accessibility. Modern classical music was seen as overly difficult and intellectually exclusive even by the middle-brow appreciators of the nineteenth-century classical music repertoire. The opposite was the case with jazz; it was quintessentially 'the people's music'.

The very claim that jazz music was good music, that it was serious and creative as well as being informal and primitive, posed a formidable challenge to the sociological and musicological theses that Adorno was advancing in respect of twentieth-century modernist music. Adorno's implacable opposition to jazz has to be seen in the context of these claims. In his 1936 paper 'On Jazz' (T. Adorno 1989) Adorno did his best to deconstruct jazz music and its claims to seriousness, and to depict it as the very antithesis of anything avant-garde or progressive. He denied its claims to be improvisatory in any serious sense and he threw doubt even upon its claims to be truly primitive or to be of genuinely African origin. For Adorno, the

161

mass popularity of jazz has quite a different meaning from the one its devotees would claim. He saw jazz, like all the products of the 'mass culture
industries', as realising, aesthetically, the technologies of control and domination characteristic of mass industrial and mass political modernity (J.
Bernstein 1991). He perceived, in jazz music, a masochistic submission to
the dominating force of the collective over the individual. He drew on a
Freudian psychoanalytical language to condemn jazz as 'castration' music or
as an aesthetic realisation of an onanistic, narcissistic and sexually regressive
consciousness. All its claims to musical inventiveness, its syncopation,
arrangements and orchestrations, he judged to be inferior derivatives – even
trivialisations – of what classical composers had invented decades earlier and
used more 'meaningfully'. Adorno did not ever soften the savagery of his
onslaught on jazz in any of his later writings even though, by the time of his
death in the late 1960s, a great deal more avant-garde jazz had appeared and
the jazz scene was no longer as dominated by the dance bands as it had been
in the 1930s and 1940s.

Some have seen Adorno's critique of jazz as the product of an artistic
snobbery, a prejudiced judgement by a defender of the classical European
tradition; to such critics he was an implacable opponent of American culture
because he was European, or of black music because he was white. All such
judgements seem to me to be wide of the mark. Adorno's treatment of jazz
has to be seen in the context of his treatment of mass culture generally. This
is a central theme of his sociological analysis of modern culture. To make his
own claims stick concerning the culture industry and the effects of commodification upon subjects in modern society, it was necessary to deconstruct
those claims being made for jazz in relation to modern art music.

In the 1936 paper 'On Jazz', Adorno begins by acknowledging 'its decidedly modern character'. Musically, he argues, this 'modernity' refers to the
characteristic sound and rhythm of jazz. Syncopation is its rhythmic principle. It occurs in a variety of modifications, such as

> the displacement of the basic rhythm through deletions (the
> Charleston), slurring (Ragtime); 'false' rhythm – more or less a
> treatment of common time as a result of three and three and two
> eighth-notes, with the accent always on the first note of the group
> which stands out as a 'false' beat from the principal rhythm; finally,
> the break, a cadence which is similar to an improvisation, mostly at
> the end of the middle part two beats before the repetition of the
> principal part of the refrain.
>
> (T. Adorno 1989: 45)

In all of these syncopations, Adorno argues, the fundamental beat is rigor-
ously maintained and marked over and over again by the bass drum. While
the rhythmic phenomena may bring variety into the accentuation and

phrasing in the music, they remain essentially ornamental and superimposed on the basic timing which is unaffected by them.

> Thus the principle of symmetry is fully respected, especially in the basic rhythmic structure. The eight-bar measure and even the four-beat half measure are maintained, their authority unchallenged. Simple melodic and harmonic symmetrical relationships correspond to this as well, broken down in accordance with half and whole closures.
>
> (T. Adorno 1989: 46)

Adorno uses this opposition between superficial irregularity and underlying conformity to establish the groundwork of a musicological critique of jazz. Jazz music is seen as constituting, in its distinctive sound, an amalgam of deviation and excess on the one hand and utter rigidity on the other. One of its vital components, according to Adorno, is the vibrato which causes a tone that is rigid and objective to tremble as if standing alone. This ascribes subjective emotions to the note without this being allowed to interrupt the fixedness of the basic sound pattern, just as the syncopation is not allowed to interrupt the basic metre. Adorno generalises the point to argue that the characteristic sound of jazz owes much to the manner in which the music generates a rigidity of form which it causes to shimmer and vibrate; that is, jazz achieves its most decisive effects 'through producing interferences between the rigid and the excessive' and it is this – even more than the distinctive use of instruments such as the saxophone – which Adorno sees as fundamental in jazz. However, Adorno is also careful not to identify jazz music solely with its surface appearance. In short, he distinguishes between jazz proper and music which appropriates a jazz style for its own different purposes. The music of Kurt Weill makes use of the pervasive basic rhythms of jazz and the sound of the saxophone, but Adorno does not identify it with jazz. Quite apart from the fact that Weill's practice of rhythmically profiling his melodies is, according to Adorno, alien to jazz practice, there is the question of how the music actually works.

Adorno insists that jazz is a commodity in the strict sense. Its marketability permeates its production. It is the laws of the market and the distribution of competitors and consumers which condition the production of jazz. Those elements in which immediacy appears to be present – the improvisatory moments, the varieties of syncopation, etc. – are added to the rigid commodity form in order to mask it but without ever gaining power over it. Jazz, argues Adorno, seeks to improve its marketability while masking its commodity character. Moreover, the mask itself, those moments of excess, of vibrancy, are precisely what increases that marketability, just as the stripping off of that mask – which in Adorno's phrase is 'a pasted on ornament' – would threaten marketability.

Jazz music permeated all social classes and was credited with being a music of the city, appreciated at both ends of the class divide. This, too, was something of a problem for a Marxist thinker. The appeal of jazz to the upper classes in society is specifically theorised by Adorno in terms of its careful disguising of the rigidity of authority by the immediacy of the primitive and the excessive. He argues that the bourgeoisie's contemplation of its own alienation is made endurable only so long as that which is alienated achieves sufficient distance and appears in the guise of the unconscious and of the primitive:

> To it [the upper class] jazz represents, somewhat like the evening clothes of the gentleman, the inexorability of the social authority which it itself is, but which is transfigured in jazz into something original and primitive, into 'nature'. With its individual or characteristic stylistic moments, jazz appeals to the 'taste' of those whose sovereign freedom of choice is legitimated by their status.
>
> (T. Adorno 1989: 49)

The greater the mass appeal of jazz – the more deeply it penetrates society – the more completely banal it becomes and the less it can tolerate any true freedom or the eruption of originality. Adorno insists that the pieces which play a decisive role in jazz's broad social appeal are the 'technically backward boorish dances' which are easily understood and rhythmically trivial and in which the individual or distinctive moments are minimal. 'The more democratic jazz is the worse it becomes' (T. Adorno 1989: 50).

Adorno is particularly scathing of the argument that jazz represents some elemental force which can revitalise decadent European music. He dismisses the claim as pure ideology. All of the formal elements of jazz have, in any case, been abstractly preformed, argues Adorno, in accordance with the laws of the market and with the character of jazz works as exchangeable commodities. Adorno dismisses the claim for a vitality introduced into music by the African or black associations of jazz; he likens the relationship between jazz and black people to that between salon music and the wandering fiddle players – the gypsies – who, according to Bartók, are supplied with this music by the cities:

> The manufacture of jazz is also an urban phenomenon, and the skin of the black man functions as much as a colouristic effect as does the silver of the saxophone. . . . There is nothing archaic in jazz but that which is engendered out of modernity through the mechanism of suppression. It is not old and repressed instincts which are freed in the form of standardized rhythms and standardized explosive

outbursts; it is new repressed and mutilated instincts which have stiffened into the masks of those in the distant past.

(T. Adorno 1989: 53)

To this Adorno adds a second argument concerning the black origins of the music. Insofar as there were genuinely African elements in early jazz, these suggested the singing of servant girls and the music of slaves. If this was the vitality with which American music sought to revivify itself, it was not a vitality drawn from the wild but from 'the domesticated body in bondage' (T. Adorno 1989: 53). Its apparently liberative gestures – those improvisatory movements which account for its success – express only the attempt to break out of the fetishised commodity world without ever changing it. The formula to which Adorno repeatedly returns is that of the commodity that must be simultaneously 'just like' all the others and yet 'original' – the hit tune that must unite an individual characteristic element with utter banality on every other level.

Adorno identifies the 'individual characteristic element', what one might term the 'virtuosic element', in jazz with performance and with the art of the arrangement that is associated with performance. What is essentially banal, as composition, is given a 'make-over' in reproduction. The one who arranges the music is a key figure here and is usually close to those who perform the music. Critics of Adorno's ideas on jazz have sometimes resorted to arguing that he treats jazz as 'composed' music rather than music in which 'performance' and improvised virtuosity is central. The 1936 paper reveals the extent to which Adorno has been falsely represented on this point:

Jazz seems to be progressive in two directions – both different with respect to the developmental tendency specific to music. One aspect is the reintroduction into the composition of those who are repro-ducing it. In 'artistic music' both [the composition and those who are reproducing it] are hopelessly alienated from one another; the instructions for playing the 'New Music' allow no room for freedom in the process of reproducing it – indeed the interpretation disap-pears completely behind the mechanical reproduction. In jazz it seems as if the reproducer has reclaimed his rights vis-à-vis the work of art – man has reclaimed his rights over the object.

(T. Adorno 1989: 55)

Adorno's criticism of the claims of jazz performance centre on the fact that he believes this claim to freedom to be illusory. The interjection of the performer/arranger in jazz does not permit any real altering of the material in order to realise a genuine subjective freedom. The new colour and rhythm are merely inserted along with the banal, just as the jazz vibrato is inserted into the rigid sound and the syncopation into the basic metre. Adorno refers to the freedom of the arranger/performer as a 'tugging at the chains of boredom without the power to break them'. In Adorno's view, the subject who does not succeed in breaking through in the composition certainly does not do so by means of the arrangement; the latter may serve to disguise the inhuman imposition of the commodity and thereby prolong the inhumanity surreptitiously by so doing.

The second claim for the progressive character of jazz music concerns the working process which is involved in the production and reproduction of jazz. Again, Adorno acknowledges that jazz appears to be progressive here when compared with so-called serious music. Jazz presents itself not as an isolated solo compositional process but as an obvious division of labour.

> Somebody comes up with the 'invention'; another harmonizes it or elaborates upon it; and then a text develops and the rest of the music is written and seasoned with rhythm and harmony; perhaps already by the arranger at this point; finally, the whole is orchestrated by a specialist.
>
> (T. Adorno 1989: 56)

However, Adorno does not accept this claim for the progressiveness of jazz practice as valid. He sees co-operation in the division of labour in jazz not as the workings of an organic interacting collective but as the mechanical subjection of material – often provided by 'amateurs' and those outside the mainstream profession – to various treatments from specialists (orchestration, arrangement, etc.) that are external to it. In a genuine division of labour, the creative process would be spontaneously initiated and developed within the collective through the interactions of the members, through their responsivity to each other. The mere subjection of material to treatment by a variety of specialists denotes only a mechanical assembly process which might be likened to the treatment that raw materials undergo in manufacture as they are passed along the conveyer belt. To Adorno, who was drawn to the ideal of collective creation in art, 'the division of labour in jazz merely outlines the parody of a future collective process of composition'. This argument underlines Adorno's notion of there being an isomorphism between structural relations at the level of praxis – that is, in the production of the music – and structural relations among the elements of the art work itself.

The role of the enthusiast and amateur is perceived by Adorno to be an important one in early jazz. He is careful to distance himself from what he calls 'the mythology of jazz' which sees invention as originating with the uncompromised and unsullied person, the authentic 'soul' of the black man, or whatever. He dismisses all such claims as ideology and mythology – and not just here. It has to be pointed out that, far from being racist in making such remarks, Adorno is being entirely consistent with his critical philosophy of modern music. He makes exactly the same move against the claims of Wagner in *The Ring* concerning the pure, unsullied and uncompromised nature of Siegfried.

The amateur in jazz is a key actor both as the bearer of that mythology and as 'guarantor for the apperception of the product'. Adorno likens the jazz amateur to the businessman who thinks he is transformed into a poet on the occasion of his birthday celebrations and who speaks, not like a naive or natural poet, but in imitation of famous poets. The jazz amateur, claims Adorno, imitates the clichés of current jazz music (T. Adorno 1989: 58). What he brings to the music is a consequence of the social mutilation and dislocations of mass society. The very position of the amateur, whose helplessness as an 'outsider' intersects with his helplessness as a subject in mass society, is important in the production of commercially successful music. Adorno sees the position of the jazz amateur as giving rise to a definite psychological and musical set. He characterises it, somewhat dismissively, as the mastery of a hysterical lack of restraint which enables such a person to express emotions that he does not and never will suffer, and to invest the production and invention with extra-musical associations that training tends to eradicate in professional musicians. 'Helplessness' is the characteristic element which Adorno believes to be key to jazz expression, the helplessness that derives from the fear of social power and the desperate attempt to adapt oneself to it. It is this very helplessness which Adorno believes to be so important an ingredient in achieving commercial success. He argues that it is every bit as important as the mundane consciousness of the jazz habitué who deals in the professional production of the 'banal'. At a musicological level, Adorno interprets the 'whimpering vibrato' and the 'wailing saxophone' as expressions of this helplessness (T. Adorno 1989: 60).

Even in the early 1936 paper, Adorno acknowledged that there were not only different types of jazz but differences in quality, too. He observed that the day of the amateur and dilettante appeared to be passing: at one end of the spectrum, jazz music was achieving a kind of 'stabilised' form in which it presented itself as 'symphonic', as 'autonomous art', and in the process abandoned all its former claims to collective immediacy and spontaneity. To the extent that jazz takes this direction it increasingly submits itself to the standards of 'artistic music'. The musician that Adorno had principally in mind as a representative of 'stabilised jazz' was Duke Ellington. Adorno saw Ellington's 'tasteful' jazz as an appropriation of the conventions of musical impressionism, of the style, that is, of composers such as Debussy, Ravel and Delius. He saw the most striking influences in Ellington's harmonies, in the nine-note chords and 'stereotypical blue chords' characteristic of Debussy. Even Ellington's treatment of melody shows the influence of musical impressionism. 'The resolution into the smallest motif formulae, which are not developed dynamically but rather statically repeated, and which are only rhythmically reinterpreted and appear to circle around an immovable centre, is specifically impressionistic' (T. Adorno 1989: 59). Adorno argues that all the more subtle features of 'stabilised jazz' refer back to this style which, he notes, may be making its way into the broader social strata of society through jazz. However, he sees the appropriation of musical impressionism as depriving jazz of its formal sense. Here Adorno resorts to an argument that recurs throughout his work and which is applied to different contents. He rejects any music which appears to him to inhibit any true development:

> If in Debussy the melodic points form their colouration and temporal surfaces from out of themselves following the constructive command of subjectivity, in jazz they are harnessed, like the mock-beat of 'hot music', into the metric-harmonic schema of the 'standard' cadence of the eight-bar measure. The subjective-functional distribution of the melody remains impotent by being recalled as it were by the eight-bar condensation, into a melodic soprano form which merely toys with its particulars rather than composing a new form from them; this is true in the case of the complex harmonies when they are caught again by the same cadence from which their floating resonances want to escape. *Even yesterday's music must first be rendered harmless by jazz, must be released from its historical element, before it is ready for the market* [emphasis mine].
>
> (T. Adorno 1989: 59–60)

Adorno locates jazz in two stylistic traditions, salon music and the march. He claimed that the origins of jazz reach deep into the salon style and that the *expressivo* of jazz stems from this tradition; 'to put it drastically, everything in it wants to announce something soulful'. If the salon style is responsible for the supposedly individual element in jazz, which Adorno sees as merely a socially produced illusion of freedom, the march represents a 'completely fictive community which is formed from nothing other than the alignment of atoms under the force that is exerted upon them' (T. Adorno 1989: 61). Adorno generalises the argument to suggest that all dance, as synchronised movement, has something in common with the march. In the admixture of salon music and the march, bourgeois individuality, as expressed in movement – the casual gait of individuals from the salon – appears to oppose the strict order of the march, to release the dancer from the prison of strict form and give expression to the arbitrary nature of everyday life, a life which, Adorno argues, is not escaped through dance but playfully transfigured there as a latent order. Jazz music is best suited to accompany contingent actions that are prosaic and mundane, scraps of the everyday, a chance word, people doing the most ordinary things. Adorno argues that this contingency is frequently erotically coded. He suggests that the symbolic representation of sexual union is the manifest dream content of jazz.

The interplay between the individual element and the form in jazz is deconstructed by Adorno in an insightful discussion of the rondo component in jazz: that is, the division into 'couplet' and 'refrain' (verse and chorus). The former represents the contingency of the individual in everyday life, the latter the constraint of the society or collectivity. Adorno argues that the individual in the audience experiences him or herself as a couplet-ego and then feels transformed in the refrain, merges with it in the dance and finds sexual fulfilment. The production process, he argues, realises the primacy of the refrain over the couplet in that the refrain is written first and as the principal component. This deconstruction is an example of the novel ways in which Adorno applies the analytical techniques drawn from his general musicological theory. Through his analyses of the music of composers like Beethoven, Mahler or Schoenberg, the musical subject is identified with the element, the individual note or motive, and society or the collectivity is identified with the musical form. His critical focus is always the relationship between the two; in music which he opposes, form imposes its authoritarian order upon the elements which are subsumed by it. Such a situation reflects the overwhelming force of the collective in relation to the individual. The unfreedom of the individual, reflected in the unequal relationship of couplet and refrain which in Adorno's musicology refers to a subject that is the 'victim' of the collective, is finally treated by Adorno in terms of the notion of the sacrificing of the individual to the power of the collective. This is a theme which he had explored in an essay on Stravinsky's music in which he discussed *Le Sacre du Printemps* (T. Adorno 1980) which makes use of syncopation and jazz technique. In *Le Sacre*, Stravinsky makes the subject of the work a human sacrifice – that of the principal dancer.

> The objective sound is embellished by a subjective expression, which is unable to dominate it and therefore exerts a fundamentally ridiculous and heart-rending effect. The elements of the comical, the grotesque and the anal which are inherent in jazz can therefore never be separated from the sentimental elements. They characterize a subjectivity that revolts against a collective power which it itself is; for this reason its revolt seems ridiculous and is beaten down by the drum just as syncopation is by the beat.
>
> (T. Adorno 1989: 67–8)

The line between jazz and popular music generally has always somewhat blurred; its fecundity as a musical form was impressive – ragtime, blues, bebop, swing. Of course, there have always been those who have attempted to effect a more restricted definition of jazz and a clearer distinction between real jazz and popular music. Notwithstanding the fact that there is a vast difference between the best work of jazz musicians and the worst of the popular music scene, hard and fast distinctions are difficult to sustain. It is interesting to note, in this connection, Duke Ellington's hesitations over the term 'jazz'. In his later life he eschewed the problem of definition altogether, claiming that jazz was embedded in the history of its performers and performances (T. Gracyk 1992: 537).

If an accessibility and a popularity that crossed class boundaries was what characterised jazz music, so-called serious modern music – the music of Schoenberg, Berg and Webern, for example – was marked by the opposite: by its more or less complete inaccessibility to most people and its remoteness even from many of the audiences who traditionally appreciated classical music. Moreover, the development of this music was taking it further away from what most people sought in music, from what Adorno referred to as 'music's animal warmth' (T. Adorno 1980: 109). He is actually commenting here on what he sees as the bleakness of modern social reality and the necessary bleakness of a music that is equal to the task of comprehending it in the very act of resisting it. The coldness or restraint of Schoenberg is an attitude equal to the threat and terror of modernity. Remoteness is, for Adorno, a condition of resistance in the modern world. In the introduction to *The Dialectic of Enlightenment*, Adorno and Horkheimer (1986) had discussed the difficulties of mounting an effective critique of Enlightenment thinking while using a language shaped by such thinking. The very way of constructing sentences, the relations of determinism, causality, implication, inhering in habits of discourse, in language itself, would keep surfacing to mock and to confound all attempts to undermine the edifice. Only by developing speech that was as distanced from and as resistant to the world that was being opposed, could one hope to mount a serious critique of what existed. Language, therefore, both in the special sense of musical language and in the more general sense of 'natural language', is always in danger of betraying the truth (T. Adorno 1993). Only through the most strenuous efforts can the subject hold sufficient distance from the world to avoid being sucked into it and washed clean of the power of resistance. In its reconstruction of its language, its material and in its consequent remoteness from the forms of traditional and conventional music, modern music conserved and concentrated resistance to the world, a resistance which, in its very inner structure, yielded 'true' knowledge of the world.

Adorno's philosophy of modern music did not permit a sympathetic understanding of jazz as a type of music. At the time his principal observations on jazz were made – in the 1930s and 1940s – the more conventional and highly arranged forms of jazz music played by the big dance bands were in vogue. However, Adorno lived until the late 1960s, and must have witnessed the considerable development that jazz underwent in those thirty years, and yet he apparently never altered his wholly negative opinions about jazz. He remained convinced that what he heard in the jazz music of his day was the very antithesis of the modernist project in music to which he was committed. It was not just that jazz enjoyed mass popularity and was suspect on that ground alone (as music that was absorbed by the world and therefore incapable of resistance, something he attributed to all mass culture); it was also that Adorno heard jazz as music with characteristics that were the very opposite of those that its devotees sought to claim for it. Thus he believed that jazz was essentially a formulaic music, a ritualised and impoverished performance, 'fashion' without substance (T. Adorno 1982b: 119–32).

If one turns to Adorno's specifically musical criticism of jazz, there is relatively little when one contrasts it with the detailed discussions of actual compositions which fill his books on Wagner, Mahler, Berg and so forth. Instead, Adorno resorts to a number of generalised and negative characterisations of jazz as music, rather than offering, as in the case of the classical composers, analyses of specific works. Jazz is first of all music which he sees as impoverished, containing little of musical interest in the way of harmony, melody, and metre.

The arguments concerning the poverty of musical material in jazz and the stereotyped and rigid application of its basic techniques, including 'syncopation, semi-vocal, semi-instrumental sounds, gliding, impressionistic harmonies and opulent instrumentation', are simply reasserted in the later paper on 'Perennial Fashion – Jazz' (T. Adorno 1982b: 121). Adorno paints a picture of the endlessly repetitive sameness of the music. Such difference as there might appear to be, as between different examples, is likened to the superficial differences among variants of the same basic car; you get the same basic car whatever the minor differences in styling or features. Jazz is fashion, according to Adorno, and as with all fashions what is important is show and not the thing itself. The studied effect, the solo instrumental, is polished with all the flair of the circus act and incorporated as a more or less self-contained entity without possessing any meaningful relationship to the composition as a whole. The 'cliché forms' in jazz are all seen by Adorno as interchangeable, with no organic or developmental coherence.

Again, the arguments for the spontaneity and improvisatory qualities of jazz are dismissed by Adorno as bogus. Jazz, as he sees it, is not so much a composed music in itself but a special treatment of the material of 'light music'. Specifically, Adorno sees jazz as the dressing up of 'the most dismal products of the popular-song industry'. It is the 32-measure song which he sees as the basic material of jazz. Even where there is real improvisation in jazz, the sole material, according to Adorno, remains popular songs. The improvisations are then reduced to 'a more or less feeble re-hashing of basic formulas in which the schema shines through at every moment . . . the range of the permissible in jazz is as circumscribed as is any particular cut of clothes' (T. Adorno 1982b: 123). Adorno would not allow that the rhythmic and colouristic techniques of jazz were in any way original but claimed that all such techniques had been invented and superseded in serious music since Brahms.

171

Adorno's critique of jazz, however, is entirely consistent with his general critique of both modern music and the culture industry. Schoenberg, no less than Stravinsky and jazz, is accused of constructing music that no longer recognises history. For Adorno, a music that 'recognises history' would have to be one in which the elements or parts developed freely towards the construction of a whole. In the case of music totally organised from above, music in which there is no freedom of the elements to develop in relations with each other, music in which each element is like a self-contained monad unaffected by its neighbours, there could be neither spontaneity of the elements nor development and, therefore, no history. Schoenberg's twelve-tone technique constructed, in the tone 'row', a rigid and fixed relationship among the twelve notes of the full chromatic from the very outset of a composition. In Adorno's philosophy this pre-figured ordering and its serial presentation was an abandonment (whether willed or not) of the 'subject' and of 'expression' in favour of an omnipresent musical constructivism, as surely as was Stravinsky's 'rhythmic-spatial' music in which, Adorno claimed, the parts were 'static blocks' of sound juxtaposed without motivic-thematic development. Notwithstanding the fact that Schoenberg and Stravinsky are analysed as the poles of modern serious music and distinguished from jazz, Adorno's analysis sought to expose what he saw as the potentially fatal convergence of all three in the totalitarian extinction of the subject. Jazz, too, was the totally planned construction of effects. Planned production violated the principle of emergence by preventing all that is uncontrollable, unpredictable, incalculable, in advance, and thus deprived life of what is genuinely new, without which the historical is not possible.

Adorno continued to hold to his views concerning claims about the African roots of jazz and the arguments that this music developed as an original and localised expression with strong ethnic roots long before the culture industry got hold of it and manufactured the smooth sophistication of the big bands. Whatever was wild, untrammelled, original or even African in this music had, according to Adorno, been destroyed by the culture industry when the music had been appropriated as the basis of a mass culture. Adorno passes over, here, what is an important issue concerning the roots of music like jazz or even rock music as protest, and the manner in which cultural appropriation – what Hebdige calls 'defusion and diffusion' – takes place (D. Hebdige 1979: 93). It is a point to which I return later in this chapter. For Adorno, what is important here is not whatever the music might once have been for specific social groups but its parasitic appropriation by the culture industry, which subjects every cultural element to competition on the culture market. The various techniques, rhythmic, colouristic, harmonic and melodic, are then sorted out – through being market-tested – and kaleido-scopically mixed into ever-new combinations, without there taking place even the slightest interaction between the total scheme and the no less schematic details. All that remains is the results of the competition.

Once the culture industry has generated its 'winning' schemata, it can continuously reshuffle the elements into the 'ever-new' without any danger of anything really changing at all. In this way, it can bring off its most successful trick, that of 'pseudo-individualisation', arranging the 'standards' in ways that appear as new and different, whether tailored for specific artists, audiences or performances. Adorno seeks to expose all such surface appearances as phoney; the deviations are just as standardised as the standards from which they are derived. He is no less scathing of the claims that jazz might make to being artistically avant-garde, to transcending its basis in nineteenth-century tonality.

> Anyone who allows the growing respectability of mass culture to seduce him into equating a popular song with modern art because of a few false notes squeaked by a clarinet; anyone who mistakes a triad studded with 'dirty notes' for atonality, has already capitulated to barbarism.
>
> (T. Adorno 1982b: 127)

Adorno even offers a psychoanalytic explanation of the jazz phenomenon with its rigid formulas. It represents, according to him, the sado-masochistic identification with the aggressor, with the totalistic force of the collectivity; it is nothing less, he claims, than a 'castration' ritual, a masochistic submission to emasculation. He cites one critic who likened the soaring trumpet of Louis Armstrong to the vocal sounds of the castrati (T. Adorno 1982b: 130).

It is important to set Adorno's critique of jazz in the context of his critique of modern music and his critique of the culture industry generally. In radio, the film industry, the variety act, cartoons — everywhere — Adorno saw the culture industry as the enemy of humanity and true feeling. There is no doubt, however, that the attacks on jazz seem more strident than those of other products that Adorno designates as part of the culture industry. In part this may be due to the fact that music is Adorno's speciality; in part, however, it probably reflects the fact that whereas opponents were less likely to challenge his placement of the variety act or the Hollywood star-wrapped movie, claims were frequently made for jazz which challenged the assumptions he made about its character as modern music as well as its relationship to the culture industry.

Theodore Gracyk has offered a spirited rebuttal of Adorno's arguments concerning jazz (T. Gracyk 1992). Adorno's habit of classifying non-classical music as jazz-based, apparently in the belief that jazz was the dominant and paradigmatic form of popular music during his lifetime, is criticised by Gracyk. 'Jazz was never synonymous with popular music and, with the emergence of bebop and later, rock and roll, jazz became decidedly less popular' (T. Gracyk 1992: 527). Jazz, in the normal sense, includes Miles Davis, Louis Armstrong, Charlie Parker; but it is a distortion to classify such performers with Sammy Davis Jnr, Dean Martin, Buddy Holly or the Beatles. The excellence or otherwise of any one could hardly be compared with that of the others. Ironically, it is a characteristic of the authoritarian personality to minimise the differences among the range of things to which one is opposed and to insist that they are all fundamentally the same, and equally bad.

There are two issues here, those of differences in quality – for example as between particular composers or musicians playing essentially the same broad type of music – and the qualitative differences among types of music. Adorno does concede that jazz musicians differ in quality; he acknowledges that musicians such as Charlie Parker made better music than many others; but for him the fact that there is 'good bad music' only underlines the extent to which qualified musicians have sold out to the culture industry. As to the qualitative difference among types of music, while the most subtle differences are entertained when dealing with classical music, jazz is viewed as being indistinguishable within the 'filthy tide' of entertainment music.

Those knowledgeable about jazz can, without difficulty, demonstrate the dubious and often wrong assertions that Adorno makes about jazz as music. Gracyk refutes a number of Adorno's specific claims. Adorno's belief that the sole material of jazz is the 32-measure popular song is wrong, argues Gracyk, even if we confine our attention to jazz before Adorno's death in 1969. Thus, of Louis Armstrong, a musician referred to by Adorno, Gracyk points out:

> Near the apex of his development, Louis Armstrong extended the New Orleans tradition with his Hot Five and Hot Seven recordings (1925–1927). Yet, at that time, Armstrong had little exposure to popular mainstream standards and did not write thirty-two measure tunes. In fact, his weakest recordings of the period are frequently of music composed by others, and Armstrong's strongest originals are head arrangements that draw upon blues progressions. The masterful 'Potato Head Blues' is neither the standard twelve nor thirty-two measure tune, and the highly admired 'Weather Bird' (1928) is based on King Oliver's sixteen-measure tune. In fact Armstrong's breakthrough as a jazz soloist did not derive from the popular standard tunes of his day.
>
> (T. Gracyk 1992: 532)

Gracyk goes on to consider those cases where celebrated jazz musicians do work with standard popular songs. A bedrock of popular songs may well support the art of Charlie Parker. However, while 'Thriving on a Riff', 'Chasin' the Bird', 'Ah-Leu-Cha' and 'Constellation' are based on Gershwin's 'I Got Rhythm', they are not a mere ornamentation of the original song. Gracyk argues that it makes about as much sense to argue that these songs are restrictive of the music of Charlie Parker as it would to claim that the use of sonata-allegro form was restrictive of Beethoven's symphonies. Schonherr's paper, 'Adorno and Jazz: Reflections on a Failed Encounter' (1991), makes a similar point in his discussion of John Coltrane's version of the Richard Rogers standard 'My Favourite Things' from *The Sound of Music*. Schonherr argues that it serves as an example of the successful transformation of aesthetic kitsch into the musical language of the avant-garde.

> Within a period of six years he freed this tune from all functional-harmonic and metric simplicity. The contrast to the original shows most radically in the recording from 1966, within which the deconstructed thematic material only resurfaces fragmentarily through the largely atonal improvisations. The treatment of this piece documents beyond the biographical implications also a musical self-reflection on the history of jazz and its aesthetic procedures, which converge in the nineteen-sixties to a large extent with those of contemporary music.
>
> (U. Schonherr 1991: 92)

Gracyk considers the examples of jazz musicians who consciously abandoned popular song material and its standard chord progressions, such as Miles Davis's 'Kind of Blue' (1959) and Ornette Coleman's 'Free Jazz' (1960). Both, he claims, avoid popular song composition and abandon standard tonality:

> Coleman's group in 'Free Jazz' also rejects all the pre-determined chord progressions of popular songs and improvises on a few short original themes, but where Davis plays trumpet, saxophone, and piano in the foreground, as individual soloists, Coleman downplays the convention of the foreground solo and offers thirty-six minutes of collective improvisation among as many as eight players at a time. In addition, in many pieces by Charles Mingus and Ornette Coleman, varying tempos and unpredictable rhythmic fluctuations replace a steady beat.
>
> (T. Gracyk 1992: 533)

Gracyk's examples are largely taken from the post-swing era, whereas Adorno's writings on jazz (between 1933 and 1941) belong to that era. Nevertheless, Louis Armstrong also belongs to it, and there were others in that time which deserved more critical attention from Adorno. In any case, by 1960 there were plenty of examples to indicate that 'Jazz had no essential reliance on composed songs and that it did not require diatonic tonality'. Of course, Adorno does not allow himself to be so easily caught. Here and there he does acknowledge departures from the rigid conventions imposed by the culture industry. These are claimed (like the eccentricities of Orson Welles) to be a contrived type of deviation which helps reinforce the rigid schemata which it only appears to challenge. Adorno insists that when jazz avoids popular song-forms, diatonic scales and a monotonous beat, its innovations are merely a recycling of styles that have been made before, in serious music, and are now unchallenged conventions (T. Adorno 1982b: 123–4).

Gracyk points to the differences between the tradition of classical composed music and that of jazz. He accuses Adorno of treating jazz as though it should be listened to in the way that he listened to classical music, and judged accordingly. Adorno never learned to listen to jazz, and never credited either the autonomy of jazz players nor the high degree of social co-operation and reflexivity that was necessary to make good jazz. Adorno offers nothing in the way of a study of the culture of jazz and jazz musicians nor an account or analysis of how they think concerning the business of making music. In classical music, the interpretation of a score makes the performance appear to be a secondary act of duty and conformity in the service of the written composition itself, which is seen as somehow primary. Jazz has never been comfortable with that kind of division between performance and composition, with its implicit downgrading of the former. Jazz musicians have often seen the history of jazz as a history not only of great performers and those who modelled themselves on them, but also a history of great performances through which new music was made and old music made new.

Schonherr disputes Adorno's claim that the musical interaction of instrumentalist and collective in jazz represents a 'parody of a future collective process of composition'. He insists that all the evidence suggests that it represents a form of communication free of domination, and offers the following account by the jazz musician Charles Mingus about the active involvement of musicians in the composition process. Schonherr claims that it was typical, even paradigmatic, for aesthetic production among avant-garde jazz musicians in the 1960s:

> I lay out the composition part by part to the musicians. I play them the 'framework' on piano so that they are all familiar with my interpretation and feeling and with the scale and chord progressions . . . each man's particular style is taken into consideration. They are given different rows of notes to use against each chord but they choose their own notes and play them in their own style, from scales as well as chords, except where a particular mood is indicated. In this way I can keep my own compositional flavour . . . and yet allow the musicians more individual freedom in the creation of their group lines and solos.
>
> (U. Schonherr 1991: 88)

176

No matter how persuasive the examples that Schonherr, Gracyk and others are able to bring to bear against Adorno's negative critique of jazz, it is by no means clear that the theory can be brought down by such rebuttals, or even that those self-same arguments do not end up by offering some degree of support for Adorno's critique of the culture industry. Adorno's views on jazz are integral to his treatment of the culture industry generally. The critical defence of jazz offered by Gracyk and others can be seen to demand, in opposition to Adorno, a repositioning of jazz in relation to the culture industry. What Gracyk in effect points to is a growing division between jazz on the one hand and rock music, rock and roll, country and western music and popular music styles of all kinds. The strongest examples he offers, Miles Davis and Ornette Coleman, belong to the late 1950s and 1960s, in which this separation becomes clearer; moreover, it is a separation that coincides with the decline of the mass culture appeal of jazz. One might want to conclude that when jazz proved to have a genuinely independent and expressive voice of its own it was no longer usable by the culture industry and was increasingly ignored by it. Gracyk does not seriously deny the close connection between jazz and popular song and dance music in the 1930s and 1940s, nor even the 'pseudo-individualisation' of its products as claimed by Adorno. The effect of his critique, so it seems to me, is to suggest that Adorno underestimated the potential of jazz to emerge from the grip of the culture industry and to develop, as a cultural process, its own forms of resistance. It argues for a more subtle, less monolithic view of the dynamics of cultural processes such as jazz and their relationship to the culture industry.

In their analyses of the emergence of youth culture styles in the 1960s, Hall and colleagues at the Centre for Contemporary Cultural Studies opposed the view that these cultures were created by the commercial world as distinct from being exploited by them (S. Hall *et al.* 1976). They argued that subcultural styles in music and dress arose as genuine forms of resistance, as part of an ongoing class situation, but that they were quickly appropriated by the culture industry and, in Hebdige's memorable phrase, 'defused and diffused', stripped of everything unacceptable to a mass audience, smoothed and glossed and then widely disseminated. Even the rich could come to adopt hair styles and make-up that could be labelled 'punk' (D. Hebdige 1979: 93). What may have begun as a genuine expression ends up as fashion. However, while this is to recognise the power of the culture industry, it also discloses its dependence upon a process of culture creation beyond the compass of its direct control; it raises the question of the boundaries of the culture industry and of the 'commerce' that takes place with whatever lies beyond those boundaries.

For Adorno, asociability is an attribute of jazz and the culture industry generally. This asociality is key to Adorno's radical critique of the culture industry. Its point of departure is Marx's analysis of the fetishism of commodities. Imagine (ideal-typically) a process of social production such as that which might said to obtain in so-called 'simple' societies where goods are produced and consumed in local communities to meet known local needs and not manufactured for their exchange value on a mass market; such products can be seen as mediated by the integral social relations through which they are both produced and consumed – that is, the sociality of such a community is inscribed in its products. To be conscious of each pot, pan, spear or mask is at the same time to be conscious of the social relations through which each thing is made and used. But in an industrial society which produces goods through an alienated labour process for sale as commodities on a mass market, the products themselves appear, to the individual, estranged from the social relations through which they are produced. To the consciousness of the 'individual', commodities appear as more or less autonomous things endowed with all kinds of qualities. The forceful and exploitative relationship of capital to labour in the production of commodities – a process which in Marx's analysis is inherently de-sociating and fragmenting – reappears in the compelling power of the monolithic and reified world of commodities over the consumer, de-sociated and de-individuated before it.

The de-sociation involved in commodity production leaves a mass of individual consumers facing a monolithic economic order of commodity production. The vital link between commodity and consumer upon which capitalism depends is the asocial affectivity of 'motive', rather than the social affectivity of 'value'. Commodities can realise their power, can maximise their value in exchange, only through their capacity to stimulate and engage motives (R. Witkin 1997). The value of a commodity can therefore be measured by the magnitude of the 'desired effect'. All the machinery of advertising and publicity is put to work to stimulate and arouse the needs to which the manufactured world of commodities and their effects answers.

And yet, as Schonherr points out, Adorno has provided an example of the non-ideological use of 'cultural trash' in his praise of Mahler's alliance with vulgar music – an alliance which he sees as subversive and not as submissive. Surely the same argument might be made out for jazz (U. Schonherr 1991: 88). The same point concerning Mahler is made, too, by Paddison who provides, as a further example, Adorno's treatment of the music of Kurt Weill, whose style he described as:

> a montage-style, which negates and at the same time raises to a new level the surface appearance of neo-classicism and juxtaposes and cements ruins and fragments up against one another through the 'addition' of wrong notes, it composes out the falseness and pretense which today have become apparent in the harmonic language of the nineteenth century.
>
> (M. Paddison 1996: 100)

Adorno clearly did recognise the possibility of working meaningfully with regressive material. However, the claim made by Schonherr and others that jazz can be seen to be doing this would no doubt have been rejected by Adorno. The compositional process was all-important to him and he had a strong sense of what, as composed music, for him separated Mahler or Weill from Duke Ellington or Louis Armstrong. The claims of Schonherr and Paddison, however, are based more upon their sense of jazz music in its culture and practice and their belief that its critical and subversive potential has been underestimated by Adorno.

At the opposite pole, that of rock music and jazz, Paddison cites Sandner's claim that 'in the history of both jazz and rock music there is to be seen an almost obsessive pressure from the ' "subculture" towards high art music' (M. Paddison 1996: 100). This pressure can be seen as the result of an increasing degree of self-reflection within certain kinds of more radical popular music. Increasingly this music draws on sources within twentieth-century art music and develops a critical orientation. Frank Zappa's rock music of the 1960s is offered by Paddison as a key example:

> With Zappa, it is not only that his music reflects contemporary American reality, but that it does so with such imagination, intelligence and irony and with such awareness of the extraordinary variety of material and techniques at his disposal.
>
> (M. Paddison 1996: 101)

But, as Paddison points out, the most pessimistic aspect of Adorno's critique derives not so much from the attack on jazz music or popular music generally – there is a sense in which Adorno sees popular music and serious music as two halves of the same reality – as it does from Adorno's thesis that music divides between music that accepts commodity status and commodification and submits to the manipulative power of collective forces, and self-reflective music which resists those forces. In reality, both can be seen as impotent. The former is impotent because it is a lackey of the culture industry; the latter is impotent because it is an exile with no appreciable impact on anything. Paddison accepts this thesis and therefore believes that even if it is the case that popular music develops this critical self-consciousness, it cannot escape the impotence which confronts the avant-garde as surely as it does the purveyors of kitsch.

In an interview with Volpacchio, Frank Zappa was asked whether he saw the collapse of functional tonality and common time as the single most important development in modern music. He replied:

> No. The single most important development in modern music is making a business out of it . . . you have reached the point where you can't just sit down and write because you know how to write

and you love to write and eventually somebody will listen because they love to listen and maybe somebody will play it because they'll want to play it. That is gone. The point where anybody who composes has to deal with the mechanics of the performance world, especially as it is characterised in American society, has to have a major impact on what you write. For example, one of my pet theories is that the leading cause of Minimalism is reduced budgets for rehearsal and reduced budgets for ensemble size. . . . How can a person be concerned about atonality versus tonality when the real question is how do you get anything played? Whatever it is.

(F. Volpacchio 1991: 125)

10

TAKING A CRITICAL LINE
FOR A WALK

I have been conscious throughout my reading of Adorno of the tension between the theorising of modernism that I developed in my book *Art and Social Structure* (Witkin 1995) and Adorno's rather different treatment. The judgements Adorno makes about works of art and music – and especially about whole traditions – leave me uneasy. In this last chapter I shall explore this tension in order to point up some of my difficulties with respect to Adorno's theorising of modernism. This is certainly not intended to be a 'proper' critique – something that a serious thinker like Adorno truly deserves. What is offered, rather, is a more modest thing altogether, a line of argument – a critical line – which I propose to take for a walk. It can be seen, perhaps, as a contribution towards a possible critique. However, it may well be the case that in walking this critical line I shall end up doing as much to buttress Adorno's conclusions as to challenge them.

Adorno is very certain about what is the right way to look at a work of art or to listen to a musical composition. For him, there is not only good music and bad music, there are good and bad modes of listening to music. One can listen with a concentrated and whole-hearted engagement with the work as an interdependent totality, or one can listen 'regressively', indulging oneself in a distracted fetishisation of particulars or in having one's emotions stimulated and manipulated. The culture industry and all its works were identified in Adorno's mind with regressive listening, while serious music was associated with concentrated and engaged listening. However, it is even possible to listen to so-called good music in a regressive way if it has been colonised by the culture industry. Adorno detested the fashionable appropriation of the classical concert repertoire by middle-class 'taste publics' and even extended his distaste to the man on the Underground who whistles a tune from a Brahms symphony. He saw this as a kind of commodification, a fixation on, and appropriation of, isolated particulars abstracted from the whole. It was not really different from the mode of listening that is demanded by entertainment music which he saw as actually made of up such isolated particulars.

Time is of the essence

Temporality is a pivotal concern of Adorno's philosophy of music. It is inseparable from his notion of what is 'social' and what is 'creative'. Adorno's interest in time was centred on what he saw as the *emergent* character of the present. As in George Herbert Mead's philosophy, the present, for Adorno, is not a knife-edge present, a pointillist present, but a changing, a becoming. Such a process of becoming was seen as dialectical, as an emerging from (what is also becoming) the past. The present is brought into being through negating – and being negated by – what is, and what therefore becomes, in the process of being negated, the past.

This emergence, this temporality, is integral to sociality which Adorno sees in terms of the 'going out' from the self to the other and in the mediation of the self by the other. Temporality is constructed by social relations. Holding, as he does, to such a strong identity between sociality and temporality, the notion of a music which turned its back on time was inseparable, in Adorno's philosophy, from the idea of a music that had surrendered to the asocial forces, which he saw as threatening modern existence in every sphere of modern life.

A music that is truly social (and, therefore, socially true), in Adorno's analysis, is one in which the elements manifest sociality and temporality in their relations with each other. A composition, for Adorno, is thus an interdependent whole, a developing process, a becoming. It has history within it and is transformed by the outer historical movement in which it participates. The receiver can only appreciate such a process through actively and sympathetically participating in its development, from the inside, as it were; this demands from the receiver – to borrow a phrase from Polanyi – an 'indwelling'. Any such indwelling presupposes a concentrative and absorbed mode of listening in which no element, be it a rhythm, a melody or a phrase, takes precedence over the developing totality. Thus Adorno could object to a radio treatment of Beethoven which encouraged children to think of the music as made up of themes with more or less unimportant bits in between them. He deplored the tendency to 'fetishise' parts of the work – that is, to isolate them from the whole.

In Adorno's analysis, so long as individuals act freely and spontaneously and enter into real dialectical relations with others, there will be temporality and an historical dimension to action. Any system of relations in which the individual is totally subsumed by the collectivity, and his or her relations with others mechanically determined, is a de-sociated and atemporal reality, a structure from which all change and development have been expunged.

In the shift to a more abstract level at which experience can be ordered – a level which I have theorised as intra-actional as opposed to inter-actional – the modernist subject centres itself in the constitutive process in and through which the sensibility and agency of the subject is formed. At an intra-subjective level of experience, there is no dualism to divide the world into self and other, now and then, here and there. The stream of events that makes up the experience of the subject in the whole range of life-world contexts is present in the same experiential frame. But this level of experience can only be reached through the bracketing or suspension of the ordinary world of interactional relations – through the negation of the temporal, historical world, that is – and through the pursuit of an atemporal (more accurately, a polytemporal) confluence at the level of the sensuous understanding. In pursuing his project, however, Adorno draws a number of conclusions about modernist art which may well prove wrong. We have no reason to suppose that the types of inter-actional relations existing between individuals will be equivalent to those *intra-actional* relations obtaining between the elements of experience in different life-worlds which are brought together in constituting the subject. It is Freud's argument that at deeper – we might say more subjective – levels of consciousness, consciousness is governed by the 'primary process' (S. Freud 1949: 27–34) which he claimed was undifferentiating as between here and there or now and then, and which is a confluence of events drawn from contexts that may not be temporally or spatially continuous with one another, that may be separated by decades and by continents.

Such is the consciousness of dream states. Relations among the sensuous elements constitutive of the subject may well correspond to those typical of dreams. Such relations might be described as polytemporal; they might plausibly be identified with imagination, spontaneity and creativity. Certainly, this is what Ehrenzweig does when he applies Freud's concept of the 'primary process' to an analysis of creativity in visual art (A. Ehrenzweig 1967: 257–79). It was to the model of the deeper, more subject-centred levels of consciousness that many modern artists turned in their search for more truthful modes of ordering experience. The unity that they sought at the intra-subjective level distanced them further from the functional, historical and interactional world; that world had fragmented life-worlds to the point where it became a matter of urgent necessity to undertake the journey into the constitutive foundations of the subject.

A world of intra-actional and intra-subjective events is a world in which the agency and sensibility of the individual are constituted as *capacities*. The strengthening of this synchronic level of experience may be positively viewed as a strengthening of capacity, of sensibility and agency, and as a realising of its independent and creative possibilities at the level of social action. *It may also be seen as a necessary basis for a reconstruction of relations at an interactional level*: that is, for a reconstruction of temporality and of the historical. If the view I am advancing here is correct, then Adorno's critique of many developments in modernist art must be viewed as suspect. We can best pursue the argument by considering the case of 'atemporality' in modern art.

It has been a key aspect of the development of modernist art that events that are temporally and, therefore, spatially distanced from one another are brought into the same experiential space. In a Cubist painting of common-place things, objects and parts of objects may be juxtaposed in ways that would be impossible in a so-called realistic space; different views of an object which could only be had *sequentially* and which could not therefore realistically appear in the same visual plane are made to disclose the consti-tutive machinery of the perceptual process itself. In collage/montage, the disjunctive juxtaposition of temporally, spatially and socially disparate worlds performs the same feat of bringing objectively disjunctive experi-ences into a unitary perceptual frame. In literature, the temporal construction of narrative events undergoes similar radical changes. It can be clearly seen in the experiments interfering with linear time and temporal relations in Proust, Joyce and Beckett, and in the concern of 'stream of consciousness' writing to capture the phenomenal flux of events as they rico-chet through the consciousness of living subjects; a flux that weakens and at times dissolves distinctions between 'here and now' and 'there and then' that describe the way the world is organised 'out there'.

The experiments of the Surrealists and the Futurists bring about an implosive collapse of linear continuities in space and time. All this experi-mentation was accompanied by a new interest in non-rational, non-cognitive modes of experience and by an increasing turn towards the sensuous world of the unconscious and a growing interest in the culturally exotic or primitive. The collapsing of times and spaces within the work of art brought the latter closer to the representation of the constitutive consciousness of the subject.

However, what occurred within the work of art occurred in the context of an aesthetic politics that was key to its realisation. The political dimension is powerfully stressed in the use of the term 'avant-garde'. Modernist artists were closely identified with this term and were often grouped as members of aesthetic 'movements' that issued manifestos and sometimes staged public demonstrations or attracted public attention. Poggioli identified, as a key feature of such aesthetic movements, their unrelenting hostility to tradition and of any claim that the past might have upon the shaping of the present. The violent hostility to tradition, to pastness and even to age itself, together with the worship of youth and energy that characterised Futurism as an avant-garde movement, has to be seen as rejection not simply of the past but also of the entire historical project that unfolds from it (G. Poggioli 1968). It can be seen as an attempt to pull up historical development by the root, to jettison historical construction and to re-make the world through the consciousness of a subject who is present-centred (albeit in actively negating the past) rather than past-centred. Energy, passion, aliveness were clearly identified by these artists with a liberation from the historical and all it constructs. It is thus a liberation from the 'ego', the latter's dislodgement from its secure foundation in bourgeois society – hence the unrelenting drive in modernist art towards the unconscious forces that Freud spoke of as primeval.

The pursuit of the 'unconscious' and of the 'primitive' is pervasive in early modernist and avant-garde art. Adorno was ambivalent here, too, but mostly he was hostile and suspicious in respect of its manifestations. The attempt to dive beneath the rational historical ego into a pre-dialectical primitivism represented, at its best, a cowardly desire to escape from history rather than confronting it and at its worst an unmasking and celebration of the 'violent savage' that he saw as the true character of bourgeois domination. The victims of this savagery are mocked in the modernist music of composers such as Stravinsky, argues Adorno. He is in no doubt that the evocations of the primitive in Stravinsky are a triumphant celebration of the victory of the collectivity over the individual: that is, of the annihilation of the latter as a sacrificial victim. Similarly, he is in no doubt that the 'genuine emotional shocks of the unconscious', represented by a woman's nightmare search for her lover and her discovery of his murdered corpse in Schoenberg's *Erwartung*, are a manifestation of compassion with the plight of the victims in modern society. He believes the same compassion is at the heart of Berg's music, too. Ultimately, Adorno holds us within the compass of his hearing of this music and of his implicit theory of agency. He hears the music as conditioning the sensibility of the subject – as readying the subject. His critiques of specific musics really stand or fall on the efficacy of his theory of agency, its claims concerning the way in which music works, the way in which it reflects and shapes the sensibility of subjects. It remains open to us as listeners to consider whether engagement with the music actually allows us to perceive it as working upon us in the way that Adorno suggests.

We can draw a distinction here, however, between the 'historical' as a word describing development or progress through time and history itself as a record of events. Avant-garde artists did not ignore the past, either in respect of the examples and models provided by other artists in the past or in respect of events themselves that happen to have taken place in the past. This was merely the culmination of a long-run tendency in modern art. Linda Nochlin has observed, in respect of nineteenth-century realism and history painting, that depictions of the past increasingly came to centre on capturing the presentness of past events (L. Nochlin 1971). In modernist art, a present-centred consciousness might appropriate anything at all from the past and bring it, like the disjunctive times and spaces of a montage, into the frame of the present. It is the historicality of past events that is extinguished, not the events themselves. It was a central feature of all avant-gardist movements of modern art that generated the aesthetic ferment that surrounded Adorno in his youth, that they 'turned their backs upon the historical' and that – with remarkable parallels to contemporary Einsteinian physics – they 'spatialised' time.

Adorno thus made a number of decisions concerning works of art – both their production and their reception – that were crucial for his critique. At the level of reception, he valorised a type of listening and attention characterised by a seriousness and an indwelling in the work of art as an integral 'event-world'. Such a mode of listening, however, is itself a relatively modern phenomenon. It may have originated as recently as the late eighteenth century. Tia DeNora's historical study of the construction of Beethoven's reputation among his aristocratic Viennese patrons discusses the emergence of just such a listening culture in the context of the contribution it made to the cultural construction of the authority of the artist as genius (T. DeNora 1995). Against this kind of concentrative listening, Adorno set what he saw as the type of regressive listening which involved the easy appropriation of aesthetic materials divorced from serious context, and which worked through their sensuous effects, their capacity to manipulate emotions in the listener or to provide distraction. In short, Adorno saw regressive modes of listening as centred on egoistic and personal gratifications, and he saw serious listening as concerned with meaning and with social consciousness. The latter dealt in truth and in morality, while the former was self-indulgent and morally vapid.

At the level of production Adorno valorised works of art that he saw as meeting the fundamental conditions of part–whole relations that I have discussed in terms of 'sociality'. At the micro-level, this meant music in which the elements developed (necessarily) in response to those that preceded them: that is as part of a continuous becoming. At the macro-level, this process was governed by the orientation towards the construction of the totality. Historicity in the work was bound up with both these aspects of sociality. He rejected music which violated either the condition of spontaneous development from the elements or the condition of integral totality – approached negatively, of course.

The drama of part–whole relations serves Adorno here as a litmus test for determining the moral value of the work of art in both production and reception. Thus, the lack of any kind of meaningful interdependence of whole and parts in a composition, the focus on isolated particulars, the silver of the saxophone, the drum-break, the climax to the variety act or the circus performance or whatever, by definition invites regressive and fetishised reception. Similarly, in a work of art where the elements or parts are dialectically mediating and part–whole interdependence is central, then a fully engaged and concentrative reception is called for in order to immerse oneself not in isolated themes but in the art work as a total event-world. So many of Adorno's specific judgements about works of art or performances are made on the basis of this type of thinking that it is necessary to examine it critically. After all, not only does it permit Adorno to dismiss the 'filthy tide' of popular entertainment and of mass culture but it stands behind his judgements about some of the most important movements of modernist art.

Commodification and the liberation of the subject as 'sensible agent'

Adorno is often counterposed to Lukács, in respect of their ideas about modernism. Lukács is seen as an implacable opponent and Adorno as a defender and friend of modernism. The picture is by no means that simple. There were developments that were key to modernist art to which Adorno reacted in a very negative way. One of these was the use of collage/montage, the practice of assembling together in the same experiential frame objects and materials that, to rational cognition, belong in different experiential contexts. Techniques of collage and of photomontage have been widely used in modernist art from the time of the early work of Picasso. They were exploited by the surrealist artists and poets to produce more or less fantastic or absurd compound images made up of components that could not belong together in any rationally coherent way. The construction of paradoxical forms, such as those of surrealist art, could engender tensions and anxieties in the viewer which are reminiscent of the impact made by charged dream imagery. Walter Benjamin, who was strongly attracted to surrealism and collage/montage, saw these assemblages as dialectical, as the juxtaposition of antithetical image elements giving rise to transcendent experience.

Adorno, after an initial ambivalence, came down strongly against this notion. He remained deeply suspicious of surrealist art. The juxtaposition of unrelated particulars could not be seen as dialectical but was merely the regressive model of pornography in which libido was frozen and congealed in isolated and reified forms. As with other such critical statements by Adorno, this has to be read in context. When considering the music of Kurt Weill, for example, Adorno speaks approvingly of its 'montage-like features', and there is no doubt that he has something similar in mind when praising Mahler's music. In both cases, he perceives the technique as utilised in the service of the serious art goals of which he approves. In his hostility to surrealism, however, he sees the technique as undermining the coherent and critical development of the work as an interdependent (albeit negatively interdependent) totality and as a submission to the passive and fetishistic reassembling of the elements of the status quo. Nevertheless, the move that Adorno makes in the case of claims for montage in modernist art generally extends beyond his antithesis to surrealism. We can recover them from his comments on Cubist experiments, as well as his analysis of both Stravinsky's music and jazz. Adorno was deeply rejecting of any movement which appeared to destroy the integrity of the work of art as a unitary field of dialectical mediations. Whether it was in the form of photomontage or of popular culture, the work of art as an assembly of isolated particulars spelled the end of the serious art work for him.

In *Art and Social Structure* (Witkin 1995) I offered a somewhat different view of what was involved in developments such as collage/montage. I suggested there that modernist art represented a move to a higher level of abstraction, in the sense of being a move from a concern with the world as it is distanced from the subject – *the world as seen* – to a concern with the constitutive sensibility of the subject – *the seeing-of-the-world*. To my mind, this move is decisive for the whole concept of the integrity of the art work as an interdependent structure. While what is seen, which represents a relationship between the subject and the world, can be communicated from one subject to another through being 'evoked' in the form of a picture, the reflexive awareness of one's seeing, which represents a dynamic and constructive relationship between the subject and its own experiencing, cannot be communicated at all but can only be 'provoked'.

The advent of modernism in the arts replaced the 'evocational' art, which had developed in Europe from the time of the Renaissance, with a 'provocational' art. The distance between subject and object, a distance that was exploited by an art centring on reality as the 'seen', collapsed in modernist art; the object fell back into the subject. In the very same process, a new distance was opened up in the reflexive relationship that developed between the subject and his or her 'seeing': that is, a distance that was intra-subjective. The collapsing of the distance between subject and object was achieved, in part, by annihilating the coherent interdependence of the work of art as a rational construction, its experiential unity as an inter-subjective order. We can see the obliteration of this inter-subjective object world as occurring at a number of levels: in the fragmentation and faceting of object and parts of objects in Cubist constructions, in the development of new modes of spatial representation, in the widespread appropriation of machines and machinery as a formal language in art, in the anti-art projects of certain avant-garde movements of modern art and, above all, in the resort to contradictory assemblages, to montage, in which the fusion of contradictory images heightens the sense of the resulting unity as an absolute and isolated particular. When we are deprived of the capacity to identify an object or element in terms of its relations to other objects or elements – when that object becomes an instance of the 'absolute particular' – then what we see is the seeing of things, itself. This is what is meant here by the assertion that the object falls back into the subject. At this level, the object is experienced, not as an element in a rational historical order, an inter-actional order, but as integral to the constitutive process in and through which the subject, both collective and personal, is constituted.

The power of the complex imagery of a Magritte painting has always seemed to me to lie in its capacity to provoke this sense of the 'absolute particular'. Confronted by the absolute particular the distance between the subject and the world collapses. The painting does not constitute a picture of something seen, so much as a 'machinery for doing seeing'. It does its work through assimilating itself to the constitutive sensibility of the subject through which the latter does seeing and experiencing. As a machinery for doing seeing, 'seeing' – as the perceiving subject – is effectively distanced from itself. In the imagery of dreams, seeings that belong to different contexts and which are, therefore, disjunctive with one another, are juxtaposed in complex and sometimes disturbing constructions. Such a process exemplifies something of what is meant here by a 'machinery for doing seeing'. In the juxtaposition of isolated seeings, a definite 'sensibility' is formed, a readiness or 'agency'. As soon as the focus of interest shifts from the inter-actional level of feelings to be communicated and actions to be performed to the intra-actional level of a sensibility to be formed and an agency to be constituted, the work of art as a machinery for doing seeing becomes a necessity, and such machineries, like the images of a dreamscape, constitute a juxtaposition of isolated particulars. It is the construction of such 'machineries' which I hold to be key to modernism. They are the means whereby the process of seeing and experiencing is thrust from the perceiving subject and made an 'object' of special perceptual attention.

Both musical schemes (twelve-tone method) and extra-musical schemes (Berg's use of the number 23) have abounded as constructional devices in modernist works and have to be accounted among the means used to effect such a distancing and objectification of the intra-subjective – of seeing, experiencing and the constitution of the subject. Adorno is all too inclined to equate such schemas with totalitarian and authoritarian systems that have the polar opposite function, that of closing down any such intra-subjective space, since any such space is an assertion of the autonomy of the subject and its creative role in constituting itself.

Adorno is right to see totalitarian administration as oriented to the absolute extinction of subjective freedom in that sense. However, he is wrong, it seems to me, to equate the use of abstract schemes and 'machineries' in art and music with any such totalitarian project, and doubly so in failing to recognise how vital they are to the construction of the very subjective freedom he values. He would no doubt respond that it is not the use of abstract schemes in art which are the problem, since they are always in some sense in evidence, but the use of schemes which actually do have the effect of closing down expression. He would no doubt wish to defend his objections to twelve-tone method and to serialism on those grounds.

The use of such machineries and the effective distance they open up within the intra-subjective fundamentally transforms the relationship between art work and recipient in the reception process. The recipient is required to be his or her own artist. The art work is less an object to be contemplated and enjoyed than a means for provoking, within the subject, the same intra-subjective distancing, the same process of 'seeing one's seeings', through which a sensibility can be developed, an agency constituted.

From the standpoint of a theory of reception, such a view would lead to conclusions opposed to Adorno's. The assembling of the art work as a juxtaposing of isolated particulars demands, in reception, an active and engaged contribution from the recipient whose own sensuous process is fully activated in bringing off this juxtaposition. Adorno's belief that the isolation of particulars in the work of art is linked to reification and commodification in modern life is not wrong. Paradoxically, however, the very condition he describes, that of a subject who is confronted by alien and commodified forms through which s/he is manipulated, is the very condition required for the collapse of distance between subject and object (the emergence of the absolute particular) which I have argued is necessary if art is to be a means for the establishing, at an intra-subjective level, of a machinery for doing seeing. The expressivity of the subject is realised in making use of this machinery, that is, in the making of sensibility and of agency; *the import of works of art is no longer bound within the compass of the reception of the work of art itself but extends beyond it to the aesthetic dimension of everyday life.*

Commodification and machineries of sensibility

Adorno recognises that no work of art can hold itself clear of the commodity – indeed the work of art is an 'absolute commodity' – but he does seek to set up an aesthetic posture towards the commodity by means of which the work of art, which reproduces the banality of the commodity in its inner relations, negates and distances itself from it. What I am arguing here – in an explicit reversal of Adorno's point – is that a work of art that seeks to hold itself clear of the commodity or of commodification, even by these means, might be seen as regressive, to the extent that such a work implicitly conserves, albeit through the use of the most radical means, a model of the art work that belongs to the past, to the pre-modernist period. For art to be progressive, it must surely move closer to appropriating the commodity in the way that Adorno would have dismissed as a 'false sublation' in the praxis of everyday life. I am arguing, further, that the more advanced the degree of commodification – and therefore the more sophisticated and processed the forms used as absolute and commodified particularity – the more easily assimilated they are as components for the construction of a sensuous machinery, and the more such a machinery becomes a means of intra-subjective distancing and of expressive construction available to the subject.

Adorno's pessimism and his negativity towards many developments in modernist art and music, including his concerns over serialism and twelve-tone technique, may have been the result of his holding on to a pre-modernist conception of the art work as an interdependent and more or less self-contained event-world. When one views art in that way, then a work of art which consists of isolated particulars will clearly be perceived to be inferior, to lack anything that would engage an organic and coherent subjective process. Moreover, insofar as reception of the products of the mass culture industry

190

may itself be governed by some such pre-modernist reception process, mass cultural products might, on that account, be characterised as regressive. However, Adorno's own mode of reception may be characterised as regressive: in his readings of modernist art and music, he might be said to approach such works with a pre-modernist mode of reception. If the pre-modernist work of art was an integral field of events that respected its frame, the modernist work of art is nothing of the kind. It everywhere strains beyond its frame and realises its greatest impact in the process of commodification in everyday life with which it interacts even in the very moment of its inception, when those exposed to it find it more or less incomprehensible. Should we not look for the effects of Picasso on our consciousness in the design of chairs, of curtains, the spaces of everyday life and the thousandfold commodified mediations through which his insights continue to develop their effects upon us? And should we see these not merely as 'effects upon us' but as resources through which we ourselves construct sensibility and agency? Surely it was part of the modernist project to seize hold of the process of commodification and to do the necessary work to harness its aesthetic possibilities in an active subject-centred shaping of sensibility and agency. In and through the development of such a sensibility, the subject might hope to reclaim the outer social reality from which it has been exiled by modernity.

When one takes a critical line for a walk, one cannot be certain of finding one's way home. Nothing in relation to Adorno's own positions is as simple as my line of argumentation might appear to suppose. However, my line of thinking provides a possible way of rescuing the works of neo-classical composers, jazz musicians, French music, Stravinsky and the Russian composers from the negative judgements made by Adorno concerning the moral basis of their praxis. At the same time it reinforces Adorno's claim that there is a moral dimension in aesthetic praxis.

Adorno's cultural ethnocentrism

Adorno's sense of the structural parallels between German music and German philosophy and (via Marx) modern society was profound. It was the Viennese tradition over approximately a hundred and fifty years that provided him with his analytical tools, and from his home base in that music he generalised his ideas concerning the relationship between music and society. Susan Buck-Morss identifies Adorno's own centre in German philosophy as originating in his praxis within music and, most specifically, in the influence upon that praxis of Schoenberg's music. In a remarkable passage in *The Origin of Negative Dialectics* (1977), she argues that the influence of Schoenberg upon his philosophical work is to be seen not only in the content of his ideas but in the very method of construction (one might say composition) and she deconstructs an important philosophical paper of Adorno's on nature and history as an exercise in twelve-tone construction.

It would not be forcing the analogy to argue that the structure of this essay bore a distinct correspondence to the rules of twelve-tone composition; that is, (1) the *statement* of the tone row: 'all history is natural' (hence transitory); (2) retrograde or *reversal* of the row 'all nature is historical' (hence socially produced); (3) *inversion* of the row 'actual history is not historical' (but merely the reproduction of second nature); (4) *retrograde inversion*: 'second nature is unnatural' (because it denies nature's historical transitoriness).

(S. Buck-Morss 1977: 131)

This rootedness in a revolutionary modernist music was an especial strength as well as a weakness. It was a strength because Adorno developed what is undoubtedly the most profound insight into the relationship between the structure of musical relations and that of social relations, one which was grounded in his knowledge and personal mastery of a major European music tradition. It was a weakness because Adorno did not see the need to stray too far from his home base, and other musics are often evaluated in terms of how they measure up to the ideals that describe his own tradition.

Adorno took relatively little interest in earlier music, even that written in the European tradition. Even less did he explore non-European traditions or develop an ethno-musicological perspective. From his own roots in European music he was certain of how music worked in its internal relations and of how it corresponded to social relations. No matter how perceptive his insights into Stravinsky's music, we are entitled to ask whether the purposes and functional relations of one music culture can be known through generalising from those of another very different music culture. Adorno's critical essays on Stravinsky do not discourse in any depth or at any length on the Russian tradition in music, on its cultural roots or on the priorities and values of Russian culture, on the structural affinities that such music has with French rather than German music and so forth. The more that we open up such questions, the more it appears necessary to ask whether Adorno's hearing of events and relations in Stravinsky's music does not both construct the music in terms of how it measures up to Adorno's Viennese ideals and at the same time occlude any perspective on that music that is grounded in its own cultural tradition. Why should the (motivic-thematic) developmentalism of Viennese music be the measure of musical morality and virtue while the colouristic, non-developmental traditions are castigated for their relative lack of it? Samson writes about the lack of motivic-thematic development in both the Russian and French traditions in a very different way from Adorno, emphasising the values carefully cultivated in that music and without finding it regressive as a consequence of espousing those values (Samson 1993: 58). While at first sight it might seem to be a merit that Adorno writes about specific composers, his habit of abstracting his musical antagonists from entire traditions in music and of remaining more or less silent about those traditions weakens his arguments.

Adorno's treatment of jazz suffers to an even greater extent from his musical ethnocentrism. Not only are all the old criteria as determined by Viennese composition projected onto jazz music, but Adorno makes less effort to actually get to grips with the music, to explore its variety, in the way that he did do in the case of so-called serious art music, such as the compositions of Stravinsky. There are no real analyses of jazz compositions, no detailed knowledge of how jazz musicians compose, and there is a persistent refusal to see jazz music – both performance and composition – in its own cultural context. Again, Adorno knows how it all works because Viennese classical music provides him with a model of how *all* music works, and whatever jazz musicians think they are doing at the level of innovation can be shown to be stereotypical, derivative and conventional in terms of that model, and dismissed as a consequence. Are Stravinsky and Louis Armstrong to be seen as regressive because – in Adorno's analysis – they produce commodified music alienated from any organic connection to the total life process of the subject – music which is manipulative in producing its effects upon the body of the recipient? Or are they both to be seen as regressive simply because they are not Viennese? The question may seem flippant, but one can easily imagine it being put by a critic concerned with music at the level of its various traditions.

The idea that there may be universal features of aesthetic structures that are conditioned by social relations is certainly not new with Adorno. Hegel, Wölfflin, Hauser and Panofsky also developed arguments about the homology between art and social structure, and Adorno is rooted in that German tradition, too (E. Panofsky 1972). The difference in strategy between, say, Hauser and Adorno is instructive. Hauser establishes a formal opposition between 'naturalistic' art, in which objects and events look in paintings much as they might in real life, and non-naturalistic art, in which only the most schematic, 'abstract' and formal likeness to real figures or objects exist in the painting (A. Hauser 1962). He identifies naturalism in art with bourgeois societies that are individuated and with strong middle classes; he identifies non-naturalistic art with authoritarian, autocratic or hieratic societies. Using this as a stylistic principle, he provides a broad survey of the world's art and literature from prehistoric times to the present day. In Adorno's analyses, the contrast between tonal and atonal music is central, and is comparable in some respects to the opposition between naturalistic and non-naturalistic visual art. Adorno does not survey the world's music cultures; he remains rooted in the present and in the current state of both music and society (something about which Hauser has less to say).

And yet this too can be counted as a strength as well as a weakness. The musics Adorno discusses, whether jazz, neo-classicism or serialism, are all brought to the bar of modern social and political life. It is how he sees them working in the context of the commerce that modern late capitalist societies have with works of art which constructs his discourse about them. It is this which I believe is key to Adorno's strategy in developing a sociology of music and, especially, to the boundaries he establishes for that project. All the musics he discusses are musics which are involved in late capitalist society; all are musics which have commerce with late capitalist society. His theorising of jazz or twelve-tone technique is grounded in his understanding of that commerce and of its consequences in determining the inner structure of the art work. Because Adorno had developed a general theory of the different relations that art works could have to modern society — from those he approved to those he disapproved — he could claim to know in advance what were the consequences for the social formation of the structural relations of a given type of music.

There is no doubt, too, that the Schoenberg revolution has had a key role to play in the development of other modern musics, including jazz. From the 1960s, avant-garde jazz musicians have made use of atonal developments, and twelve-tone composition became Stravinsky's late style. Adorno has some reason to suppose that the Schoenberg revolution is central to modern musics of different kinds in much the same sense that Picasso and Braque's Cubist revolution was central to the various avant-garde movements in the visual arts. It is Adorno's utter centredness in this music which informs all his speculations concerning other musics and the future of music. Schonherr points out that when Adorno castigated serialist composition in the mid-1950s as a sterile cul-de-sac, he had actually listened to very little of it. Schonherr claims, however, that the subsequent development of modern music has generally supported Adorno's judgements there. He is left sceptical but wondering as to whether his judgements concerning jazz might prove ultimately to be correct (U. Schonherr 1991).

At the very centre of Adorno's moral philosophy is the spectre of totalitarian society. Fascism of both the right and the left shaped the events of his life. The dream of purity, of perfect unity, inscribed in totalitarianism of either kind, could be seen as a pathological response to the threat to order and identity posed by modernity itself. The more that the society fragmented along the lines demanded by the division of labour and a rational-technical commodity capitalism, the less coherent the intra-subjective constitution of the subject. The substantial unity of the subject — that is, unity at the level of values — gives way to a plurality of identities which correspond to the disjunctive social worlds in which the individual is formed. It is this insight which, as I argued above, is behind sociologies such as Goffman's. The fragmentation into a plural and multi-faceted selfhood engenders a self-distancing — an irony — of the subject in respect of his or her constructed identities, a de-centring of identity which contrasts strongly with the centred and unitary subject that is at the heart of bourgeois ideology. The modernist revolution in art — especially early modernism —

reflected this condition of fragmentation, plurality and ironic self-distancing of the subject from constructed forms. It too manifested an extreme de-centring, a withdrawal of the spiritual centre from constructed forms and the setting up of distanced and resistant relations to them.

Totalitarianism, by contrast, attempts to resolve the crisis of order, not by a process of de-centring which raises the sensuous ordering of action to a higher level of abstraction, but through seeking to reimpose a centric unity on the world, a mass character, a unitary ideology and identity by bringing about the destruction of all competing sources of subjective value. Both aesthetic modernism and political totalitarianism had in common that they were responses to a crisis in which effective social action was threatened by fragmentation at the level of agency: at the level, that is, of the sensibility and capacity of the subject. Social systems as well as individuals demand coherence, a degree of negative entropy, if they are to be energised to meet the demands of action.

However, as a response to the crisis of individuation and of order in late modern societies, totalitarianism stood at the very opposite pole from modernism in the arts. The model of the unitary and homogeneous crowd governs the totalitarian ideal; it obliterates all distance between the subject and the collectivity. The modernist ideal is the very opposite: it shatters all such masses, all centric unity; it de-centres the subject even at the level of its constitutive subjectivity and prevents its incorporation as surely as totalitarianism aims at the total incorporation of the subject. The totalitarian authorities in Fascist and communist states during this century have hardly doubted the threat posed by modernism; modernist art and literature has frequently been ridiculed, banned and even physically destroyed by totalitarian regimes.

Twelve-tone machineries

Adorno's willingness to identify certain types of modern music with totalitarianism as a structural ideal and with serving the interests of totalitarian forces in modern society as a political consequence has to be seen as problematic. His method is to set music up as a drama or event-world in which part–whole relations within a musical work can be treated as a structural analogue of part–whole (individual–society) relations in society. The unfreedom of the notes bound into the twelve-tone row, their lack of mutual mediation, is equated with the unfree and non-dialectical relations of individuals in a totalitarian society. The rigidity and stereotypy that Adorno claims to detect in jazz and in the atemporality and rhythmic-spatiality of neo-classicism are similarly identified by him with totalitarian order. Adorno lumps together vastly different types of music and claims that they are all 'wrong' for the same reasons. He would no doubt defend this strategy by arguing that he is not denying the essential differences among these musics, but is seeking to expose the totalitarian 'infection' in all of them. I have argued here that his reasoning is suspect, not concerning the dangers of totalitarianism but in his attribution of complicity on the part of the musics he criticises with totalitarianism, with unfreedom.

Twelve-tone technique can be shown in a somewhat different light, for example, if we consider it in terms of the demands of an intra-subjective mode of ordering experience. The shift to an intra-subjective level of experience in modernist art and literature inevitably entailed a breakdown in the linear, sequential and historical modes of organising experience, bringing about a confluence of all that was normally held apart.

But how, at the level of aesthetic imagery, is the subject able to bring about without difficulty the confluence of what would normally be held apart? It is reasonable to suppose that, at an intra-subjective level, the unity that makes this confluence possible is a unity of *substance*; that all events, at the level of consciousness, are made out of the same material, the same 'stuff'. The discovery of this confluence – which is the realisation of an intra-subjective level of experience – is the discovery of the substantial unity of consciousness: that is, its unity as 'substance' or 'stuff' from which sensuous experience is formed. We can liken 'substantial unity' to the material substance – brick – with which we construct a building. Buildings are variegated structures in themselves and differ from each other, and yet they are all made from bricks.

A constitutive subjectivity can be represented as a unity of substance, as furnishing in all its parts the identical building blocks to be used in construction. To meet this condition of substantive unity, any of the intra-subjective elements that constitute the parts must contain all the values, arranged in the same invariant order, to be found in any of the other parts. What I here refer to as 'the body of subjectivity' is subjectivity considered as the 'stuff' from which any construction can be made, not subjectivity as the forms made with such stuff. An art which seeks to move to this level of abstraction must depict objects and events as they arise in the sensibility of the perceiving body of the subject.

Constructing an intra-subjective machinery – a machinery of sensibility – means laying down the material substance, the juxtaposition of absolute particulars, from which a sensibility is to be generated. If we make such a demand of music, that it must manifest a unity of substance, that it must be everywhere the same in the tonal materials from which it is constructed, then this ideal can be seen to reflect the type of concern with ordering represented by Schoenberg's twelve-tone technique and the music of the later serialists. To meet the condition of being 'substantially' the same, music in the European classical tradition would have to be built out of units which comprised all twelve notes of the full chromatic. Moreover, these would have to possess an invariant order, absolutely particular for any given composition.

An art that is oriented to the production of intra-subjective machineries –

machineries of sensibility – is necessarily both de-individuated and de-historicised. Such machineries are activated as integral to the constitutive sensuousness of the subject. They are machineries for the production of sensibility. They need to be seen as distinct from the sensible relations which can be made or constructed with them, from the altered relationship to life which they make possible. A radical modernist art which is oriented to provoking agency and sensibility in the subject necessarily confines itself to the problem of engineering a machinery of sensibility that is to be the instrument of provocation. Only when such a consciousness is secure (I hesitate to say 'second nature') can art redirect its projects and reclaim the interactional order, the macro-structure.

The principal revolutionary moments of modern art – those around 1910 with Picasso and Braque's invention of Cubism and Schoenberg's discovery of free atonality – were marked by the most intense efforts to bring the new modes out from the material inherited by these artists. There was no jettisoning of the past, here, in the sense of starting again, as though with a tabula rasa. Picasso was deeply conscious of what Cézanne, Manet and the early modernists had done, and could construct his work in a line of development from them; similarly, Schoenberg was steeped in the condition of Viennese music and the problems bequeathed by Beethoven, Brahms and Wagner. The very foundations of any new twentieth-century modes of aesthetic construction were laid down in the first two decades of the century in these revolutionary movements, which derived their radical innovations as radical developments in the aesthetic material bequeathed from the past. The revolutions brought about by such artists ought perhaps to be distinguished from the avant-garde movements which made use of these insights to proclaim the new as the extinguishing of the old, movements that sought to absolutise the new.

Adorno located his defence of modernism securely in the revolutionary moment of the emergence of 'free atonality' in modern music around 1910. This is the perspective in which present and past are viewed. What stretched forward for him from this point was an undermining of temporality, which he abhorred: hence his ambivalence with respect to so many of the developments that occurred in avant-garde art, from surrealist dreamscapes to Stravinsky's ballets and the works of serialist composers. For Adorno, if the Minotaur of modernity is to be slain then we cannot afford to lose the thread which alone makes it possible to negotiate the maze. Thus there is no inconsistency in the fact that Adorno can both revere Schoenberg as the father of the revolution in modern music to which he himself is committed and yet oppose the direction taken by the later Schoenberg in developing twelve-tone technique, even though he can see how the development of that technique is inherent in the musical material that composers such as Schoenberg worked with.

Adorno's conservatism and his ambivalence towards many movements in modernist art is reflected in his self-location at the revolutionary moment when the thread is still intact and the new has not yet dissolved the old – that is, the intra-subjective does not yet obliterate from view the inter-subjective, the dynamic temporality of events. It is only in and through interactional relations and the temporality they construct that the subject can realise a capacity, a sensibility or agency in *action* that has been developed at polytemporal intra-actional level. So long as the thread between the polytemporality of agency and the temporality of action is maintained intact, then the world becomes the subject's world, a world constructed through the expressivity of the subject. When the thread is broken, however, and the atemporal agency of the subject is divided from any integral and expressive temporality of social action, agency and sensibility are open to being shaped from the outside. A rupture between these two worlds leaves the subject at the mercy of collective and objective force.

It seems to me that the critical force of Adorno's insights into modernism should be located here, in the rupture between two levels at which experience is ordered: those of agency (intra-action) and of action (inter-action). Such an argument would have to be distinguished from what seems to me to be Adorno's untenable claim that the atemporality of musical relations that he perceives in the inner cells of a jazz work or a work by Stravinsky makes of that work a simulacrum of totalitarianism. I have argued, in opposition to this, that the (polytemporal) intra-subjective process leads in the opposite direction: that is, towards the constituting of a subjectivity that is both enlarged and distanced from the collectivity.

However, it may not do so – and here Adorno's argument can be (partly) recovered – under conditions where agency is disjoined from action. A rupture between the two levels of experience is, in effect, a rupture between the inner world of subjectivity and its objects. If a constitutive subjectivity which is cut off from interaction is narcissistic and de-sociated, then it makes sense to see any such rupture between these two levels of experience (agency and action) as pathological.

When Adorno seeks to analyse Stravinsky's music in terms of pathology, he does so using the model of schizophrenia, a model which is peculiarly resonant for many modern analysts who have used it as a vehicle for reflecting upon modernity (R.D. Laing 1965; G. Deleuze and F. Guattari 1984). The idea of an individual cut off from genuine dialectical relations with others, condemned to the condition which Laing described as 'shutup-ness', cut off from change, would seem to be the perfect symbol of such a rupture between a constitutive subjectivity (agency and sensibility) and the world. Adorno's claim is that the initiate can actually hear the pathology in the music.

It is possible to argue, given the line of thinking I have been walking here, that the expansion of subjectivity at the intra-subjective level can only be progressive, in Adorno's sense, if the thread is maintained and the process as a whole is driven by the expressive needs of the subject in interaction with others; that a rupture between the two means that the synchronic process will be implosive rather than explosive; that it will inscribe the forces of external and collective domination and result in an impoverishment of agency and sensibility. Whether such a view of surrealism, or of neo-classicism or of any of the other movements that Adorno judged to be regressive, is a tenable one is something that remains to be argued. It is also possible to argue, as I have done here and elsewhere, that the withdrawal to the level of a constitutive subjectivity is a necessary basis for reclaiming, revaluing and remaking the world: that is, of re-building social relations from such an intra-subjective and intra-actional ground.

Adorno's perception that serious art and the products of the culture industry are 'two torn halves that don't add up' needs to be considered in the light of the dialectical and mediated relations that exist between them. It is not just that so-called serious artists are continuously making forays into mass culture for the purpose of acquiring material – Adorno discusses this frequently – but also that the accomplishments of serious art are diffused (if also defused) in mass culture over time; the products of so-called serious modernist art enter, indirectly, into every aspect of modern design and ultimately modernism's insights become assimilated to mass culture and mass audiences. Television, radio and film have plundered the modernist music repertoire for many of the effects that they deploy in constructing presentations and in composing theme music. At the other pole, popular art continuously develops towards high art in its more avant-garde forms. Thus the label 'jazz', once applied to any dance-band music, now encompasses avant-garde music such as that of Ornette Coleman or John Coltrane; within the jazz idiom these composers assimilated many of the lessons of atonal composition. In doing so, as Adorno foresaw, their music has become virtually indistinguishable from so-called art music.

The development of a modern rational-technical capitalism tended to polarise subject and object, individual and society, through its marginalising of the sensuous life of the subject and its exiling of art and art-making to the very periphery of the institutional order of modern society. Adorno's sharp counterposing of mass culture to serious art occludes the ferment of mediations between them. It is at least as plausible to argue that mass culture plays a mediating role between an exiled subjectivity and the institutional order, that it is continuously reshaping sensibility and agency in ways that mediate the 'two halves', serious art and popular culture, 'defusing' and 'diffusing' from one to the other, ultimately bringing them closer together. If the view of modernism I have presented in this chapter is correct, then such a convergence is implicit (*pace* Adorno) in the development of commodification itself which the culture industry represents.

Whether or not further studies confirm or throw doubt upon the specific judgements that Adorno makes about particular composers on the basis of his own implicit theory of agency, his sociological studies of the modern musical art work represent the richest source of insights and ideas available to a sociology of music and to the sociology of art works generally. That is the case now and will be for some time to come. No one has done more to persuade us of the moral dimension of all cultural construction and of the sociality that is the basis of anything truly creative and liberative. One can imagine that these same insights may ultimately prove of value in the construction of a social musicology that reaches conclusions and judgements that differ greatly from those of Adorno.

REFERENCES

Adorno, T. (1956) 'Modern Music is Growing Old', trans. Rollo H. Myers, *The Score*.
——(1973) *The Jargon of Authenticity*, Routledge and Kegan Paul Ltd: London.
——(1976) *Introduction to the Sociology of Music*, trans. E.B. Ashton, Seabury Press: New York.
——(1980) *The Philosophy of Modern Music*, Seabury Press: New York.
——(1981) *In Search of Wagner*, New Left Books: Trowbridge.
——(1982a) 'Bach Defended Against His Devotees', *Prisms*, MIT Press: Cambridge, Mass.
——(1982b) 'Perennial Fashion – Jazz', *Prisms*, MIT Press: Cambridge, Mass.
——(1984) *Aesthetic Theory*, Routledge and Kegan Paul Ltd: London.
——(1989) 'On Jazz', trans. J. Owen Daniel, *Discourse*, vol. 12, no. 1, pp. 45–69.
——(1992) *Mahler*, trans. E. Jephcott, University of Chicago Press: London.
——(1993) 'Music, Language and Composition', trans. Susan Gillespie, *Musical Quarterly*, vol. 77, no. 3, pp. 401–14.
——(1994a) *Alban Berg*, Cambridge University Press: Cambridge.
——(1994b) 'Analytical Study of the NBC Musical Appreciation Hour', *Musical Quarterly*, vol. 78, no. 2, pp. 325–77.
——(1994c) 'Late Style in Beethoven', trans. Susan Gillespie, *Raritan*, vol. 13, no. 1, pp. 102–7.
——(1994d) 'Vers Une Musique Informelle', *Quasi Una Fantasia: Essays on Modern Music*, trans. Rodney Livingstone, Verso: London.
Adorno, T. and Horkheimer, M. (1986) *The Dialectic of Enlightenment*, Verso: London.
Adorno, T., Frenkel-Brunswick, E., Levinson, D. and Sanford, N. (1950) *The Authoritarian Personality*, 3 vols, Harper and Rowe: New York.
Alberti, L.B. (1966) *On Painting*, trans. J.R. Spencer, Yale University Press: London.
Arendt, H. (1973) *The Origins of Totalitarianism*, André Deutsch: London.
Armstrong, R. (1971) *The Affecting Presence: An Essay in Humanistic Anthropology*, University of Illinois Press: Urbana, Ill.
Auerbach, E. (1968) *Mimesis*, trans. Wilard R. Trask, Princeton University Press: Princeton, NJ.
Bekker, P. (1921) *Gustav Mahler's Sinfonien*, cited in T. Adorno (1992) *Mahler*, University of Chicago Press: London, p. 16.
Bernstein, J.M. (1991) *The Culture Industry: Selected Essays on Mass Culture*, Routledge: London.
——(1993) *The Fate of Art*, Polity Press: Cambridge.

Blumenfeld, H. (1991) 'Ad Vocem Adorno', *Musical Quarterly*, vol. 75, no. 4, p. 263.

Boissevain, J. (1974) *Friends of Friends: Networks, Manipulators and Coalitions*, Basil Blackwell: London.

Brand, J., Hailey, C. and Harris, D. (eds) (1987) *The Berg–Schoenberg Correspondence*, Macmillan: London.

Bryson, N. (1983) 'Image, Discourse and Power', *Vision and Painting*, Macmillan: London, pp. 133–62.

Buber, M. (1987) *I and Thou*, second edition, trans. R. Gregor Smith, T. and T. Clark: Edinburgh.

Buck-Morss, S. (1977) *The Origin of Negative Dialectics*, Harvester Press: Brighton, Sussex.

Burkhardt, J. (1981) *The Civilization of the Renaissance in Italy*, Phaidon: Oxford.

Deleuze, G. and Guattari, F. (1984) *Anti-Oedipus: Capitalism and Schizophrenia*, trans. R. Hurley, M. Seem and H.R. Lane, Athlone Press: London.

DeNora, T. (1995) *Beethoven and The Construction of Genius*, California University Press: Berkeley.

Durkheim, E. (1933) *The Division of Labour*, Free Press of Glencoe: New York.

——(1951) *Suicide*, trans. J. Spalding and G. Simpson, Free Press of Glencoe: New York.

Ehrenzweig, E. (1967) *The Hidden Order of Art*, Weidenfeld and Nicholson: London.

Fenichel, O. (1946) *The Psychoanalytic Theory of Neurosis*, Routledge and Kegan Paul: New York.

Freud, S. (1949) *An Outline of Psychoanalysis*, trans. J. Strachey, Hogarth Press: London.

Garfinkel, H. (1967) *Studies in Ethnomethodology*, Prentice-Hall: Englewood Cliffs, NJ.

Goffman, E. (1959) *The Presentation of the Self in Everyday Life*, Doubleday Anchor: New York.

——(1961a) *Asylums: Essays on the Social Situation of Mental Patients and Other Inmates*, Doubleday Anchor: New York.

——(1961b) *Encounters: Two Essays on the Sociology of Interaction*, Bobbs-Merrill: New York.

——(1963) *Stigma: Notes on the Management of Spoiled Identity*, Prentice-Hall: Englewood Cliffs, NJ.

Goldmann, A. and Sprinchorn, E. (1981) *Wagner on Music and Drama*, trans. H.A. Ellis, DeCapo Press: New York.

Gracyk, T.A. (1992) 'Adorno, Jazz and the Aesthetics of Popular Music', *Musical Quarterly*, vol. 76, no. 4, pp. 526–42.

Hall, M. (1997) *Leaving Home: A Conducted Tour of Twentieth Century Music with Simon Rattle*, Faber and Faber: London.

Hall, S., Clarke, J., Jefferson, T. and Roberts, B. (eds) (1976) *Resistance Through Rituals*, Hutchinson: London.

Hauser, A. (1962) *The Social History of Art*, 4 vols, Routledge and Kegan Paul: London.

Hebdige, D. (1979) *Subculture: The Meaning of Style*, Methuen: London.

Hegel, G.W. (1931) *The Phenomenology of Mind*, trans. J.B. Baillie, Allen and Unwin: London.

——(1975) *Aesthetics: Lectures on Fine Art*, trans. T.M. Knox, Clarendon Press: Oxford.

Hofstede, G. (1994) *Cultures and Organizations: Software of the Mind*, HarperCollins: London.

Jarman, D. (1979) *The Music of Alban Berg*, Faber and Faber: London.

Jay, M. (1973) *The Dialectical Imagination: A History of the Frankfurt School and the Institute of Social Research 1923–1950*, Heinemann Educational Books: London.

Laing, R.D. (1965) *The Divided Self*, Penguin: Harmondsworth.

Lukács, G. (1972) *Studies in European Realism*, Merlin Press: London.

——(1978) *The Theory of the Novel*, Merlin Press: London.

Mann, T. (1968) *Doctor Faustus*, Penguin: Harmondsworth.

Mead, G.H. (1967) *Mind, Self and Society*, University of Chicago Press: Chicago.

Metzger, H.-K. (1960) 'Just who is Growing Old?', *Die Reihe*, vol. 4, pp. 63–80.

Mitchell, J. (1969) *Social Networks in Urban Situations*, Manchester University Press: Manchester.

Nochlin, L. (1971) *Realism*, Penguin: Harmondsworth.

Paddison, M. (1993) *Adorno's Aesthetics of Music*, Cambridge University Press: Cambridge.

——(1996) *Adorno, Modernism and Mass Culture: Essays on Critical Theory and Music*, Kahn and Averill: London.

Panofsky, E. (1951) *Gothic Architecture and Scholasticism*, Archabbey Press: La Trobe, PA.

——(1972) *Studies in Iconology: Humanistic Themes in the Art of the Renaissance*, Harper and Rowe: London.

Park, R. (1952) *Human Communities*, Free Press of Glencoe: Illinois.

Parsons, T. (1951) *The Social System*, Routledge and Kegan Paul: London.

Piaget, J. (1970) *Genetic Epistemology*, trans. E. Duckworth, Columbia University Press: London.

——(1972) *Psychology and Epistemology: Towards a Theory of Knowledge*, trans. P.A. Wells, Penguin: Harmondsworth.

——(1978) *The Development of Thought: Equilibration and Cognitive Structures*, trans. A. Rosen, Basil Blackwell: Oxford.

Poggioli, R. (1968) *The Theory of the Avant-Garde*, Belknap Press of Harvard University: London.

Reich, W. (1965) *The Life and Work of Alban Berg*, trans. Cornelius Cardew, Thames and Hudson: London.

Rose, G. (1978) *The Melancholy Science: An Introduction to the Thought of Theodor Adorno*, Columbia University Press: New York.

Rufer, J. (1961) *Composition with Twelve Notes, Related Only to One Another*, trans. H. Searle, Barrie and Rockliff: London.

Said, E. (1992) *Musical Elaborations*, Vintage: London.

Salzman, E. (1974) *Twentieth Century Music: An Introduction*, Prentice-Hall: Englewood Cliffs, NJ.

Sample, C. (1994) 'Adorno on the Musical Language of Beethoven' (a review of T. Adorno (1993) *Beethoven, Philosophie der Musik* Frankfurt, Suhrkamp) *Musical Quarterly*, vol. 78, no. 2, pp. 378–91.

Samson, J. (1993) *Music in Transition: A Study of Tonal Expansion and Atonality 1900–1920*, J.M. Dent: London.

Schonherr, U. (1991) 'Adorno and Jazz: Reflections on a Failed Encounter', *Telos*, vol. 87, pp. 85–97.

Simmel, G. (1950) 'The Metropolis and Mental Life' in K. Wolff (ed.) *The Sociology of Georg Simmel*, Free Press of Glencoe: Illinois.

Skinner, B.F. (1953) *Science and Human Behaviour*, The Free Press: New York.

Stein, L. (ed.) (1975) *Style and Idea: Selected Writings of Arnold Schoenberg*, Faber and Faber: London.

Subotnik, R. (1976) 'Adorno's Diagnosis of Beethoven's Late Style: Early Symptoms of a Fatal Condition', *Journal of the American Musicological Society*.

——(1990) *Developing Variations: Style and Ideology in Western Music*, University of Minnesota Press: Minneapolis.

——(1996) *Deconstructive Variations: Music and Reason in Western Society*, University of Minnesota Press: Minneapolis .

Szondi, P. (1987) *Theory of the Modern Drama*, Polity Press: Cambridge.

Turner, V.W. (1969) *The Ritual Process: Structure and Anti-Structure*, Routledge and Kegan Paul: London.

Volpacchio, F. (1991) 'The Mother of All Interviews: Zappa on Music and Society', *Telos*, vol. 78, pp. 124–37.

Wagner, R. (1995) *Opera and Drama*, trans. W. Ashton Ellis, University of Nebraska Press: Lincoln, Nebraska.

Weber, M. (1946) 'Class, Status and Party' in H. Gerth and C. Wright Mills (eds) *From Max Weber: Essays in Sociology*, Oxford University Press: Oxford, pp. 180–95.

Williams, R. (1976) *Keywords*, Fontana: London.

Witkin, R.W. (1995) *Art and Social Structure*, Polity Press: Cambridge.

——(1997) 'Constructing a Sociology for an Icon of European Modernity', *Sociological Theory*, vol. 15, no. 2, pp. 101–25.

Wooton, A. (1975) *Dilemmas of Discourse: Controversies about the Sociological Interpretation of Language*, Allen and Unwin: London.

Zimbardo, P.G. (1969) 'The Human Choice: Individuation, Reason and Order Versus Deindividuation, Impulse and Chaos' in W.J. Arnold and D. Levine (eds) *Nebraska Symposium on Motivation*, vol. 17, University of Nebraska Press: Lincoln, Nebraska.

INDEX

absolute particulars 25, 41, 188, 190, 196
abstraction 13, 156
accommodation:
  assimilation–accommodation model 54–6
agency 105, 129, 156, 185, 198; action and 105, 198; individuated 105–7; music as mode of 15; sensibility and 105, 129
aggressor: identification with 73–4, 76, 144, 145, 173
Alberti, L.B. 37, 132
alienation 16, 43, 97, 100, 144–5; *see also* commodification; commodity fetishism
anomie 102
archaic, the 154; objectivity in 157–8; Stravinsky and 89
architecture: Scholasticism and 38–9
Arendt, Hannah 18
Armstrong, Louis 173, 174, 175
Armstrong, R. 156
artistic freedom 3–4, 27
Art Nouveau 77
asociality 177–8
assimilation–accommodation model 54–6
atemporality *see* time
atonalism 96; principle of centricity in 134; transition from tonalism 100–1, 106–7, 110, 134; *see also* free atonality; twelve-tone technique
Auerbach, E. 36
Auschwitz 1, 144
authenticity 25, 26
automaton, the 115

avant-garde 184–5; jazz 160, 161, 162, 173, 176, 194, 199; modernism 11; use of term 184; visual arts 194

Bach, J.S. 3; Beethoven compared 61–2
ballet *see* dance
Balzac, Honoré de 28, 94; Lukács on 41–2
banality: in art 60, 103–4; the automaton 115; Berg and 124–5; commodification and 68, 103; of conventions 57–9, 103; of jazz 164; the power of the banal 60
Bartók, Béla 149, 164
Baudelaire, Charles 60
Bauer-Lechner, Natalie 115
Beckett, Samuel 11, 56, 60, 104, 143, 184
Beethoven, Ludwig van 29–30, 46, 110; anti-harmonism 52; Bach compared 61–2; as centre of musical history 62; classical tonality 102; conventions 68–9; dissonance 90; emergence of listening culture and 186; the Eroica 64; expression 67; Fifth Symphony 29, 64–5; irony 110; 'Kreutzer' Sonata 64; late 43, 48, 51, 52–3, 59, 60–1, 65–9, 101, 103, 116; late quartets 60, 100; mature style 62–6; middle/second-period 30–1, 45, 52, 60–5, 67, 74, 101, 102, 114–15; motives 32, 87, 102; Ninth Symphony 64, 65; 'nothingness' 63–4; part–whole relations 5, 63–7, 102; 'Pastoral' symphony 28, 64; Piano Sonata Opus 111, 31, 46, 125; Seventh Symphony 64–5; sonata-